EN PLEIN AIR

Acrylic

Expert techniques and simple step-by-step projects for creating dynamic landscapes in the open air with acrylic

Mark Mehaffey

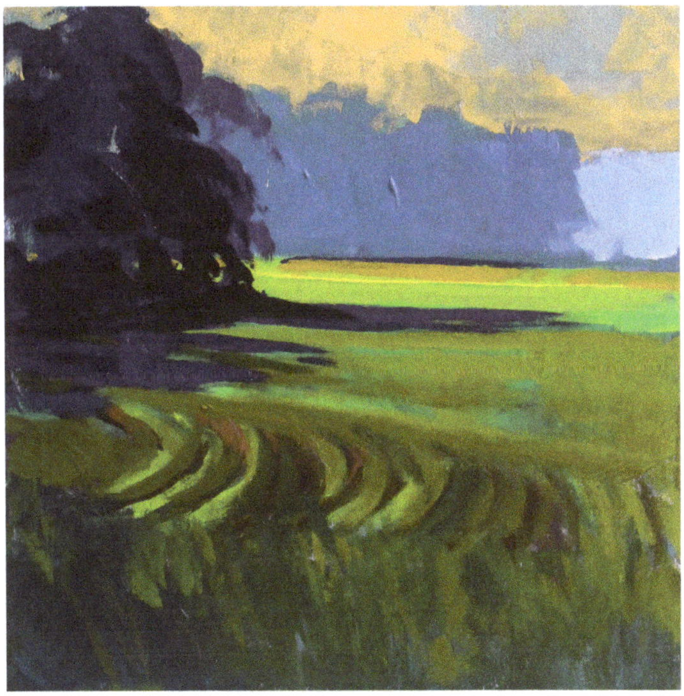

Walter Foster

Quarto.com
WalterFoster.com

First Published in 2018 by Walter Foster Publishing, an imprint of The Quarto Group.
26391 Crown Valley Parkway, Suite 220, Mission Viejo, CA 92691, USA.
T (949) 380-7510 **F** (949) 380-7575

Walter Foster Publishing titles are also available at discount for retail, wholesale, promotional, and bulk purchase. For details, contact the Special Sales Manager by email at specialsales@quarto.com or by mail at The Quarto Group, Attn: Special Sales Manager, 100 Cummings Center, Suite 265D, Beverly, MA 01915, USA.

ISBN: 978-1-63322-610-4

Digital edition published in 2018
eISBN: 978-1-63322-611-1

Text and artwork by Mark Mehaffey
Editorial and design by BlueRed Press Ltd.

Page 1, ***Sun and Shadows***
Page 3, ***Spring Crossing***
Page 4, ***Dawn Sky***
Page 6, ***Farm Country***

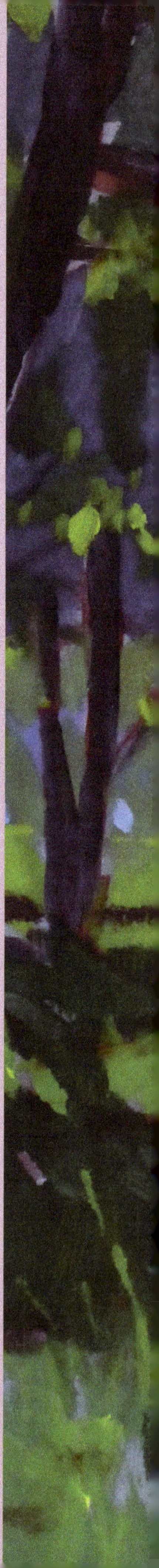

EN PLEIN AIR Acrylic

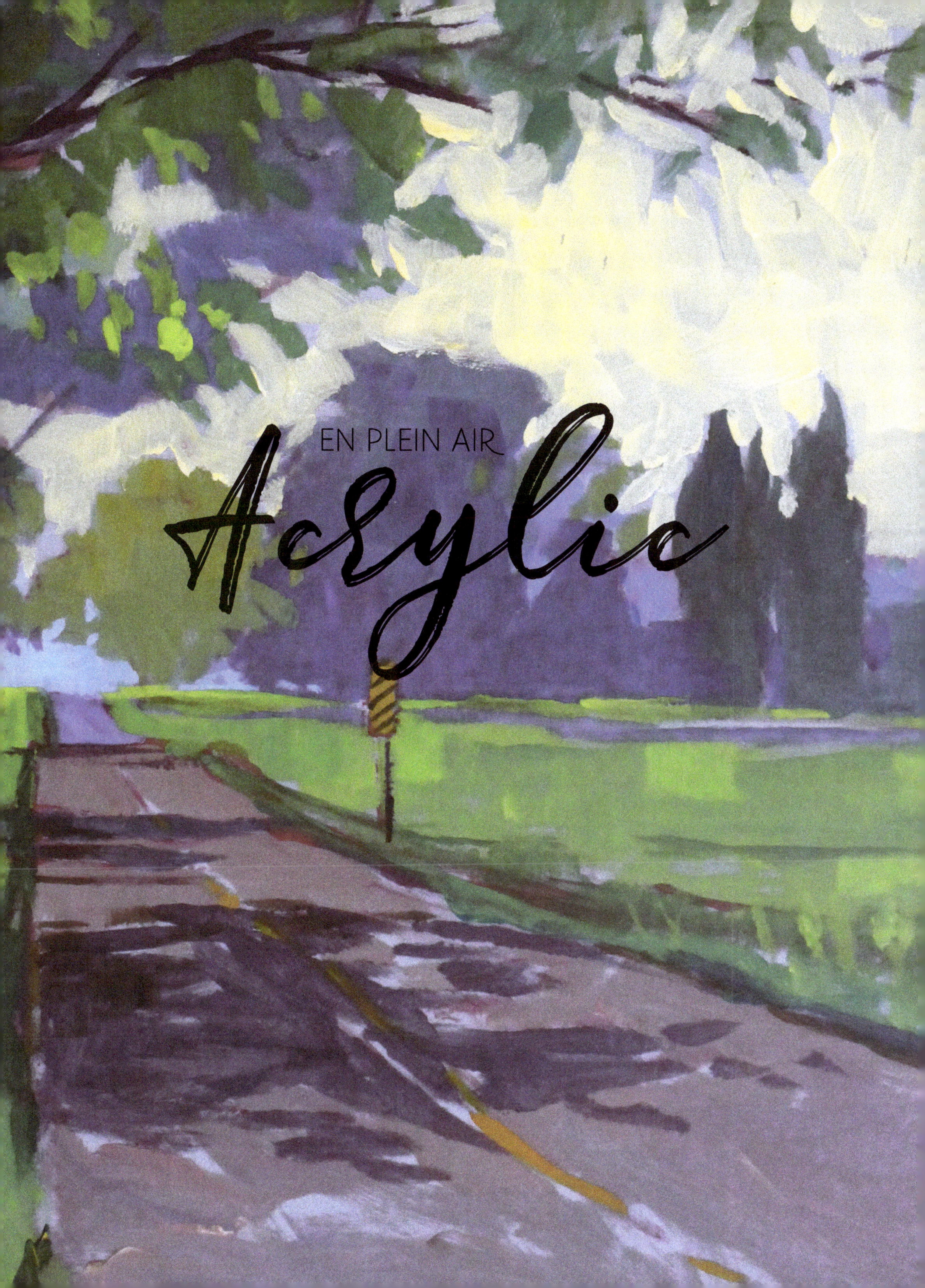

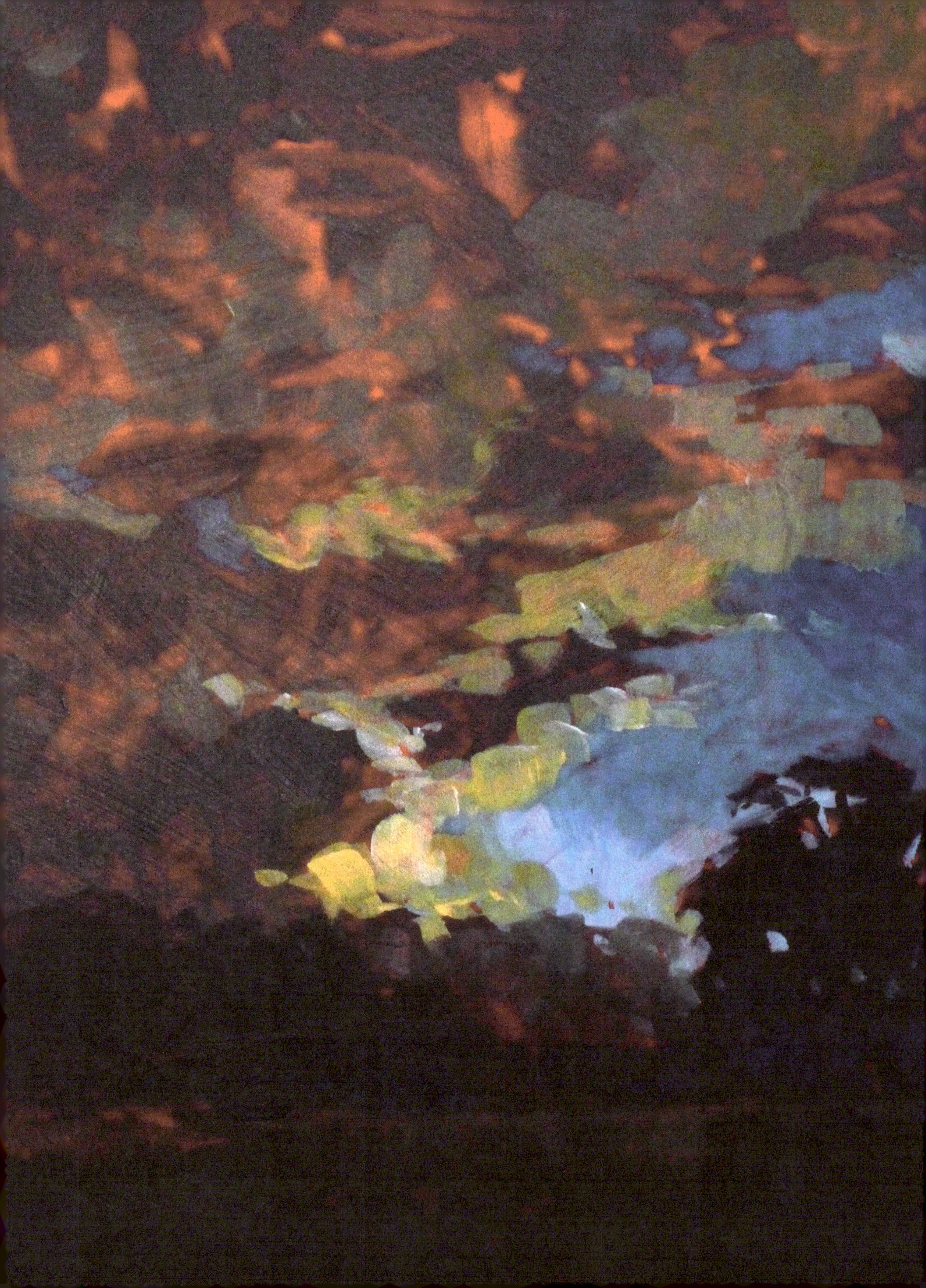

Contents

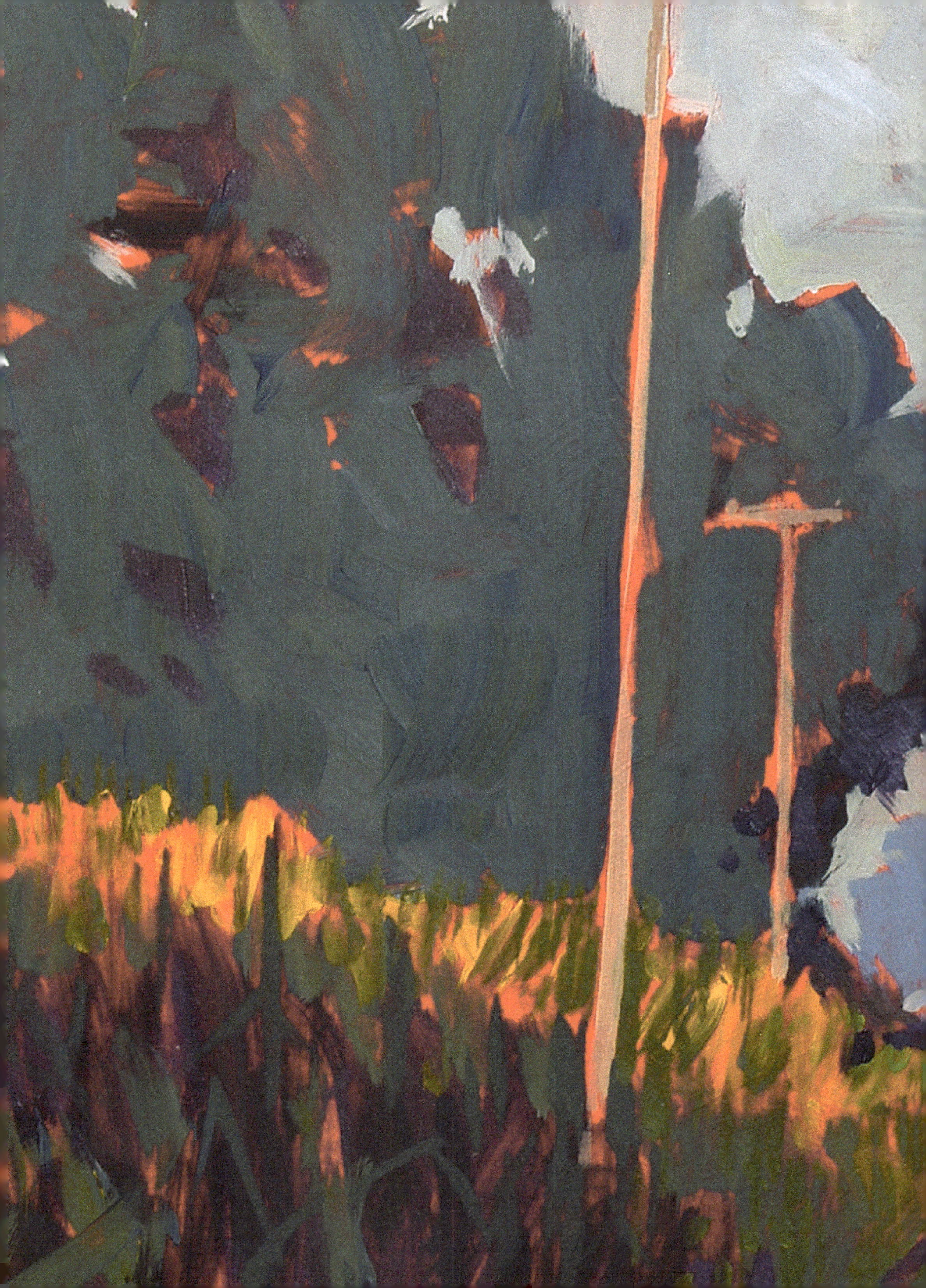

Introduction

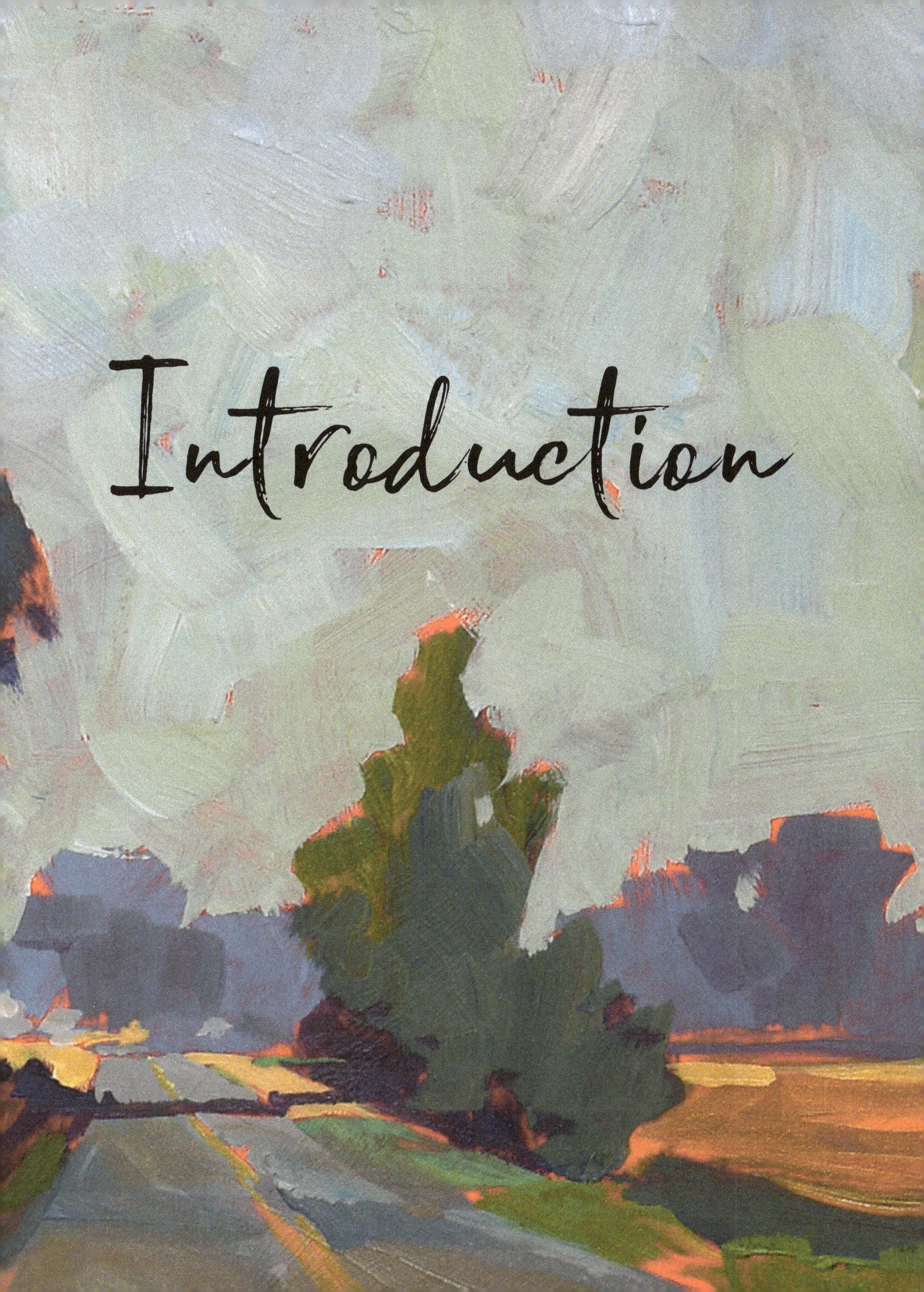

En Plein Air

French for "in the open air," *en plein air* has become the accepted term for painting out of doors.

Artists have been painting outdoors for ages. Most agree that it was the invention of the collapsible zinc paint tube by John Goffe Rand in 1841 that really jump-started the *plein air* movement. Prior to that, artists had to grind their own pigment into linseed oil and then keep the resulting mixture in glass jars—very inconvenient for carrying paint around. This changed with the invention of the capped tube. It became relatively easy for artists to carry a portable easel, a palette, a handful of brushes, and some tubes of color into the great outdoors.

The popularity of Impressionism and its practice of painting outdoors to capture the light and atmosphere of contemporary life gave rise to *plein air* painting as a movement. Claude Monet, Pierre-Auguste Renoir, and their contemporaries all saw the benefit of painting from life outdoors. From the Barbizon School in France to the Hudson River School in New York, artists have discovered and rediscovered the value of painting *en plein air*.

Today there are thousands of painters worldwide who either work both in the studio and outdoors or are solely dedicated *plein air* artists. Some view painting outside as a hobby, and some use it as a tool to inform their studio work. There are also many professional *plein air* painters who view working outside as their ultimate goal. Galleries and other venues are now also dedicated to showing and promoting *plein air* work. There are hundreds of *plein air* "events," some tightly juried; some invitation-only; and others that encourage anyone to sign up, come along, and paint. *Plein air* painting has become so popular that Eric Rhoads, publisher of *Plein Air Magazine*, has coined the movement "The New Golf."

Some artists have gravitated toward painting outdoors because they grew up fishing, camping, or hiking and view painting outside as an extension of those activities. Others enjoy traveling to new locations and the social interaction of changing scenery and painting with other like-minded artists.

Whatever your motivation, there is no better time to start than now. Read along, learn some techniques, try out new ideas, and follow the demonstrations provided in these pages. Then get outside, practice, wear out some brushes. I guarantee it will be fun!

Working Outdoors

The first thing you need to do is decide where you'd like to paint. The majority of my *plein air* work is done within two miles of my home in Michigan, where the landscape is a mix of old and new housing and farmland. In this rural setting, I find many interesting things to paint: gravel country roads, farm buildings, farm equipment, woods and fields, cars, runners and walkers, and vistas and close-ups.

In most parts of the world, you have tacit permission to set up and paint in public places. I usually don't ask, but if I'm told to move out of the way or set up in another area, I always smile and agree. If I'm in the middle of a painting, I take a photo of both the view and my work and finish later. You also have tacit permission to set up on almost any public roadway as long as you don't impede or block traffic; however, I have been asked to move further from the road by local police when I am too close to traffic.

One of my favorite places to paint is a gravel road not far from my house. It was also the preferred place for a local patrol officer to stop and catch up on paperwork. He loved one of my paintings of that road and bought it—a nice surprise that can happen when painting locally.

I love to travel and always take my painting supplies with me. It is wonderful to be invited to paint at what is—to me, at least—an exotic international destination. When traveling abroad, I always research the customs of that country to make sure I don't offend anyone or break any laws. Painting is an international language. Everyone understands the effort needed to make a painting!

Ultimately, I never trespass to paint. If I find a private location I like, I always ask permission first. No one has ever said no. Every now and then, if I complete two paintings on private property, I'll give one of them to the owner. They are always appreciative, and I always get invited back. Double-check to make sure you've not left any paper towels or equipment behind.

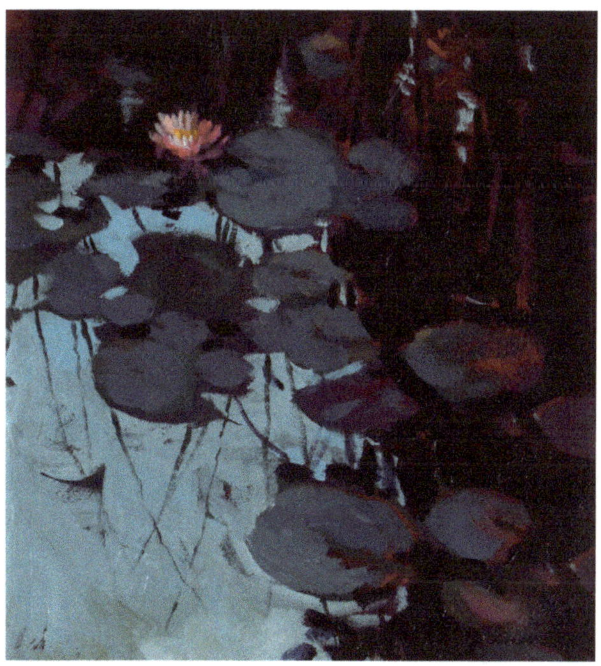

Early Morning Lily

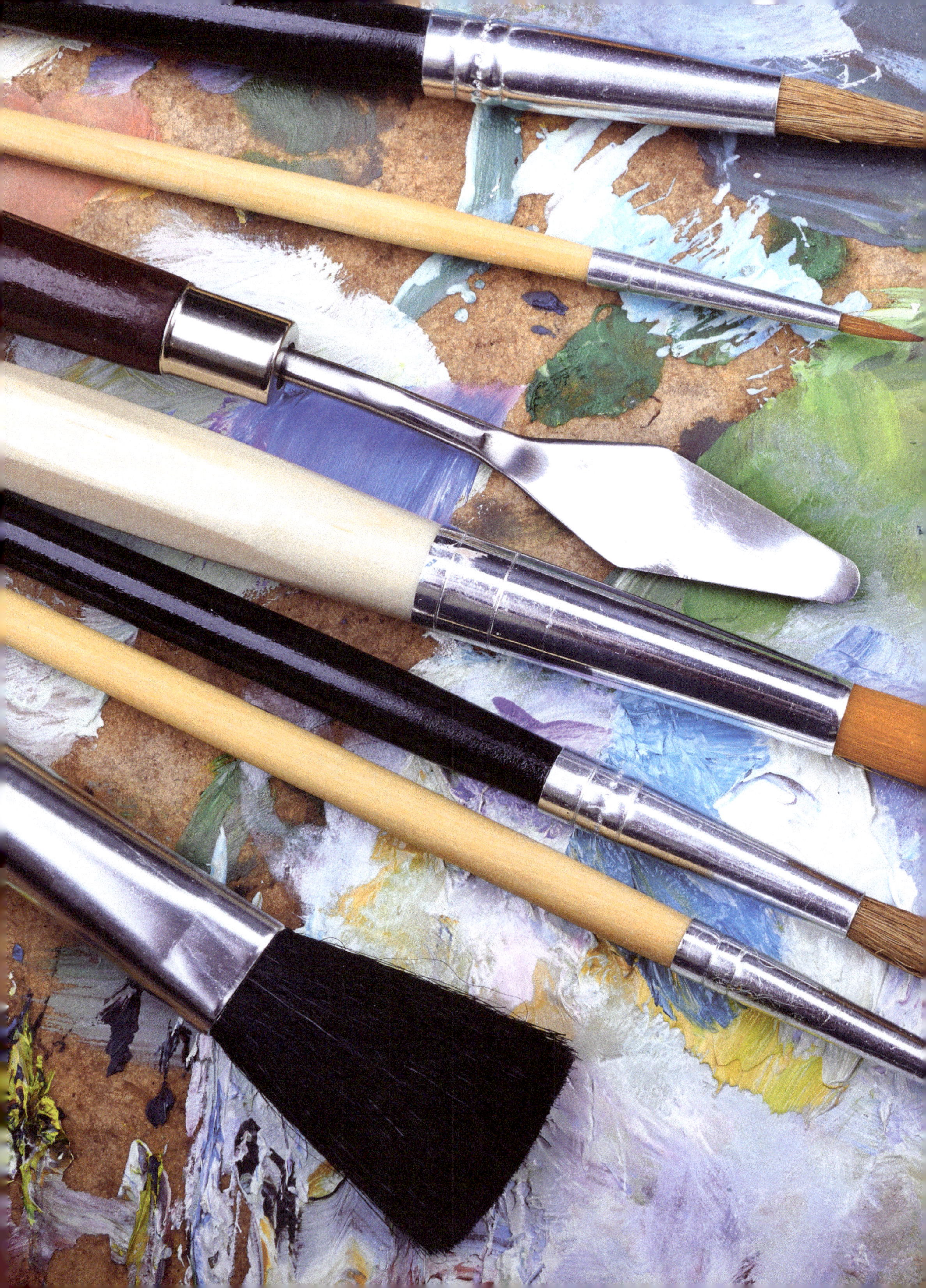

Materials & Supplies

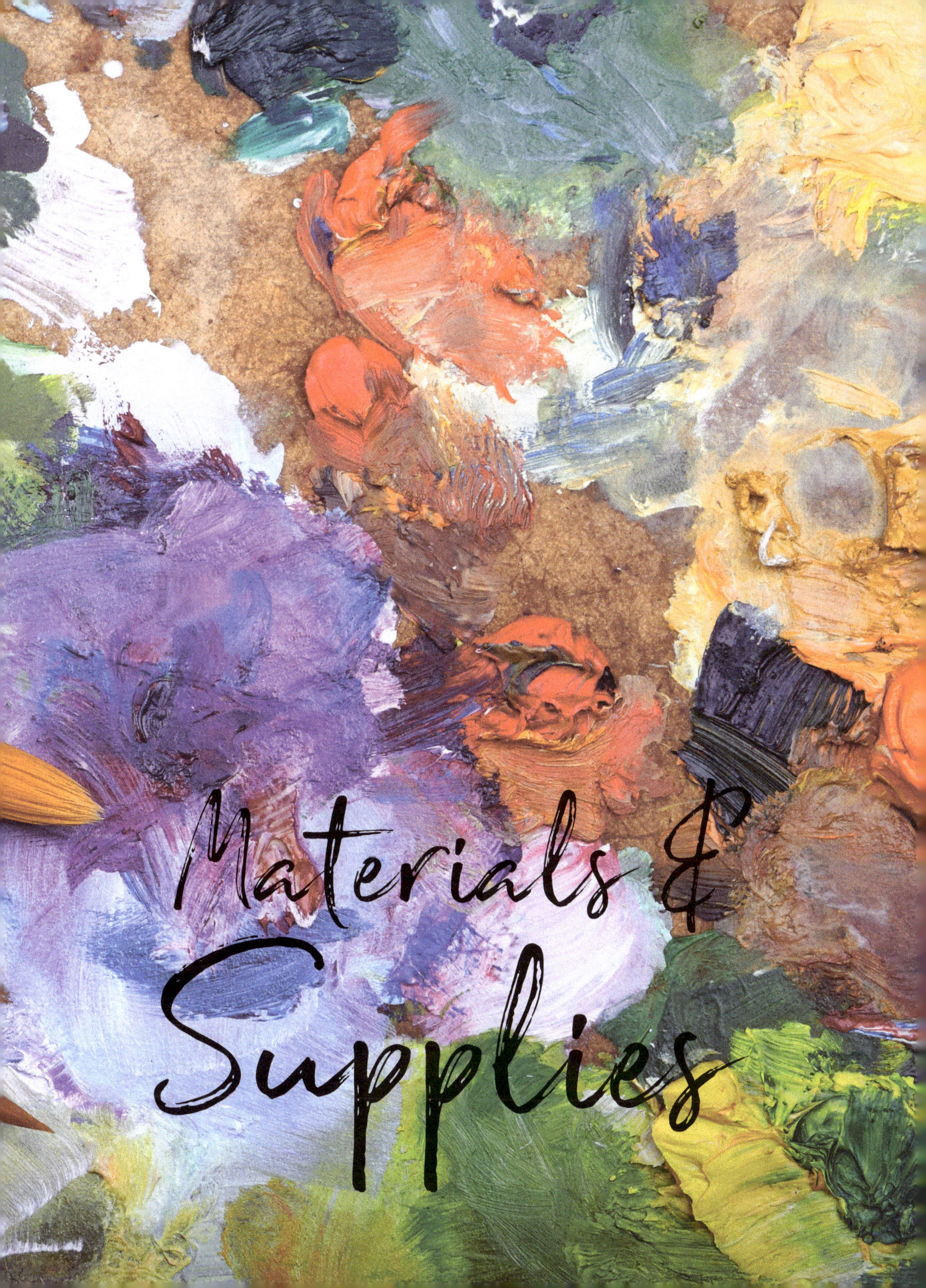

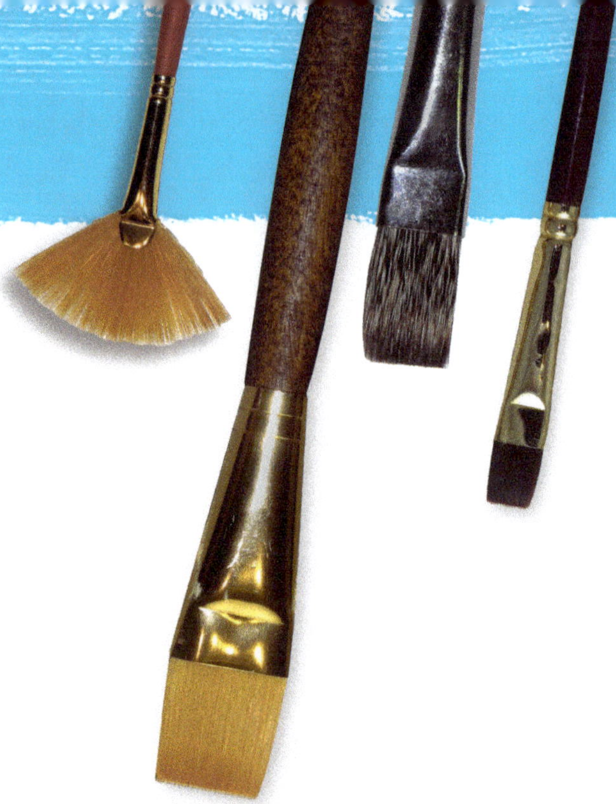

Brushes

A wide range of brush types and sizes is available. Choosing the right brush for the right task makes a difference in your painting experience. Remember that skimping on brush quality can leave unintended marks from frayed, unwieldy bristles or stray hairs that get stuck in the painting.

Brushes come in three basic hair types: soft natural-hair, soft synthetic-hair, and bristle brushes. Choosing the right brush for the right task makes a difference in your painting experience.

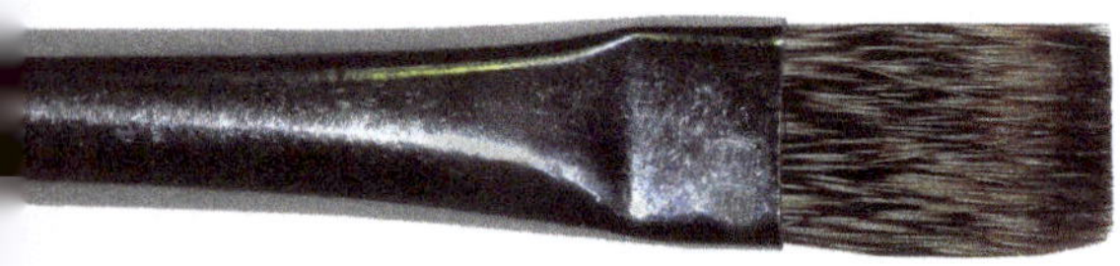

Natural-Hair Brush

Soft natural-hair brushes are made up of the hair of an animal such as a weasel, badger, or squirrel. High-quality naturals hold a good amount of moisture and are an excellent choice for watercolor. Some oil artists use natural-hair brushes for detail work, but most acrylic artists avoid them because they are delicate and damage easily.

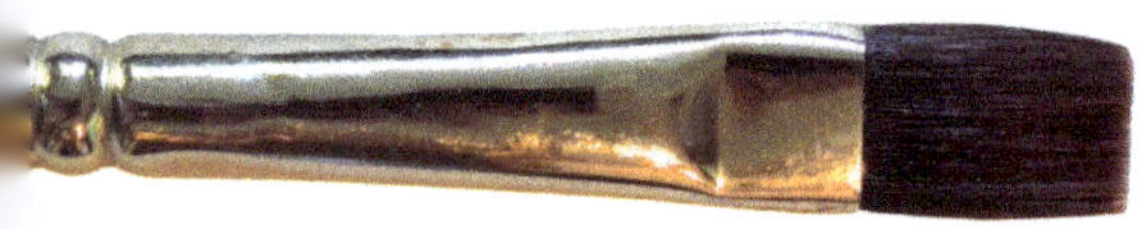

Synthetic-Hair Brush

Soft synthetic-hair brushes are made of man-made fibers such as nylon and polyester filaments. They are ideal for acrylics and serve as an excellent alternative for watercolorists when natural-hair brushes are cost-prohibitive.

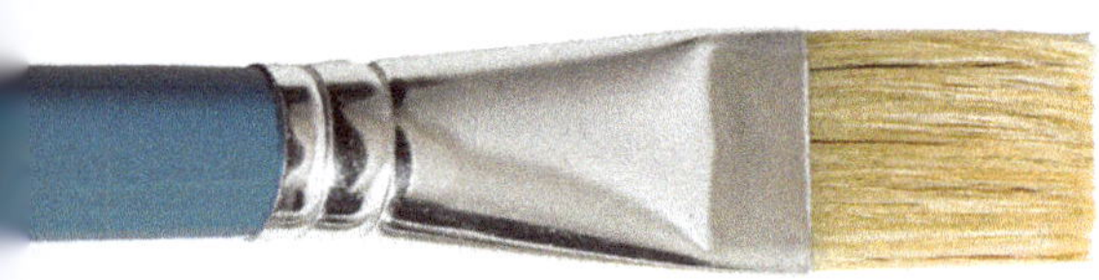

Bristle Brush

Bristle brushes are coarse and sturdy for working with thick oil and acrylic paint. Made of hog hair, they produce visible, painterly brushstrokes.

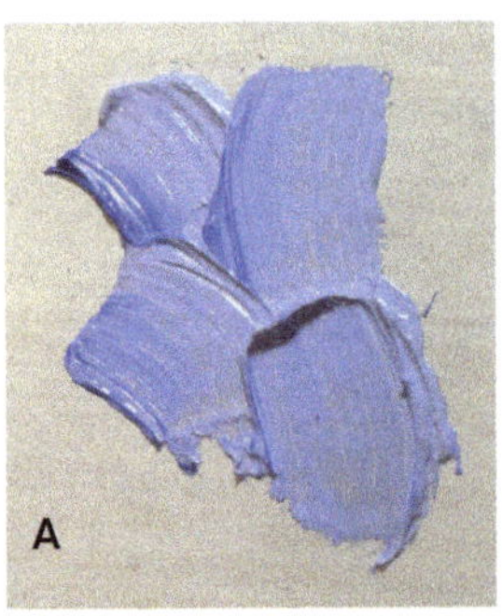

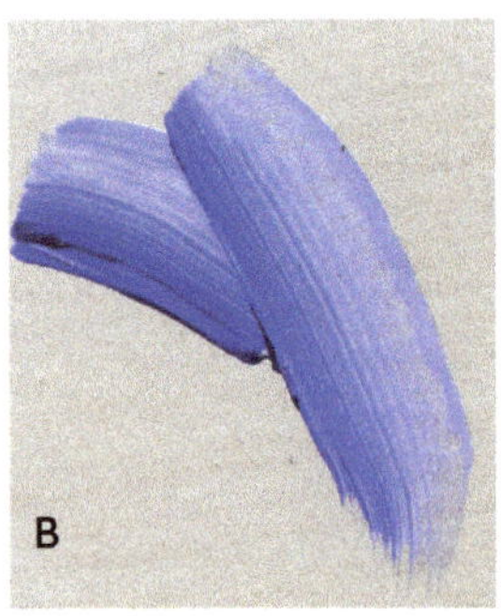

Bristle brushes are ideal for using heavy-bodied paint (A), whereas soft-haired brushes work well for feathery strokes, details, and blending (B).

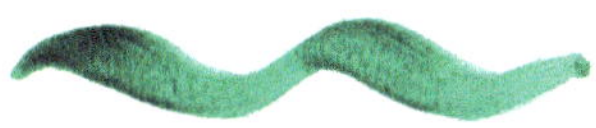

Round brushes have round ferrules and hairs or bristles that taper to a soft point, allowing for varying stoke widths.

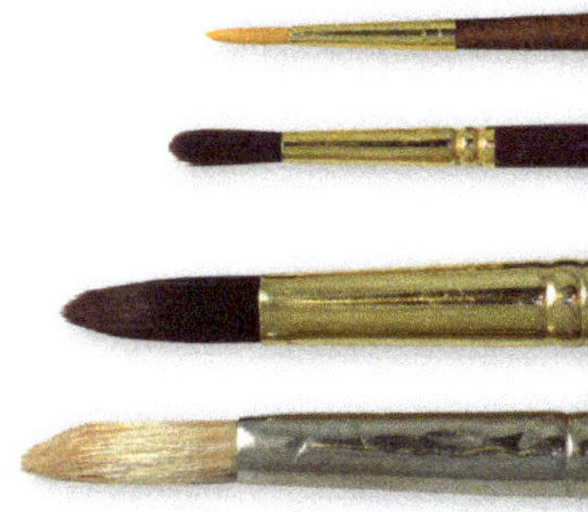

Round Brushes

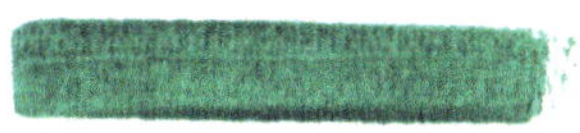

Flat brushes are referred to as "shaders" or "one-stroke" brushes; flats are ideal for creating straight edges.

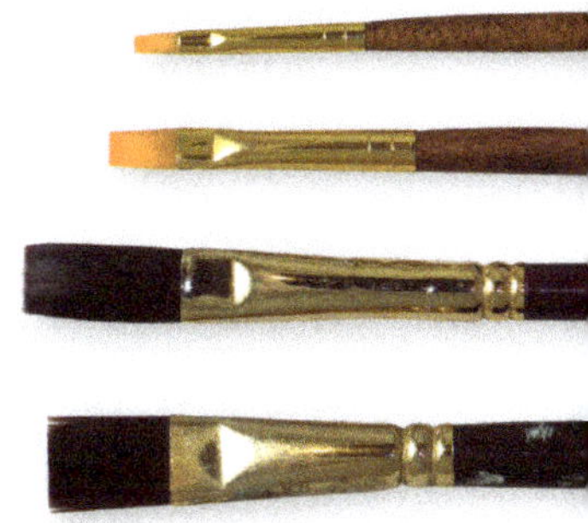

Flat Brushes

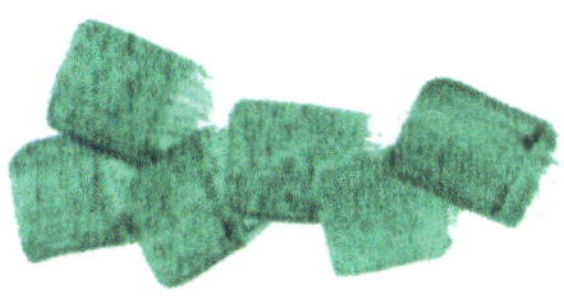

Bright brushes are flat brushes with short bristles or hairs, offering greater control over strokes.

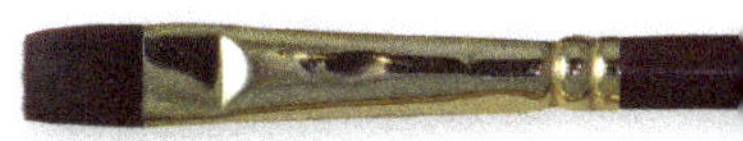

Bright Brush

Wash brushes are wide, flat brushes with soft hairs and a thin edge.

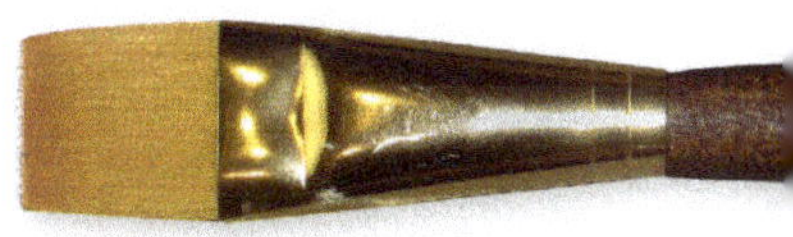

Wash Brush

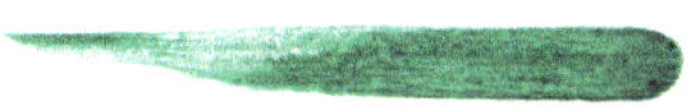

Filbert brushes act as a hybrid of round and flat brushes.

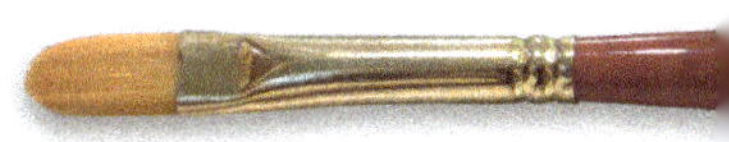

Filbert Brush

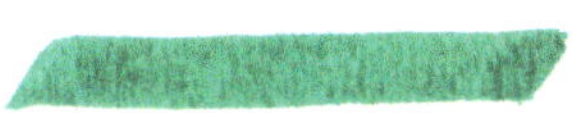

Chisel-Edge brushes are also called "angular" or "slanted"—a chisel-edge brush is a flat brush with bristles or hairs trimmed diagonally.

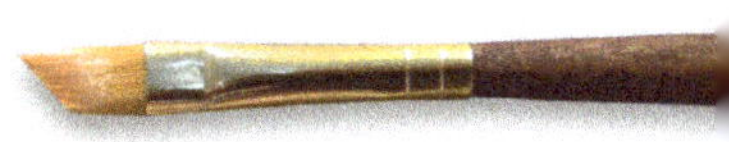

Chisel-Edge Brush

Sketchbooks and Pencils

One item I'm never without is my sketchbook. This is where I test out ideas and make decisions regarding what to include and what to leave out. This is where the simplification process begins—all the shapes are outlined and all the values are assigned (see pages 76–79). It's after this "plan" that I begin to paint.

I've been composing shapes and painting for many years. Now, more than half the time I skip the small value plan. I am experienced enough to see the finished painting and can work toward that vision. When painting on site, my energy level is high and I want to start painting right away, but there have been many times I wish I'd taken the time to plan first. Perhaps that's why I love acrylics so much. I can make a mistake, whether in terms of hue or value, let that mistake dry for a few minutes, and then make a painted correction over the offending area. If you are a novice *plein air* painter, I highly recommend that you create a preliminary value plan before you begin painting. It is time well spent.

Everyone I know who paints outdoors has more than one setup, but everyone is different in terms of materials and intentions. See what works for you. Try different easels and surfaces. Just remember: If you bring it, you have to carry it.

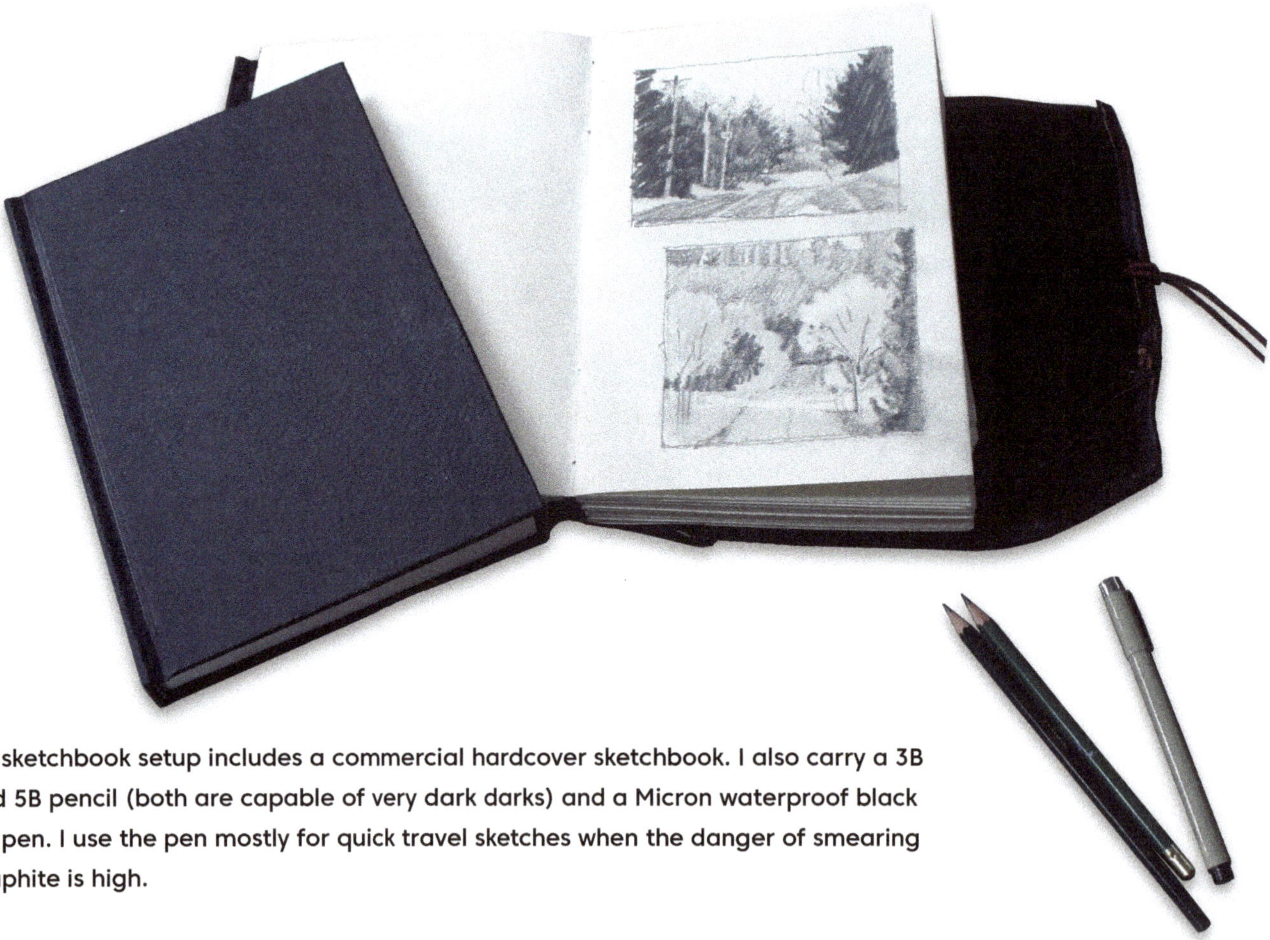

My sketchbook setup includes a commercial hardcover sketchbook. I also carry a 3B and 5B pencil (both are capable of very dark darks) and a Micron waterproof black ink pen. I use the pen mostly for quick travel sketches when the danger of smearing graphite is high.

Brushes with Brush Caddy

I carry all of the brushes shown in the photo below. Do I use them all at any given painting session? No, I do not. Most of the time, I start and complete a *plein air* painting with one brush. A lot depends on how much time I have and how many small shapes or details I want to include.

The three nylon flat brushes shown diagonally are short-handled flats. They are wonderful brushes for pushing acrylic paint. I am rough on brushes, but I have yet to wear out one of these. I always clean them properly after every painting session.

I also carry two pencils separate from those I carry with my sketchbook. More than half the time, I begin a painting by drawing with diluted paint, outlining all the large shapes. Occasionally, I find it necessary to use a graphite pencil (5B) to delineate more of the smaller shapes. This darker pencil shows up well against a light or white background. Sometimes I use a white water-soluble pencil, which shows up well against a darker background. The water-soluble lines disappear when touched with a loaded brush.

Brush cases are available through most art-supply companies. I also carry four brushes dedicated to watercolor: two round Perla by Escoda brushes in sizes 8 and 12 and two Series 995 nylon flats by Winsor & Newton. There are also a couple of smaller brushes used for details and a triangular palette knife that I occasionally use for line work or added texture.

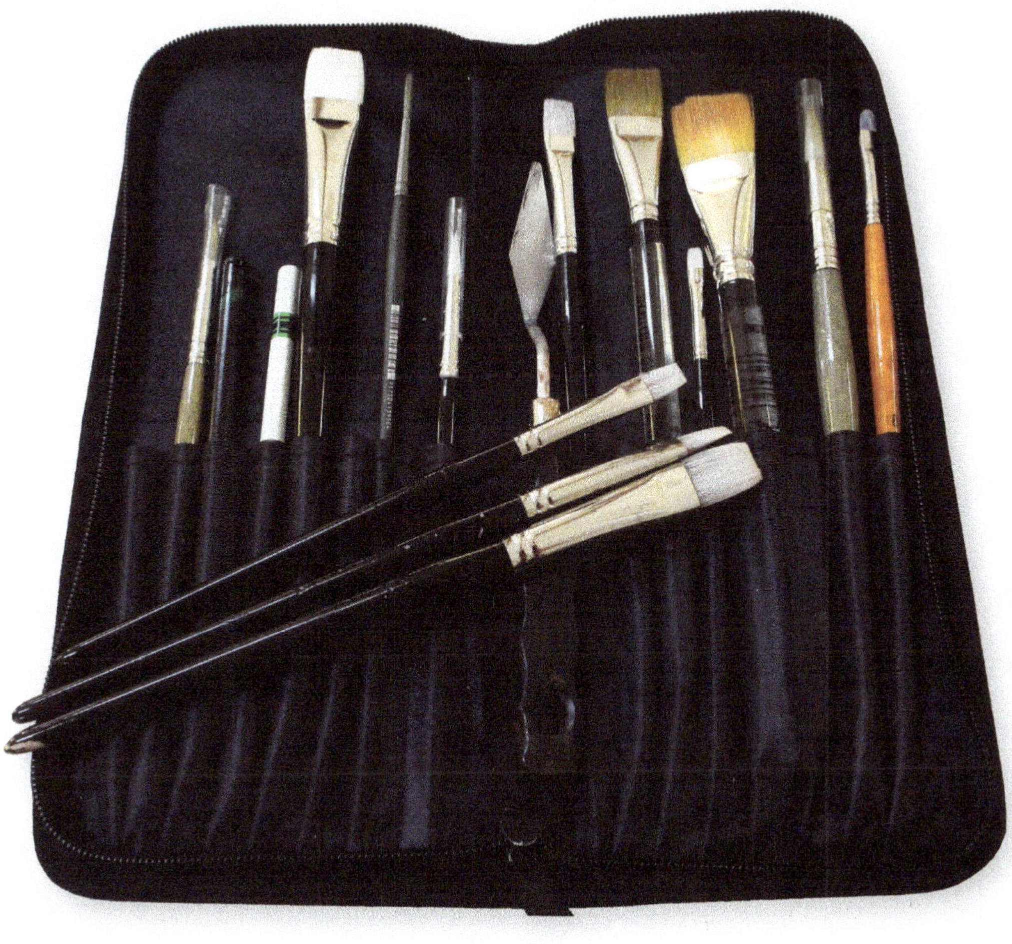

Palette

Acrylics dry fast—I love this for painting. I do not love that they dry fast on my palette. To counteract this, I use a palette that contains a sponge and a tight-fitting cover. When the sponge is moistened and covered with palette paper, it will keep the acrylic pigments wet for more than one painting session.

The gray paper under the palette is a specially made palette paper toned a neutral gray. This paper is placed on top of the moistened sponge, and when you mix a color, this gray-toned paper makes it easier to discern both its hue and value.

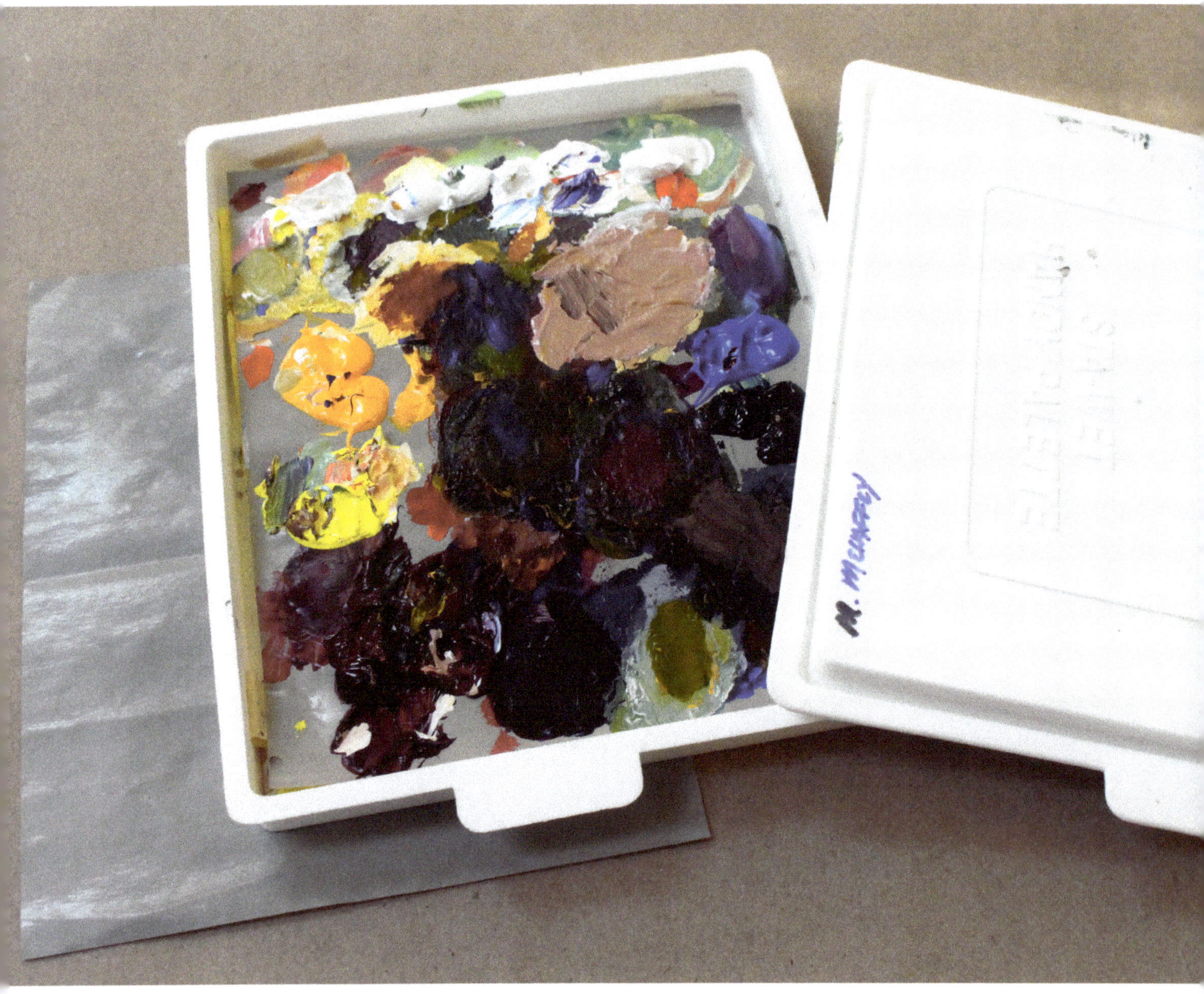

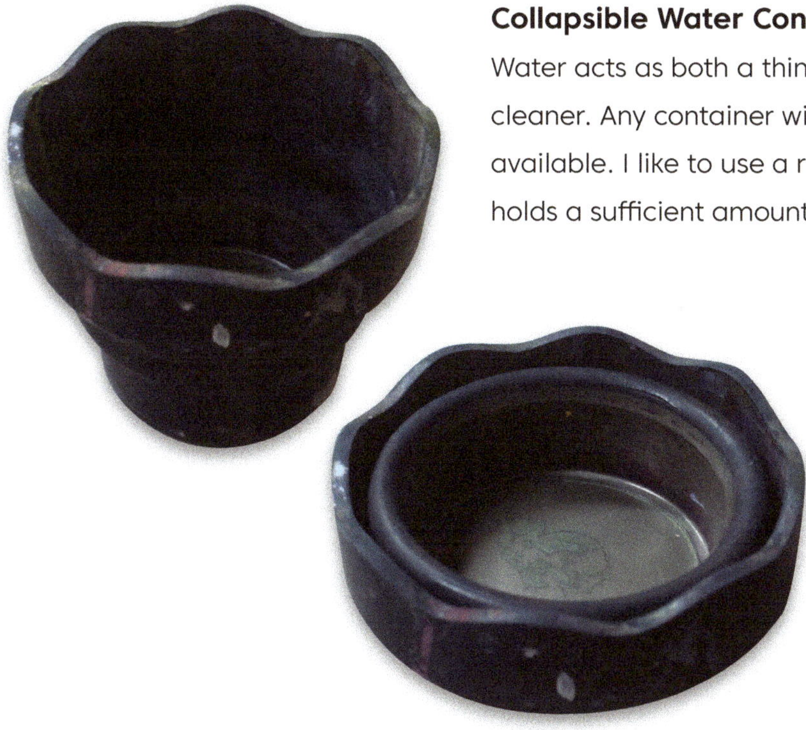

Collapsible Water Container

Water acts as both a thinner for your acrylic paints and a brush cleaner. Any container will work, and there are many varieties available. I like to use a rubber collapsible water container. It holds a sufficient amount of water and is easy to pack.

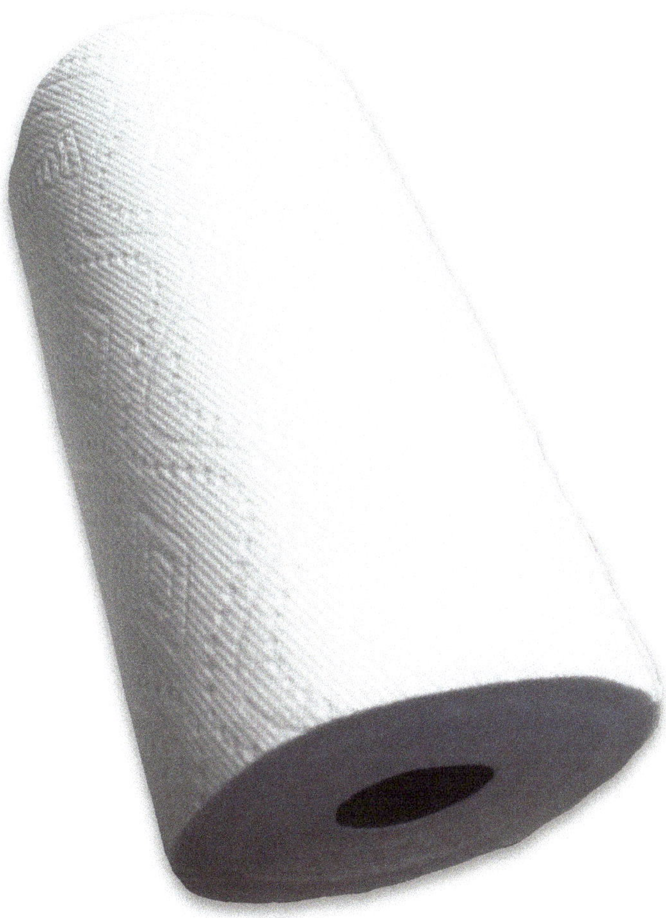

Paper Towels

I use paper towels both in the studio and in the field. A full roll is fine to carry in your vehicle but is too large to carry in your bag. I usually just tuck five or six sheets into my bag for a painting session.

The Minimalist Approach

There may be occasions when you want to paint outside, but you either don't have much time or you don't feel like carrying all your usual tools and supplies. For me, it's usually a matter of time or place. There are occasions when I only have an hour to paint, but I still go for it. Also, when packing for a trip that requires flying, I sometimes greatly reduce the painting supplies I bring. The flip side of this is the fewer clothes you bring, the more painting stuff you can pack!

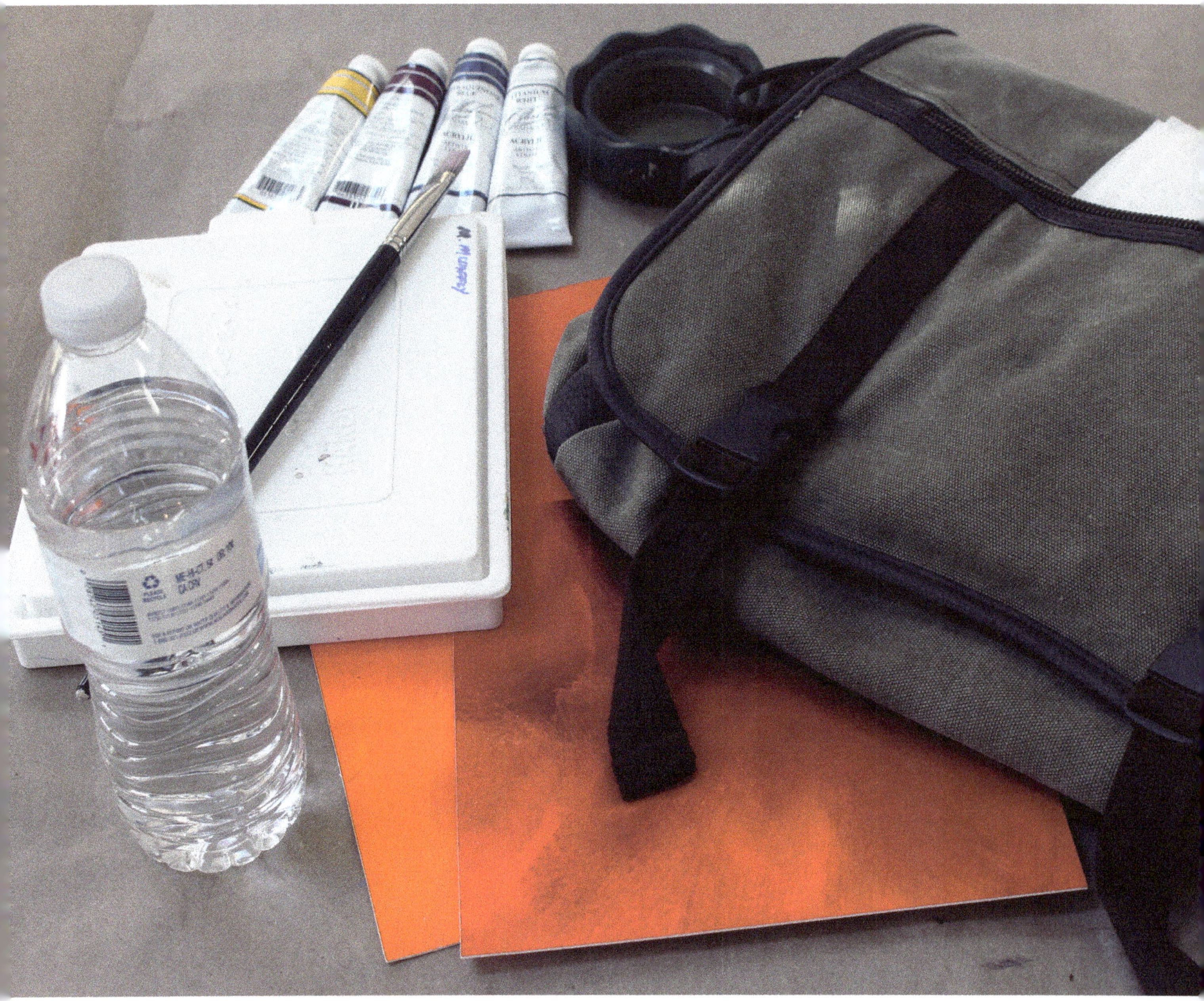

Let's take a look at what I carry for a quick outing. The only thing I've left out of the photo (opposite) is the large plastic bag I use to sit on if the ground is wet. It also forms a barrier between you and whatever bugs might be around. In certain parts of the world, that plastic bag could mean the difference between standing for a few minutes and sitting comfortably for an hour.

- Bottle of water for drinking, mixing paint, and cleaning brushes.
- Size 8 nylon flat brush, which I use both for painting and for the initial outlines. Use the largest brush you can. Although this restricts your ability to paint small shapes, it takes less time to paint only the large shapes.
- My covered stay-wet palette.
- Four tubes of paint. I only bring the three primary colors plus white. In this case, it's gamboge (warm yellow), alizarin crimson (cool red), anthraquinone blue (cool, similar to phthalo blue but darker), and titanium white. I can make browns and neutrals by mixing all three primaries. I can make a very dark mix with anthraquinone blue and alizarin. There may be some compromise in terms of how saturated (bright) your secondary mixtures may be, but remember, you don't have much time!
- A collapsible water container.
- Two painting panels made with 300-pound, rough watercolor paper (lighter in weight than almost any wood or fiber panel). I prepaint these with my favored cadmium red light base coat.
- A bag or pack large enough to carry everything. I use a messenger bag. Notice the paper towels sticking out of the front pocket. Don't forget them!

Umbrella

I prefer using the stake-in-the-ground style of umbrella rather than those that attach to the easel. I've tried both. The latter folds up and is easier to carry, but there are times it will not stay in place or is not large enough to shade both me and my painting. And if a gust of wind is strong enough to grab and toss your umbrella, it will also take your easel, your supplies, and your painting with it. A staked umbrella is larger, sits higher, and is easily angled to block the light—and it won't take your painting and supplies with it if it blows away.

The drawback of a larger umbrella is that it is another large piece of equipment to carry. If I'm traveling to a location where I can paint out of the back of my vehicle, I take the umbrella. If I have to hike any distance to paint, I leave the umbrella behind.

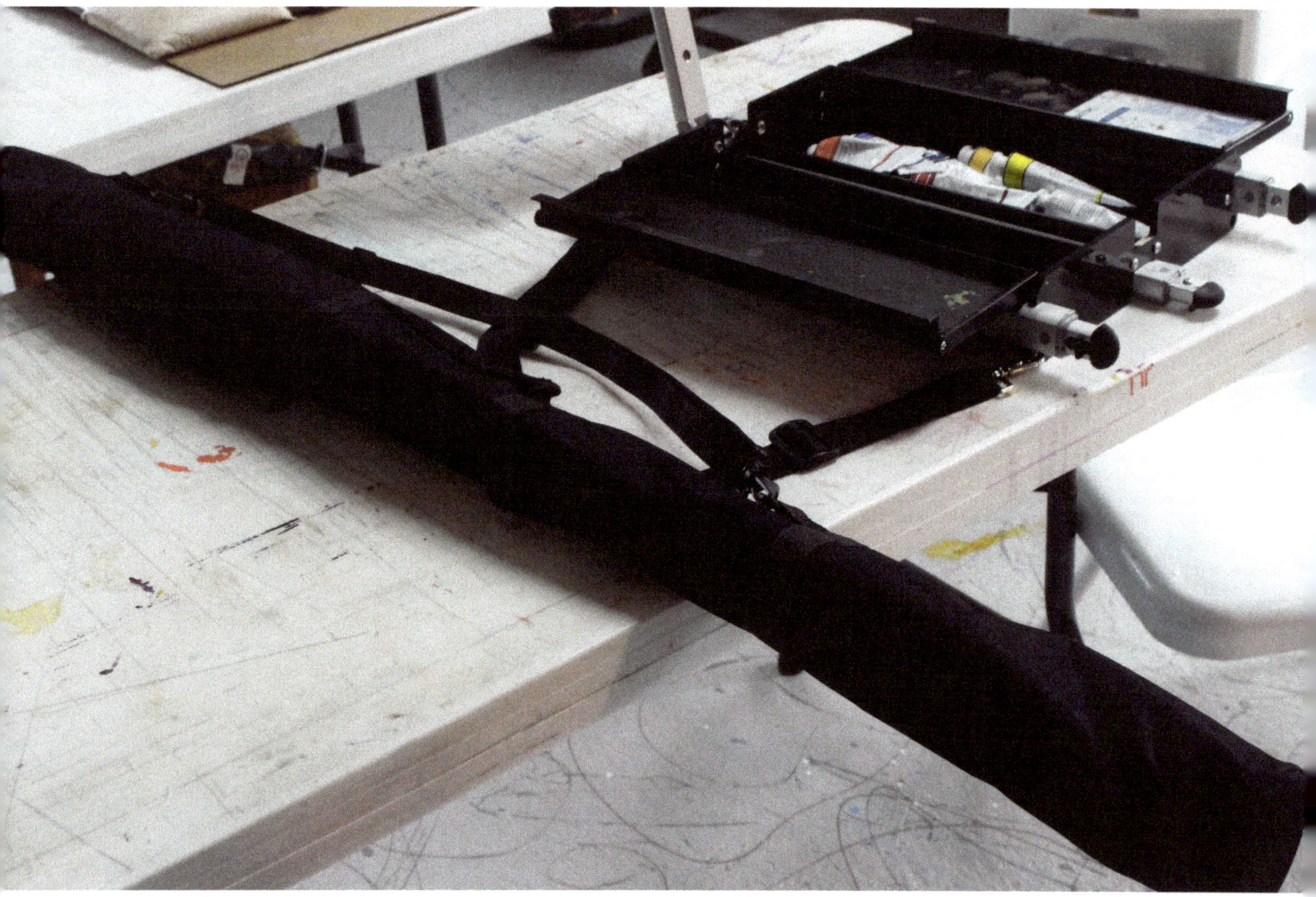

The umbrella I use is about 3 feet long and adds a considerable amount of weight to a supply load, but it provides ample shade for me and my work.

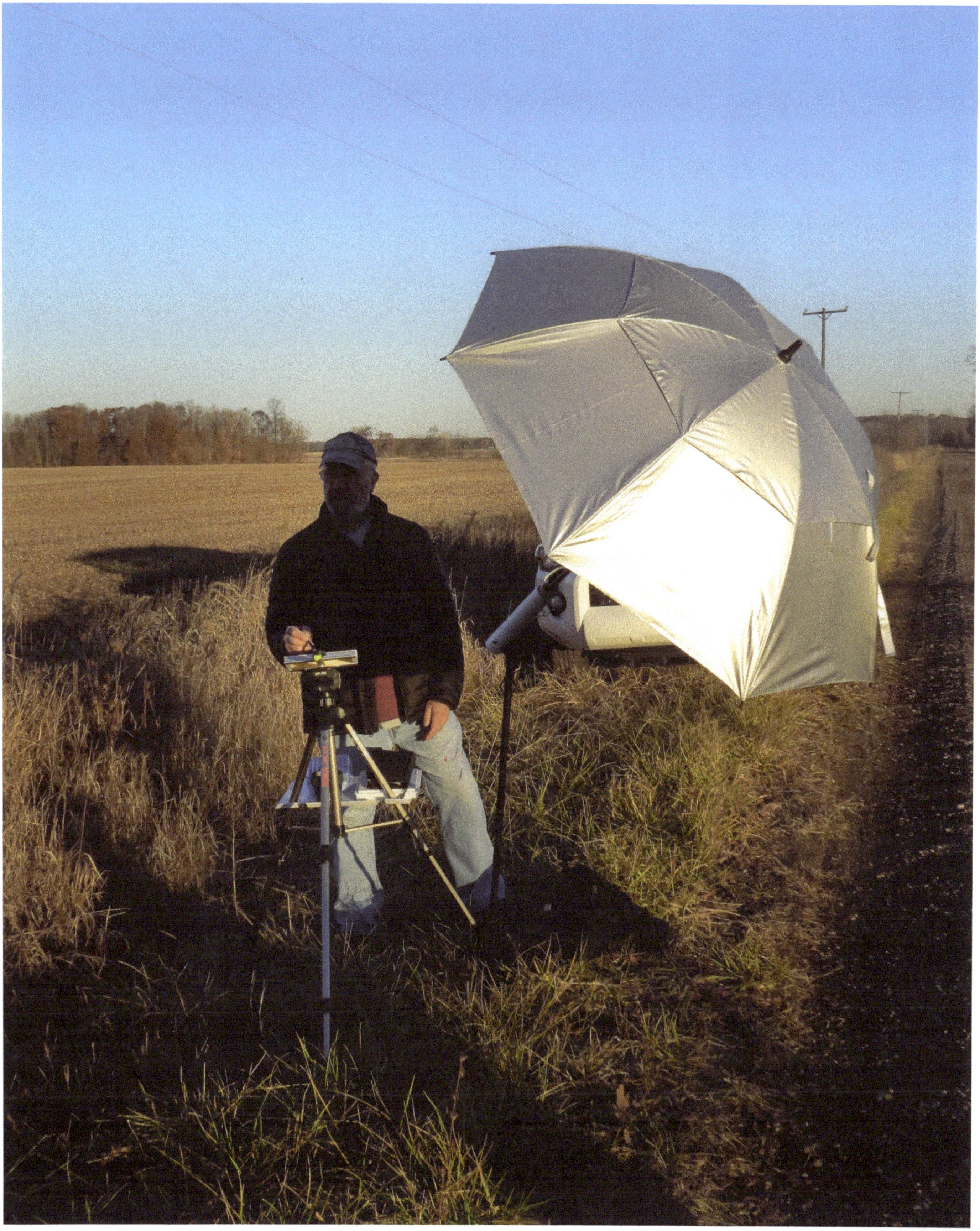

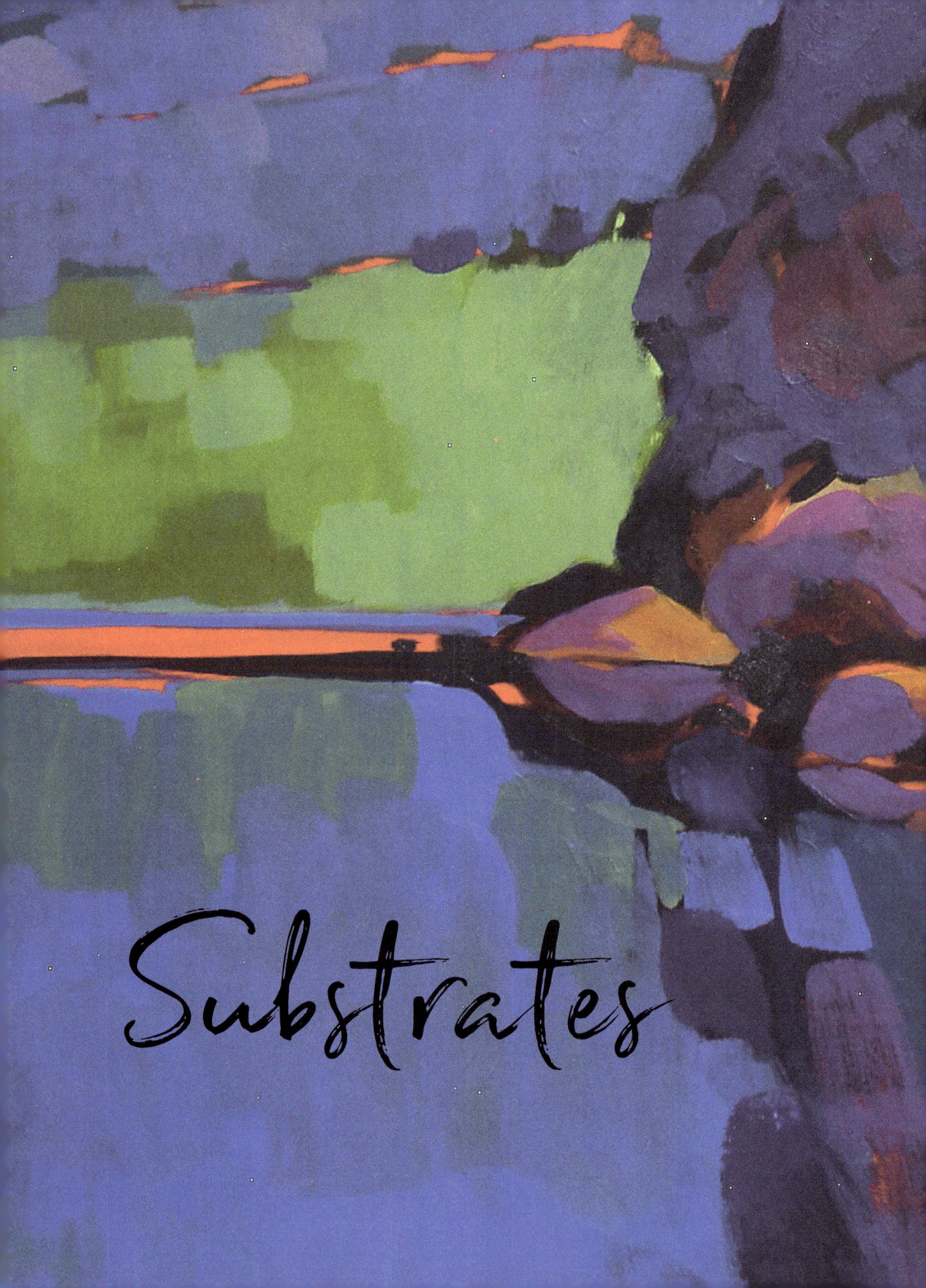

Substrates

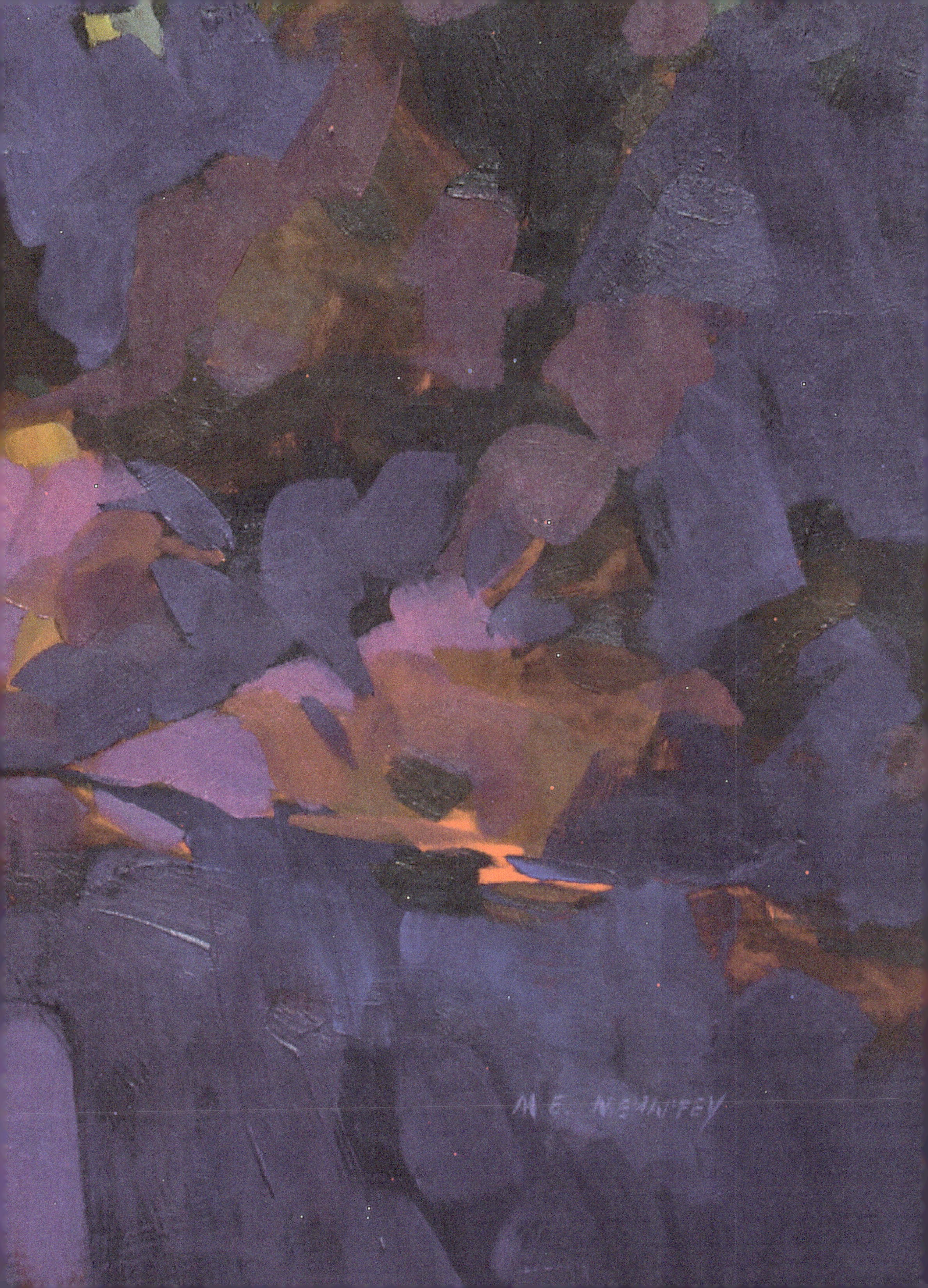

Surfaces

The list of surfaces we can paint on is long and varied. You can use just about any archival surface that accepts paint. Unlike oil paint, acrylic does not contain walnut, safflower, or linseed oils as part of their mixture. (These oils can also be detrimental to some surfaces.) While it is recommended that your painting surface be sealed (ideally with acrylic gesso), it is not absolutely necessary. Let's take a look at some of the substrates, or surfaces, that I paint on. This list is not all-inclusive—my chosen surface often depends on both the day and what I can find for a good price!

Paper

300-pound, rough watercolor paper: I like the rough surface of watercolor paper and enjoy incorporating texture into my work. I usually prepare the paper with two coats of gesso or a heavy coat of cadmium red light paint. I generally reserve this surface for when I travel. The paper is lightweight and takes up little room.

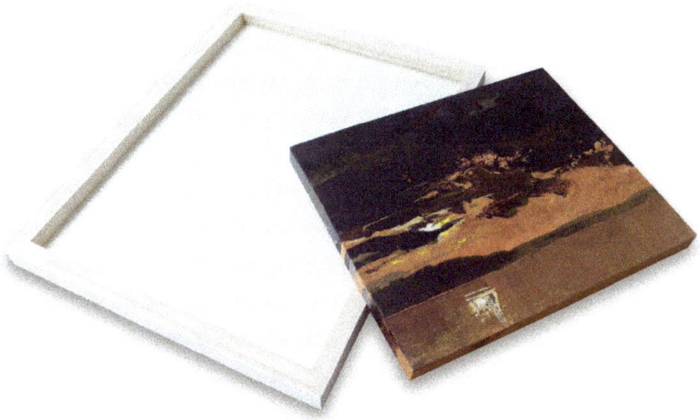

Board, Panel & Wood

Medium density fiber board: I buy fiber board from my local hardware store and have them cut it to size. I use this surface to create some added texture by applying my own coatings of acrylic gesso. Sometimes I'll cover it with white acrylic gesso, and then cover that with another color to prepare the surface.

MDF board covered with a fine-weave cotton canvas: This is a commercially available surface that comes pre-gessoed. The cotton weave can be covered with thick applications of paint or allowed to show through thinner applications. It's ready to go right from the package, saving prep time.

Hardboard: Commercial hardboard (below right) is stable and does not warp, but it is quite heavy. Hardboard can be purchased cradled with wood or as thinner uncradled boards, and it can be bought coated or uncoated. The board in the middle came pre-gessoed with a warm gray tone. It is also available in cool gray and white. Commercial hardboard comes in a variety of surfaces and is precoated. You can also buy it untreated, but I almost always coat it with white acrylic gesso; then apply a colored acrylic as a base coat.

Wood panels: Wood panels usually come with either tung wood or birchwood surfaces. Both of these need to be protected with gesso. You can buy panels pre-gessoed or gesso them yourself. The back of the panel (above) features a glued frame; this provides rigidity. The rigid surface is the one main difference between a wood panel and stretched canvas. Canvas gives and pushes back against your brush, whereas a wood panel does not. If you are a very aggressive painter or you scrub or scumble often, you may prefer this surface. Wood works best with palette-knife painting. Wood is often more expensive than canvas or paper and is usually not available in very large sizes.

Page 22, *Carmel River*

Substrates

Canvas & Linen

Canvas: Cotton canvas has been used as a support for centuries. Cotton fibers will, after a very long time, begin to deteriorate, so it's necessary to coat the fibers with something that will preserve the cotton. I use acrylic gesso. It's readily available and does not require any special handling. A lot of painters buy prepared (pre-gessoed) canvas.

I've wrapped the completed acrylic painting (above) around the edge of the canvas. Wrapping the painting around the canvas allows you to display it without a frame. Commercially prepared stretched canvas usually comes in two widths: ¾-inch and 1½-inch (or sometimes 2-inch) widths. The ¾-inch size costs a bit less.

Stretched canvas: If you search, you can usually find a package deal on stretched canvas. The downside is that it is somewhat thicker—about half to three-quarters of an inch—and occasionally the canvas will bow or buckle. The canvas keys that come with them usually take care of this issue. You also can stretch and gesso your own canvas, but this takes time.

Stretched linen: Some artists paint on stretched or mounted linen. You can find a very fine weave, but there are times when I want to either make my own textural surface or I want a completely smooth surface. Linen is also a bit more expensive than canvas and most other panels.

Commercially prepared canvas: Stretched canvas often comes ready to paint on. You can also buy untreated canvas and add your own gesso. I sometimes add a heavy layer of gesso and then texture with brushstrokes. This adds some underlying textural interest and gives added character to the piece.

Toned Substrates

Preapplying a color to your panel sets a tone for the painting. My two favorite base coats are cadmium red light and white. I do sometimes tone using a middle value (neutral, warm, or cool gray), and occasionally, I also use yellow or violet.

Using a middle-value ground color, such as cadmium red light, tells me if a stroke of paint is lighter or darker than a mid-tone. This helps me arrange and use values in a more effective fashion. In addition, cadmium red light is a warm color. If my painting is to have a warm dominance, I can leave more of the cadmium red light showing, which helps warm up the whole painting. If my painting is to have a cool dominance, I can cover most of the cadmium and leave just a small amount showing to contrast against the cool colors.

Many painters begin on a white gessoed panel and then tone it back with a wash to subdue the white surface. I sometimes do this. Sometimes I just outline my big shapes and paint right on the white, knowing that as the painting progresses, most of the white will be covered. And sometimes I leave some of the white showing.

Experiment with your underpaintings to see what works for you. I use red, white, gray, yellow, and violet often enough to know what to expect. I have learned my preferences from repetition. I like a warm or cool gray on overcast, cloudy days. I can leave some of the gray showing, and that helps me to create the feeling of clouds on a moody day.

Yellow is warm and often lighter than a mid-tone. I usually reserve yellow for sunny, bright days and allow quite a bit of yellow to show through. This also helps bias the painting toward a warm dominance. Temperature dominance provides unity in the work.

Page 28, *Light From the Right*

Working with Acrylic

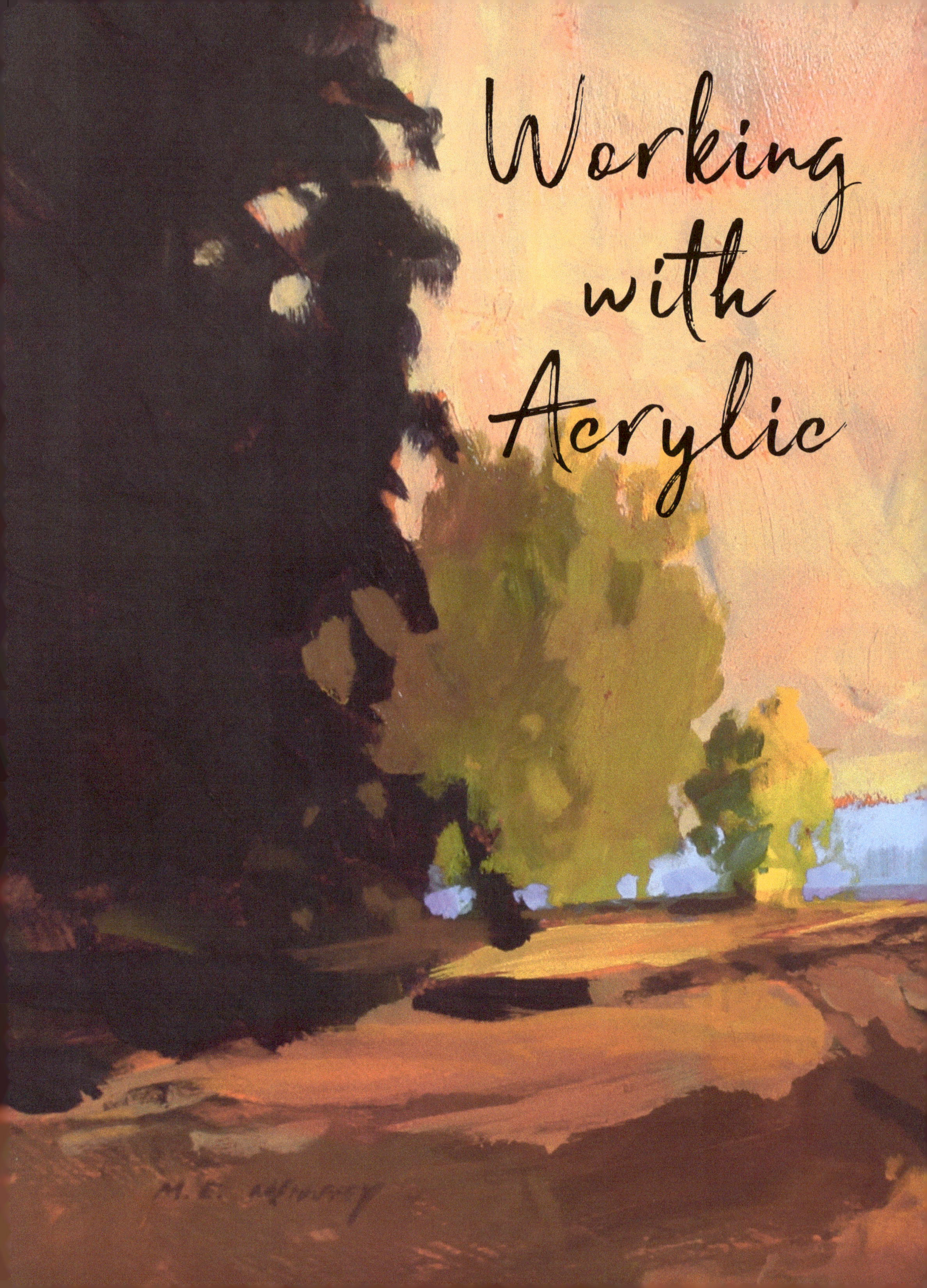

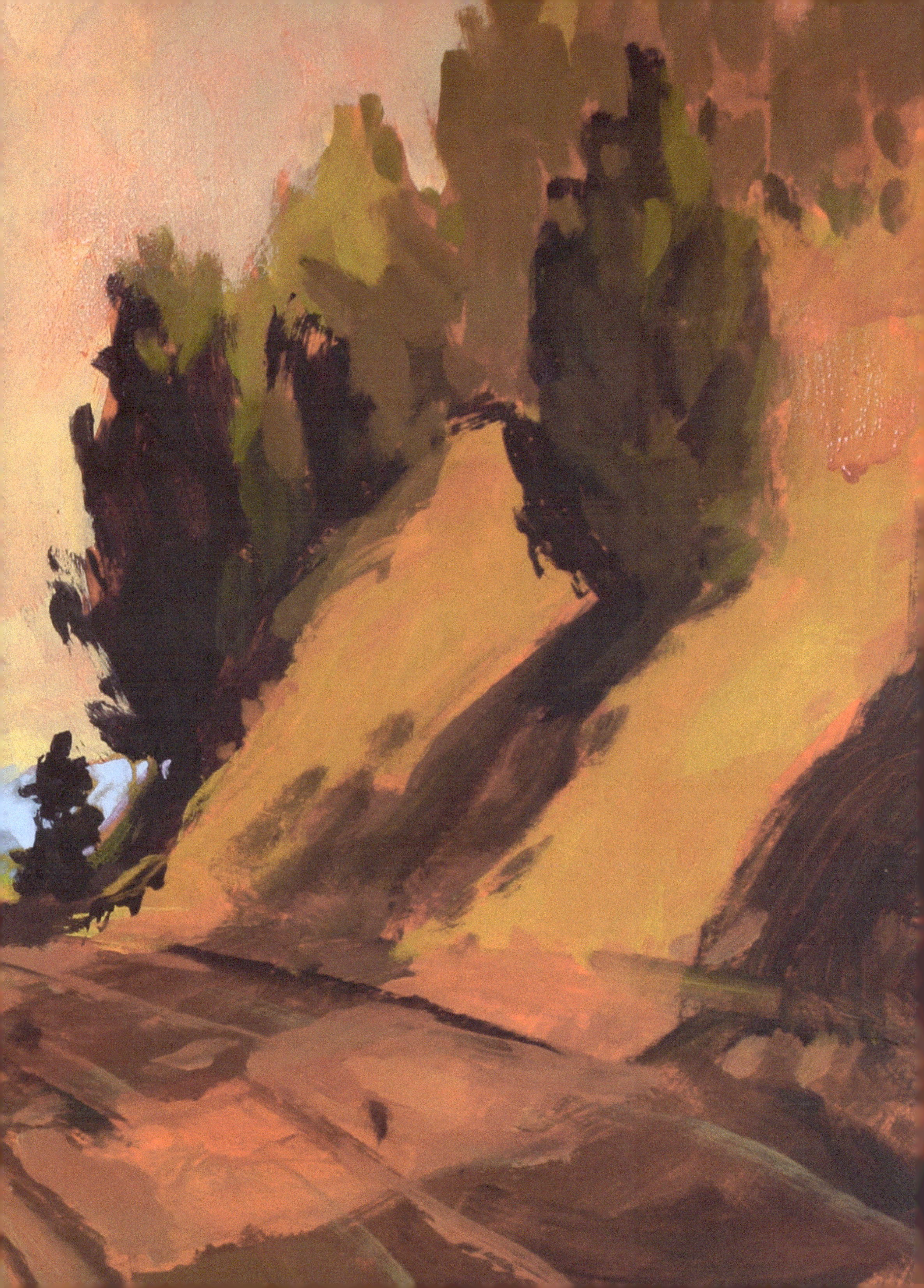

Color Theory

Acquaint yourself with the ideas and terms of color theory, which involve everything from color relationships to perceived color temperature and color psychology. In the following pages, we will touch on the basics as they relate to painting.

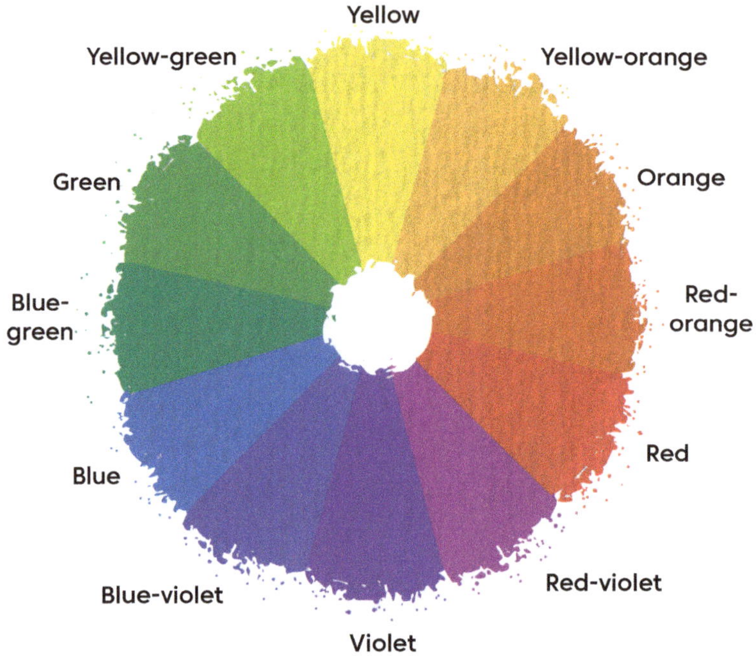

Color Wheel

The color wheel, pictured to the right, is the most useful tool for understanding color relationships. Where the colors lie relative to one another can help you group harmonious colors and pair contrasting colors to communicate mood or emphasize your message. The wheel can also help you mix colors efficiently. Below are the most important terms related to the wheel.

Primary colors are red, blue, and yellow. With these you can mix almost any other color; however, none of the primaries can be mixed from other colors. Secondary colors include green, orange, and violet. These colors can be mixed using two of the primaries. (Blue and yellow make green, red and yellow make orange, and blue and red make violet.) A tertiary color is a primary mixed with a near secondary, such as red with violet to create red-violet.

COMPLEMENTARY COLORS are those situated opposite each other on the wheel, such as purple and yellow. Complements provide maximum color contrast.

ANALOGOUS COLORS are groups of colors adjacent to one another on the color wheel, such as blue-green, green, and yellow-green. When used together, they create a sense of harmony.

A hue is a color in its purest form (A), a color plus white is a tint (B), a color plus gray is a tone (C), and a color plus black is a shade (D).

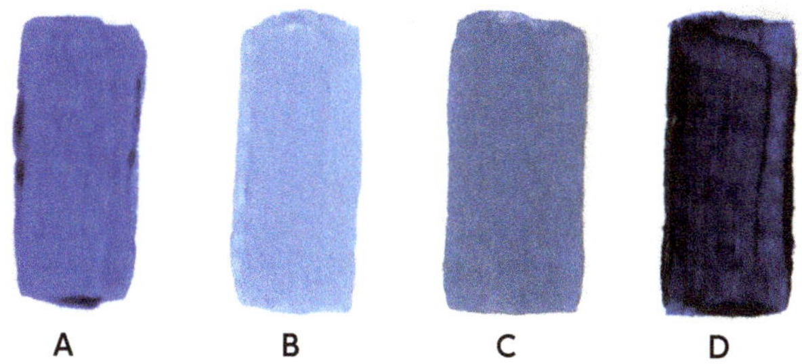

A single color family, such as blue, encompasses a range of hues—from yellow-leaning to red-leaning.

Color & Value

Within each hue, you can achieve a range of values—from dark shades to light tints. However, each hue has a value relative to others on the color wheel. For example, yellow is the lightest color and violet is the darkest. To see this clearly, view the color wheel in grayscale (a photograph or scan of a color wheel that has been changed using computer-editing software). It is also very helpful to create a grayscale chart of all the paints in your palette so you know how their values relate to one another.

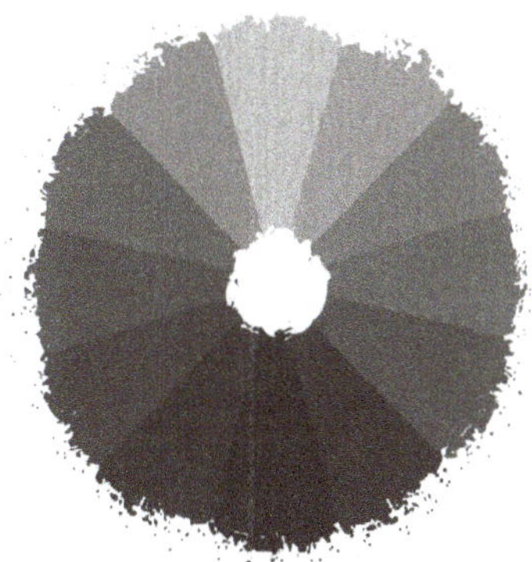

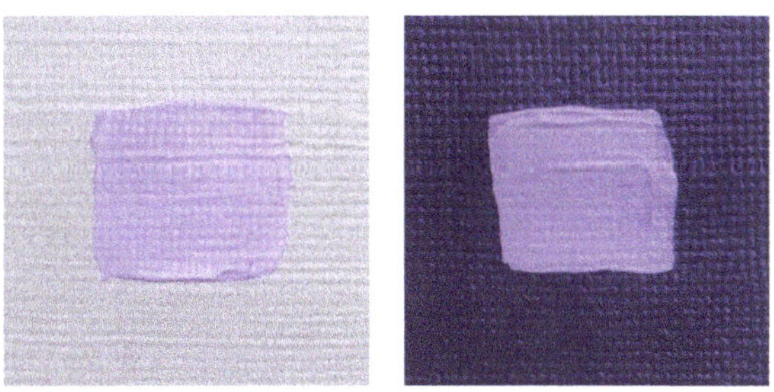

Value Relativity

Values are perceived relative to others in the same scene. A color may appear dark against a white surface or light tint, but the same color may appear light against a dark surface. Above are middle-value strokes of purple over light and dark backgrounds. The same value can appear very different depending on its surroundings.

Color Temperature

Color temperature refers to the feeling one gets when viewing a color or set of colors. Generally, yellows, oranges, and reds are considered warm, whereas greens, blues, and purples are considered cool. When used within a work of art, warm colors seem to advance toward the viewer, and cool colors appear to recede into the distance. This dynamic is important to remember when suggesting depth or creating an area of focus. For more about color temperature, turn to page 97.

Types of Acrylic

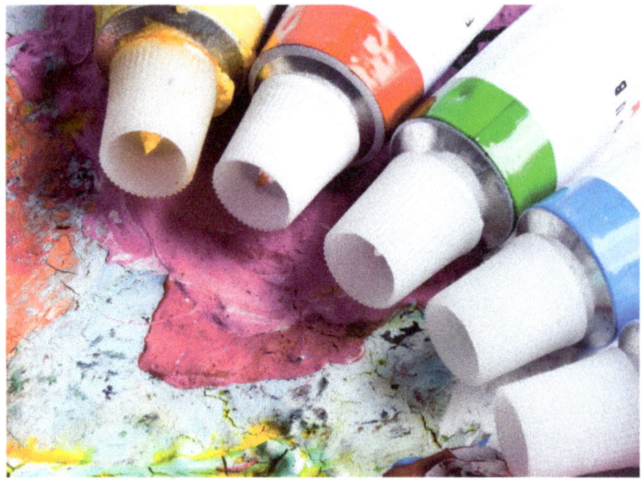

Acrylic is a unique medium with unparalleled versatility. While it has its own look and feel, it also beautifully mimics other media, such as watercolor, oil, and even pastel. Acrylic paint dries quickly like watercolor but is as permanent as oil and as vibrant as pastel. You can thin acrylic paint with water to create luminous washes, or you can use it straight from the tube to build up thick layers. And because acrylics are water-based, cleanup is simple with soap and water.

Acrylic paint, which is made up of pigment and acrylic polymer, boasts a number of positive qualities that make it a viable competitor to oil and watercolor. First, you can dilute the paint with plain water (no harsh solvents needed), but once it's dry, the paint is waterproof. Second, you can apply the paint in thick or thin layers, imitating either oil or watercolor, respectively. Third, acrylic is resistant to cracking and fading. Fourth, unlike oil, acrylic dries quickly so you don't have to wait long between applying layers.

Acrylic paint comes in tubes, tubs, jars, and squeeze bottles. Tubs and squeeze bottles typically hold thinner paints, whereas traditional tubes contain thicker paint with more body. There are several distinct consistencies (or viscosities) of paint available, from thick and heavily bodied to thin and fluid. Manufacturers also produce paints with sheens that vary depending on the light and your viewing angle.

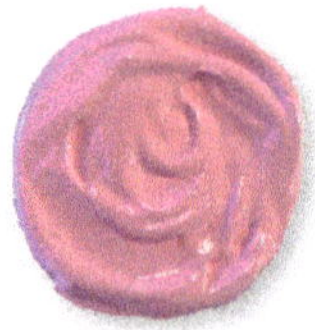

Basic acrylics have less body than oil paint but much more than watercolor washes. The gel-like consistency forms soft peaks and offers a great middle ground for artists who desire more control than fluid paints without the bulk of thick, heavy paints.

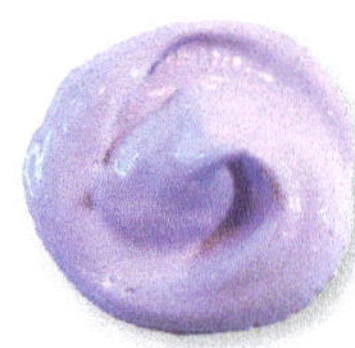

Heavy body acrylics have a high viscosity that retains brushstrokes and allows artists to form stiffer peaks of paint. This thick, buttery paint is a great choice for highly textured work that uses painting knives, coarse brushwork, and impasto techniques.

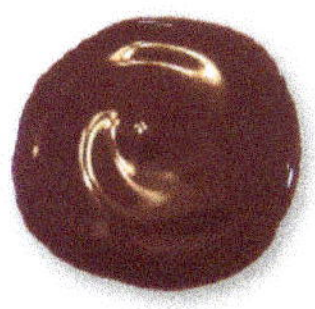

Fluid acrylics have a low viscosity, with a consistency that lies between ink and basic acrylic paint. Fluids settle to a smooth finish and do not retain brushstrokes or peaks. You can achieve wonderful flowing, drippy effects and expressive spattering with this paint.

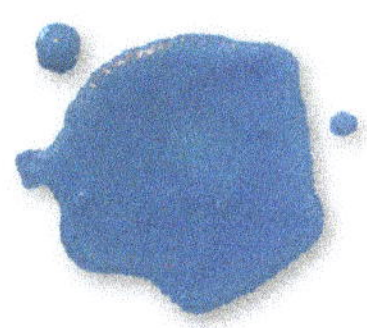

Acrylic inks, also called "liquid acrylics," are the thinnest acrylics available. They work well with watercolor techniques such as spattering and glazing. Because they are waterproof, you don't have to worry about disturbing previous layers once dry.

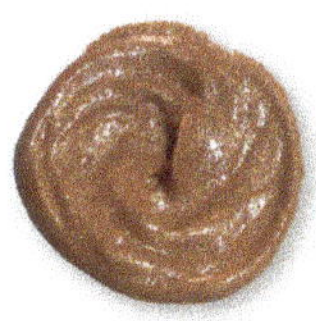

Iridescent acrylics contain mica, which gives them a metallic shimmer. Iridescent paints are very reflective and can provide exciting accents that add depth and variation to a work.

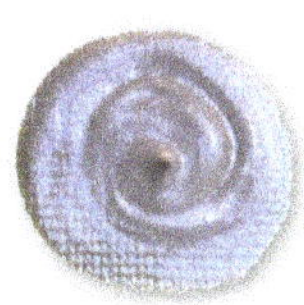

Interference acrylics are transparent paints that, depending on the light and your viewing angle, shift between a bright, reflective sheen and its color's complement. This paint works best mixed with or glazed over black or dark colors.

Acrylic Mediums & Additives

A vast array of acrylic mediums and additives allows you to experiment endlessly with the consistency, sheen, and behavior of your paint. These liquids, gels, and pastes are sure to breathe new life into your painting sessions and encourage creativity. Below are the most common types of additives and mediums, followed by the most common products available to artists today. Note that it's best to add paint to a medium, rather than medium to paint.

Liquid additives change the behavior of paint without adding binder to the mix. Often just a small amount of additive is needed.

Gel mediums are colorless substances made from the same emulsion as acrylic, so they mix into the paint seamlessly. They are excellent tools for extending and diluting paint colors, and you can also use them as collage adhesives. Manufacturers offer them in a range of viscosities and sheens to suit your needs.

Pastes are opaque mediums with fillers that allow for interesting textures. They do not dry clear as gels do, so consider this when using the pastes as a mix-in.

Flow improver is a liquid additive that increases the fluidity of paint by breaking the surface tension. Unlike plain water, flow improver helps preserve the strength of a paint color.

Retarder is a liquid additive that slows the drying time of acrylic paint. Because acrylic paint dries quickly, artists use retarders to extend their working time, minimizing wasted paint on the palette and allowing for more blending on canvas.

Acrylic vs. Oil

There are advantages and disadvantages to any media an artist chooses. Based on my observations, I would guess that the majority of *plein air* painters use oil paint.

Dry Time

Because oil paint takes such a long time to dry, it is necessary to cart along a wet-painting box to store and transport a completed painting. This is a disadvantage. However, one of the advantages of using oils is they take a long time to dry—sometimes the drying time is measured in months. Because of this quality, oil painters have plenty of time in the field to make very smooth transitions between different colors or values.

Acrylics, on the other hand, dry fast. Even the relatively new "slow-drying" acrylics dry to the touch in hours. Compared to oils, this is fast. I prefer the original fast-drying acrylics. My methods and application process have been adjusted to account for the fact that any given passage is dry to the touch within minutes. I love this. It means that I can paint a shape, even a large shape, and if I later realize it was the wrong color or value, all I have to do is wait five minutes for it to dry and then paint the correction. There are times when areas are repainted three or more times in one *plein air* session.

Varnish

Oil paintings should receive a final varnish after drying completely. Sometimes it is necessary to wait weeks before doing so. Acrylics benefit from a final archival varnish, but it is not absolutely necessary. Another plus.

Varnish usually comes in two finishes: matte and gloss. There are times when I want my acrylic painting to have a gloss varnish. It will then look very much like a varnished oil painting. I use a matte finish to seal water-media paintings (watercolor and gouache), and I sometimes use a gloss finish to seal acrylic paintings. If you don't want a shiny, glossy finish, you can combine the two finishes—one over the other—to achieve a satin finish. Make sure you spray outdoors or in a well-ventilated area; inhaling the fumes from any spray can be harmful.

Acrylic paints come in three consistencies:

- **Heavy-bodied acrylic** is the thickest and will hold brushstrokes.
- **Soft-bodied acrylic** will run, and brushstrokes will be minimal.
- **Fluid acrylic,** depending on the manufacturer, will be runny—about the consistency of cream.

Compare these two photos of *Winter Dawn*. This painting is varnished with a gloss finish and is "shiny."

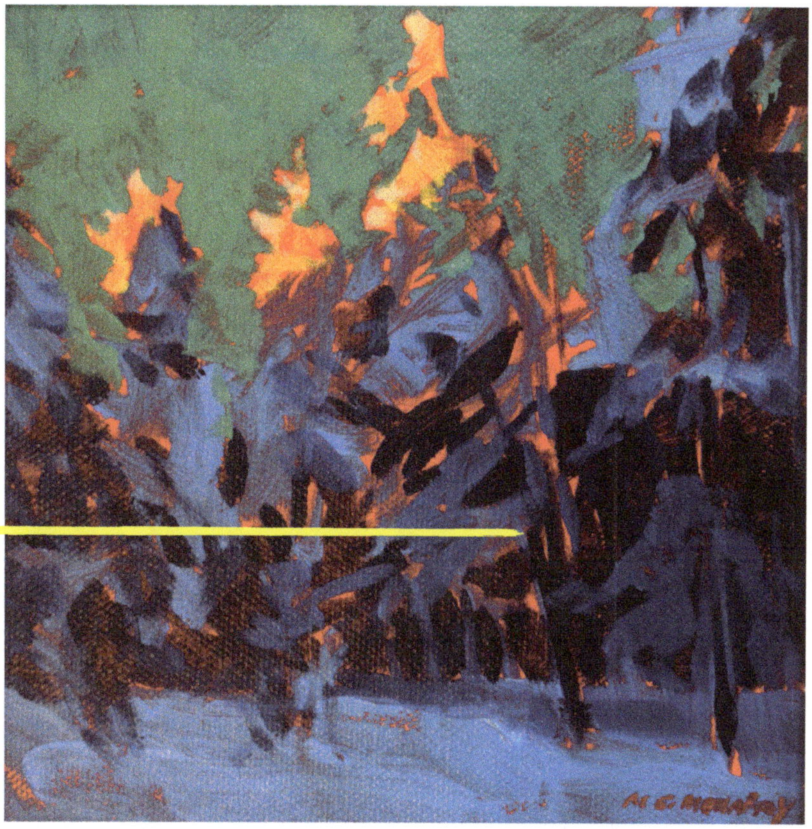

This photo was taken in my studio with no light coming in from the windows. Under these conditions, the gloss finish does not show as well as in the photo below.

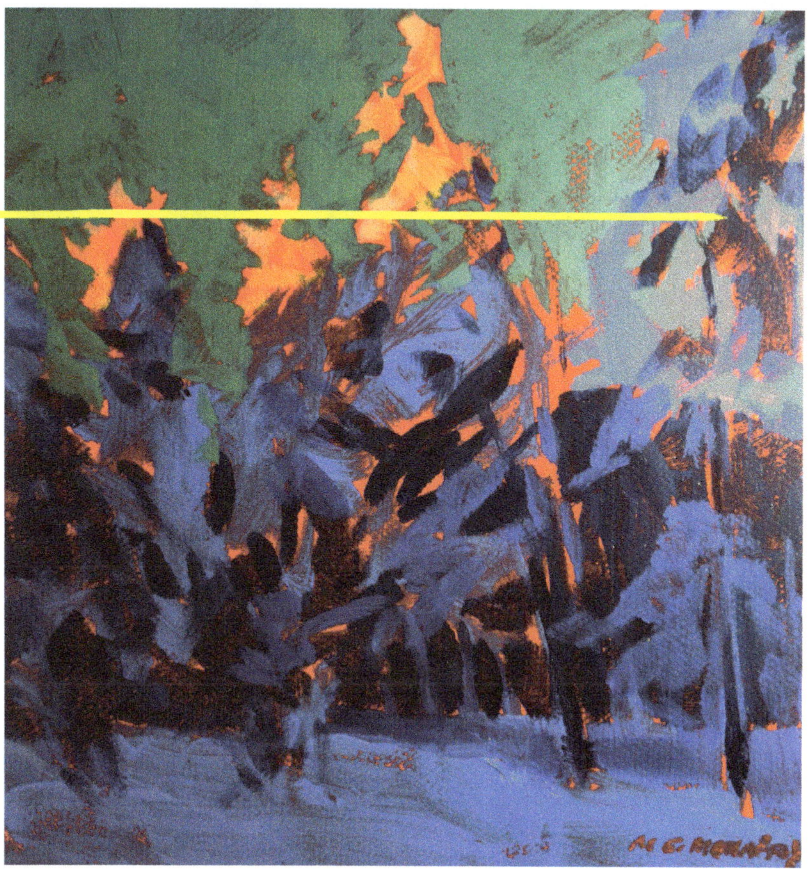

Before I took this photo, I opened the window shades in my studio and let the light stream in from the right. You can see the "shiny" effect produced by a gloss varnish.

Techniques

As noted previously, acrylics come in heavy, soft-bodied, and fluid formulas. You can use the paint straight from the tube, or you can add water or glazing medium to adjust the consistency. The following pages explore a few of the techniques I often use when working with acrylic.

Using Acrylics as Watercolors

The *passage* (meaning brushstroke or area of paint) at right was painted with acrylic thinned with water. There is virtually no difference in appearance from watercolor when painting this way with acrylic.

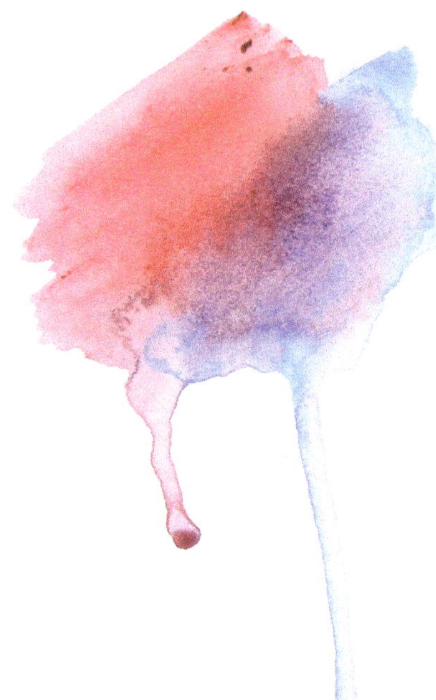

However, there is one big difference once the paint dries. Watercolor is re-soluble. You can use a wet brush to remove it or adjust it well after an area has dried. Once acrylic dries, however, it is not re-soluble. You can paint over it, but you cannot add water to adjust it. This allows the acrylic artist to use multiple layers of paint, one over the other. As long as each layer is allowed to dry first, the layers will not mix together.

Watercolor and acrylic combine wonderfully. I will sometimes take advantage of the insolubility of dry acrylic when painting with watercolor.

In my painting *Path to the Castle* (*plein air*, Scotland), I wanted to capture the early morning light. I loved the backlit trees and the resulting shadows the light created on the path. With acrylic, I could work back to front (from farthest away to closest), using layers of paint to create the illusion of light shining through. Although I could have accomplished the same look with watercolor, using acrylic made it easier. There was no intermingling of washes, thus no unwanted neutrals.

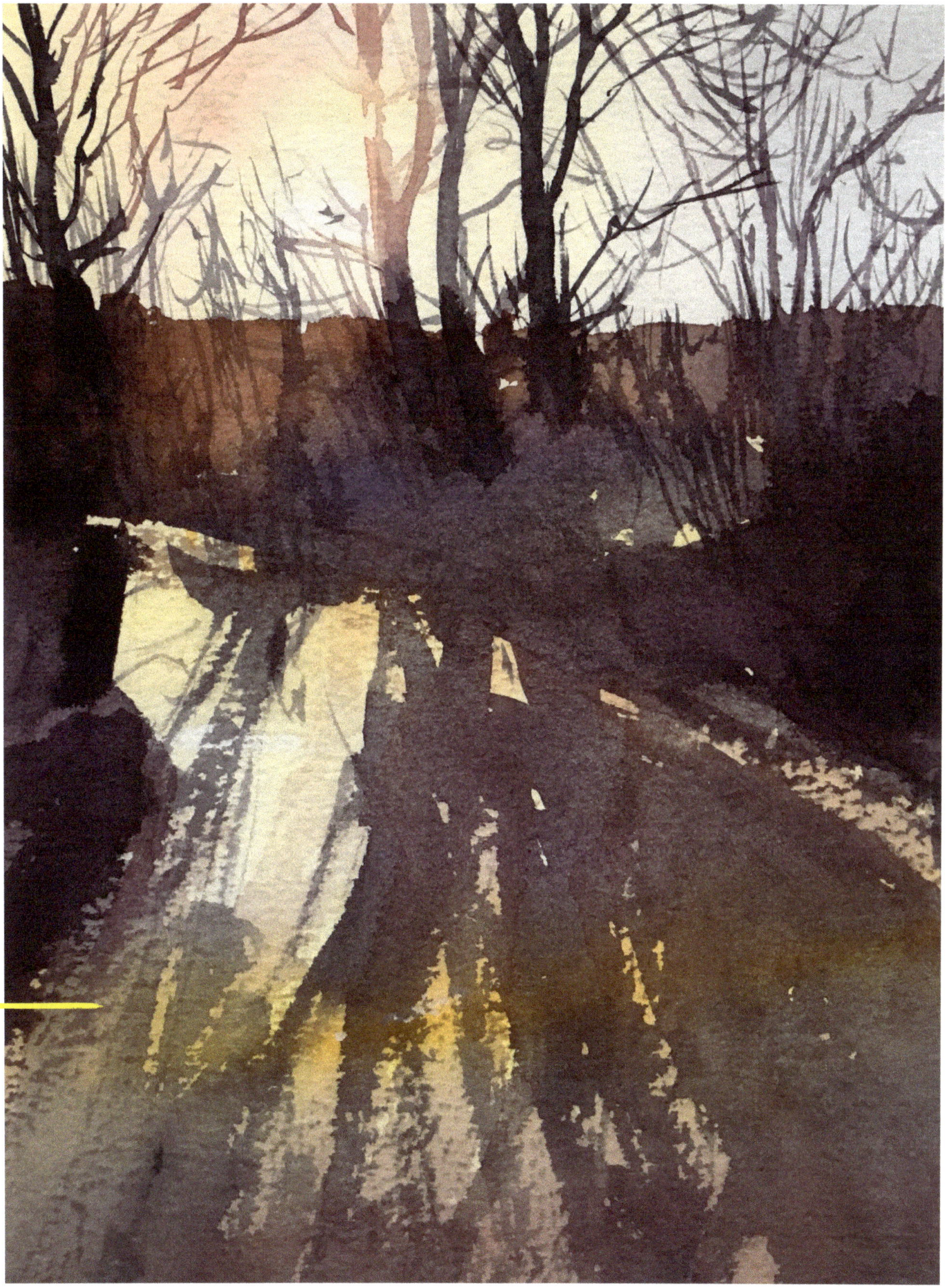

Using Acrylics as a Glazing Medium

There are times you may want to alter the color of certain shapes or completely change the overall temperature of your painting. I don't do this often, but it's nice to know you can do this with acrylic easily. You can make a glaze—or a thin, transparent mixture of acrylic—by adding water, matte, or gloss medium. I usually use matte medium mixed with enough water to make the color completely transparent.

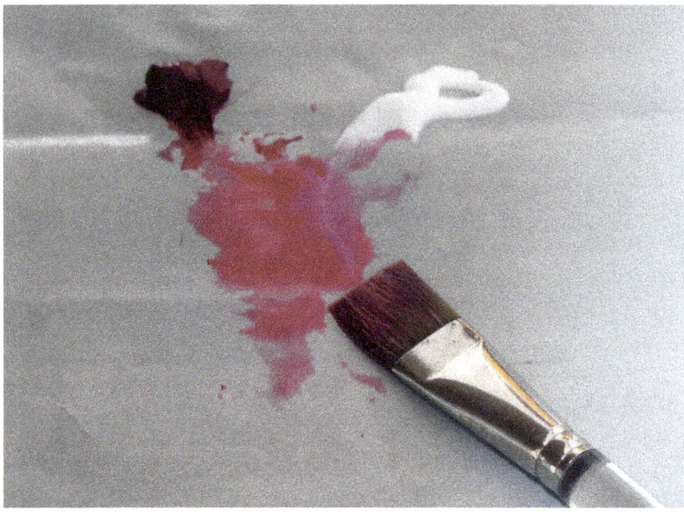

Here I mixed a glazing wash using a small amount of alizarin crimson with a bit more matte medium, plus a small amount of water. I used a soft brush—in this case a nylon flat designed for watercolor.

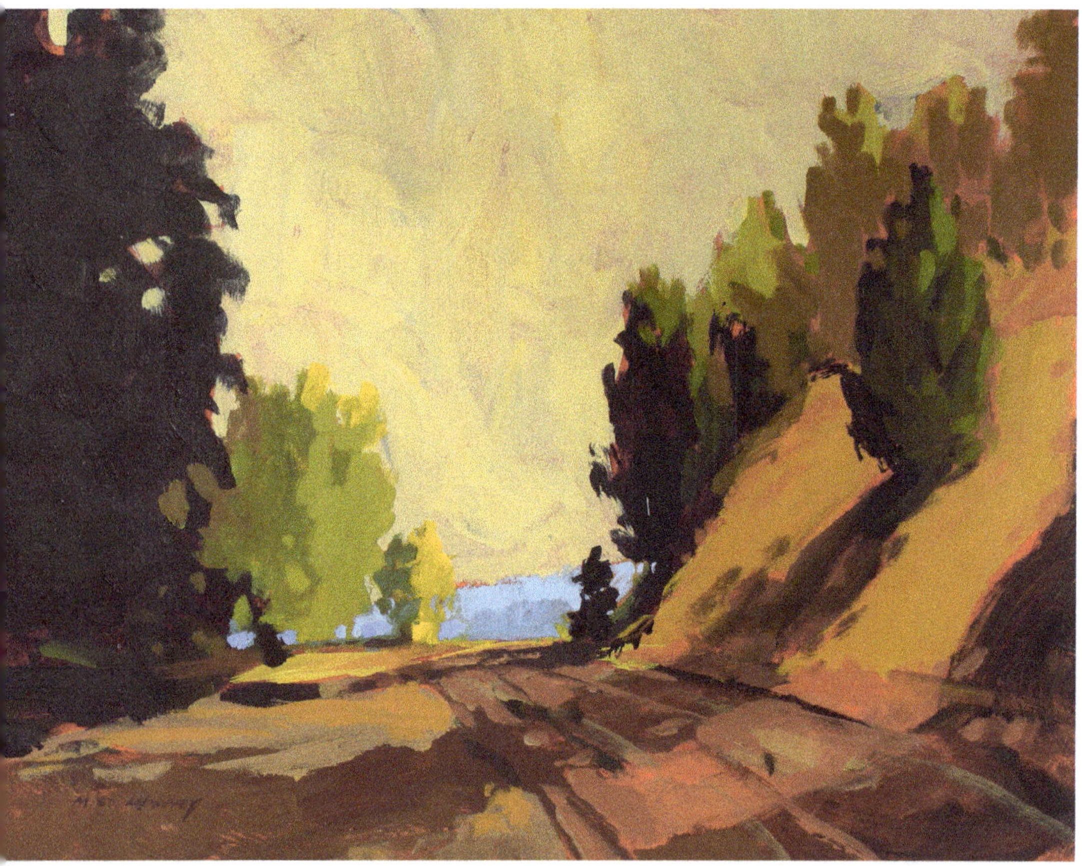

I liked the painting *Light From the Right*, but I wanted to warm it with a glaze and pull it together by adding a transparent warm wash over the whole painting. Compare the example on the left with the example on the opposite page.

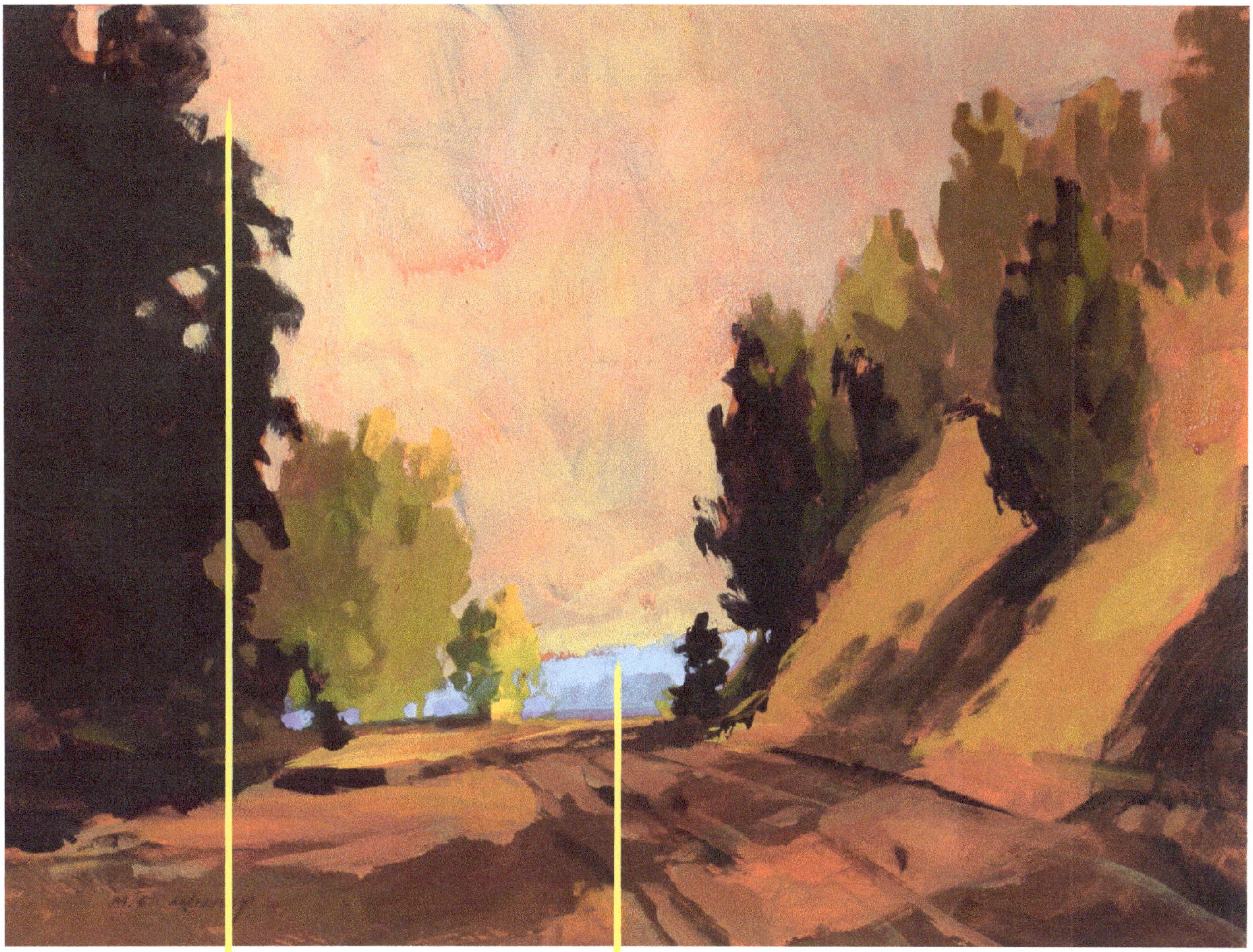

The overall painting now has a red glow.

I avoided painting over the blue on the horizon to make sure that this part of the painting stayed cool in contrast to the warm glaze.

By glazing over my painting with a warm, transparent red wash, I added a bit of drama. In addition, there are times when we just use too many different colors, which can make a painting look fractured or visually chaotic. Glazing over your work will add unity to a scene with a complex color scheme.

Thick-Bodied Acrylics

I love thick, heavy-bodied acrylic paint straight from the tube. Acrylics offer so much choice for the painter. You can apply them in thin washes, very much like watercolor; you can use a slightly heavier application for coverage; or you can use thick, heavy paint right from the tube. When using heavy-bodied acrylic, the peaks and valleys of dried paint can enliven the surface of a landscape.

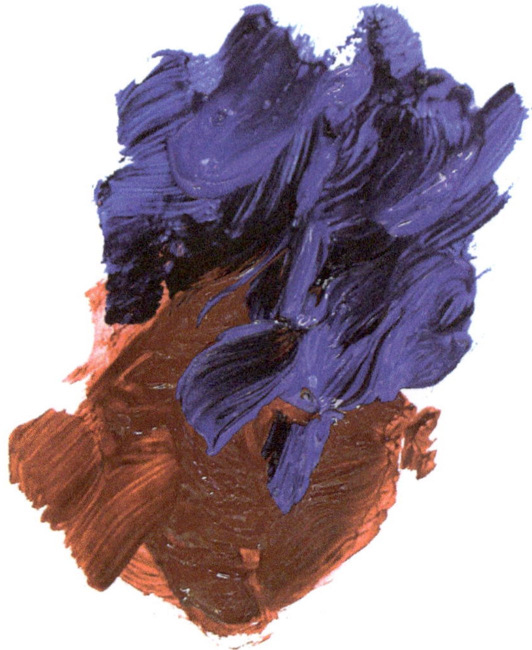

For *Winter Shadows* (opposite), I used a very thick application of paint. I loaded my brush and let the paint flow off the brush onto my canvas.

The detail below shows thick paint strokes applied with heavy-body paint. The ridges of paint add another textural element of interest.

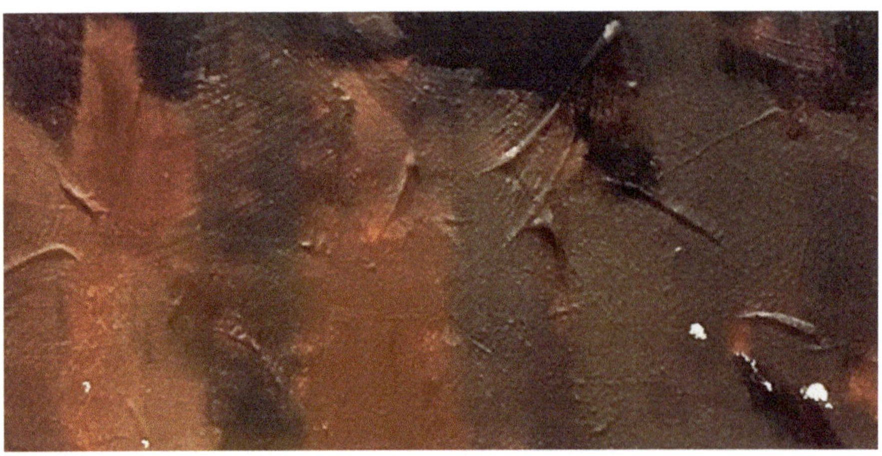

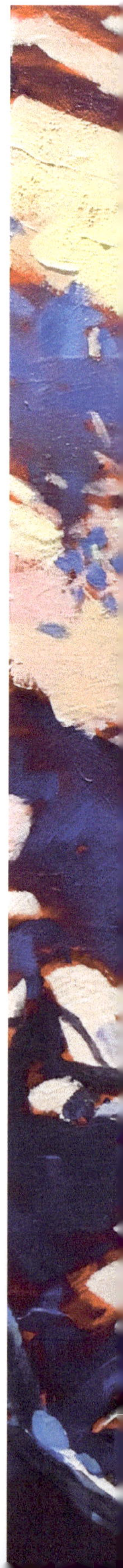

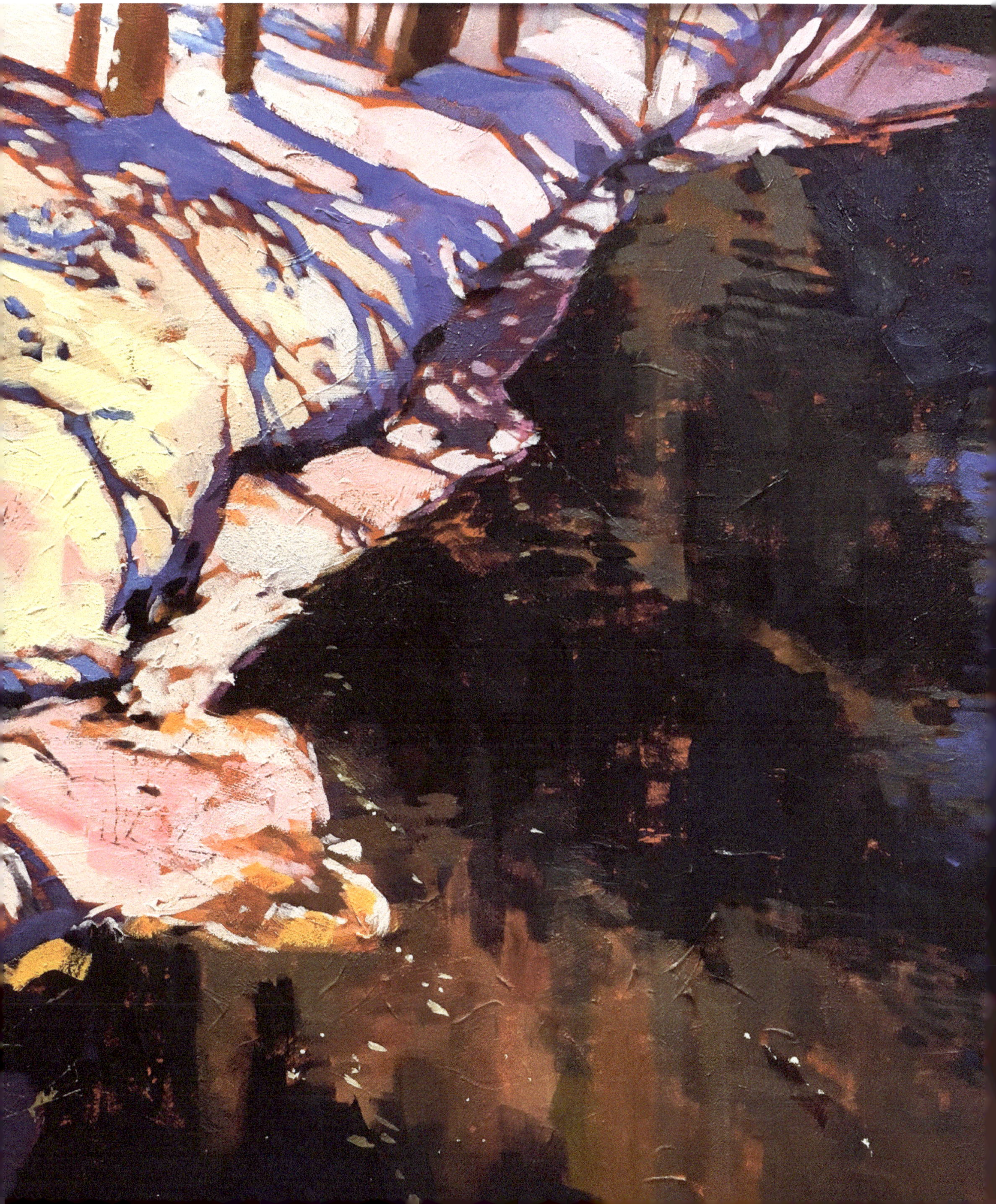

Scumbling

You can see the effect that scumbling with a dry brush gives to the blue area below. I painted a few strokes of cobalt blue, allowed that to dry, and then used alizarin crimson to scumble over the blue. This produced a violet hue. Depending on how heavily you load your brush and how much you remove with a paper towel, you can control the transparency of the scumbled area.

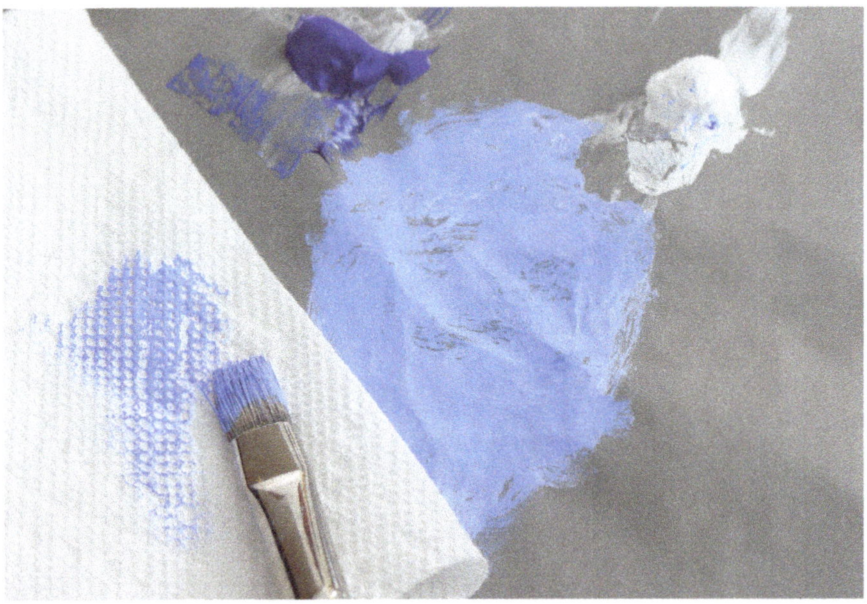

You can control how much paint you add to your painting by first drying or rubbing your brush on a paper towel. The more paint you remove from the brush, the less will go onto your painting.

This is the painting before scumbling. I felt that the oak tree was too dark and dominant. I wanted to push it back visually and create a landscape with more atmosphere. Scumbling was the answer.

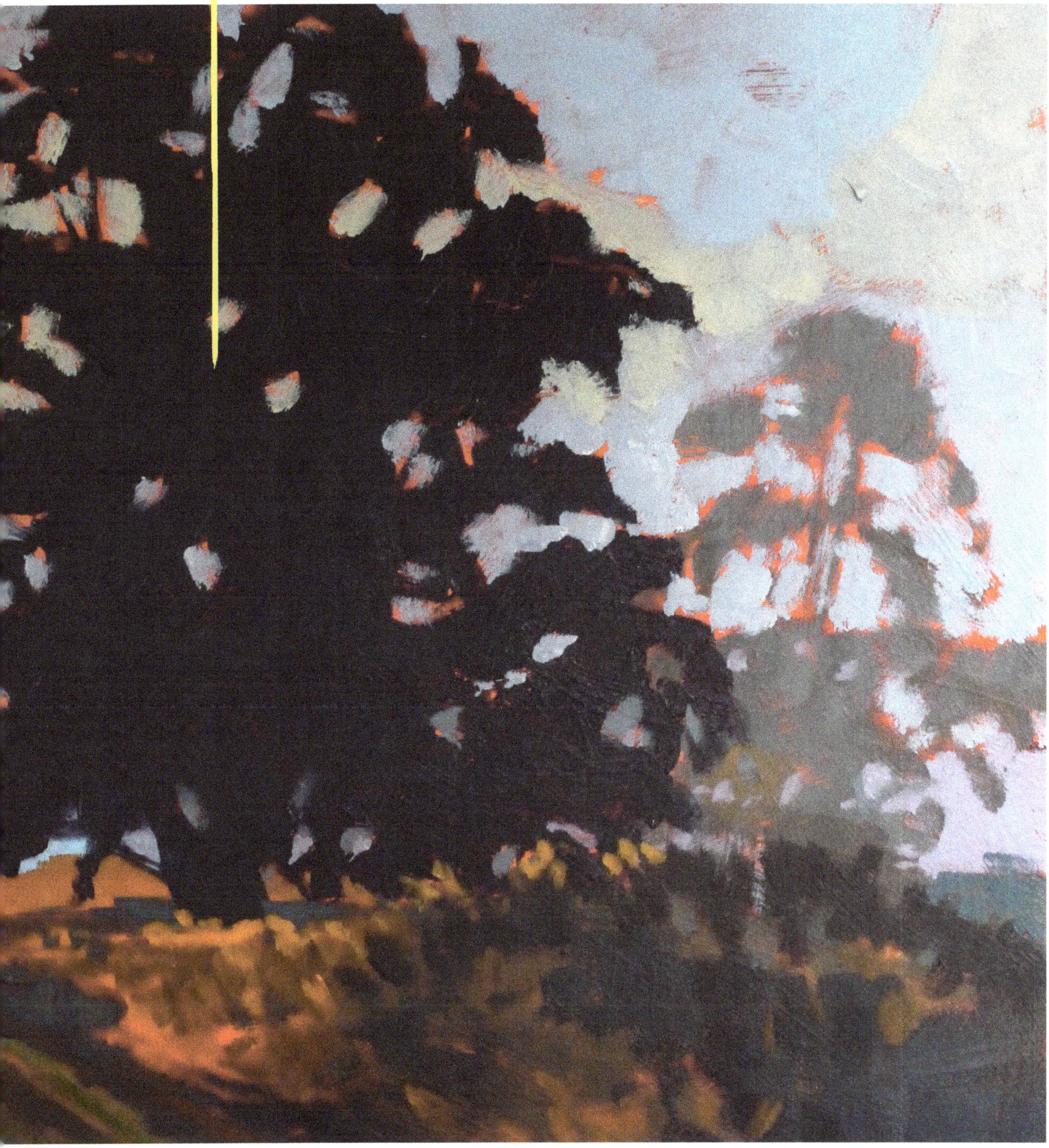

I used a hard scrub to get the dry paint to come off my brush. I had to reload, redry on my paper towel, and reapply numerous times to complete the alteration. I created more atmosphere and mystery with scumbling. Another technique for your toolbox!

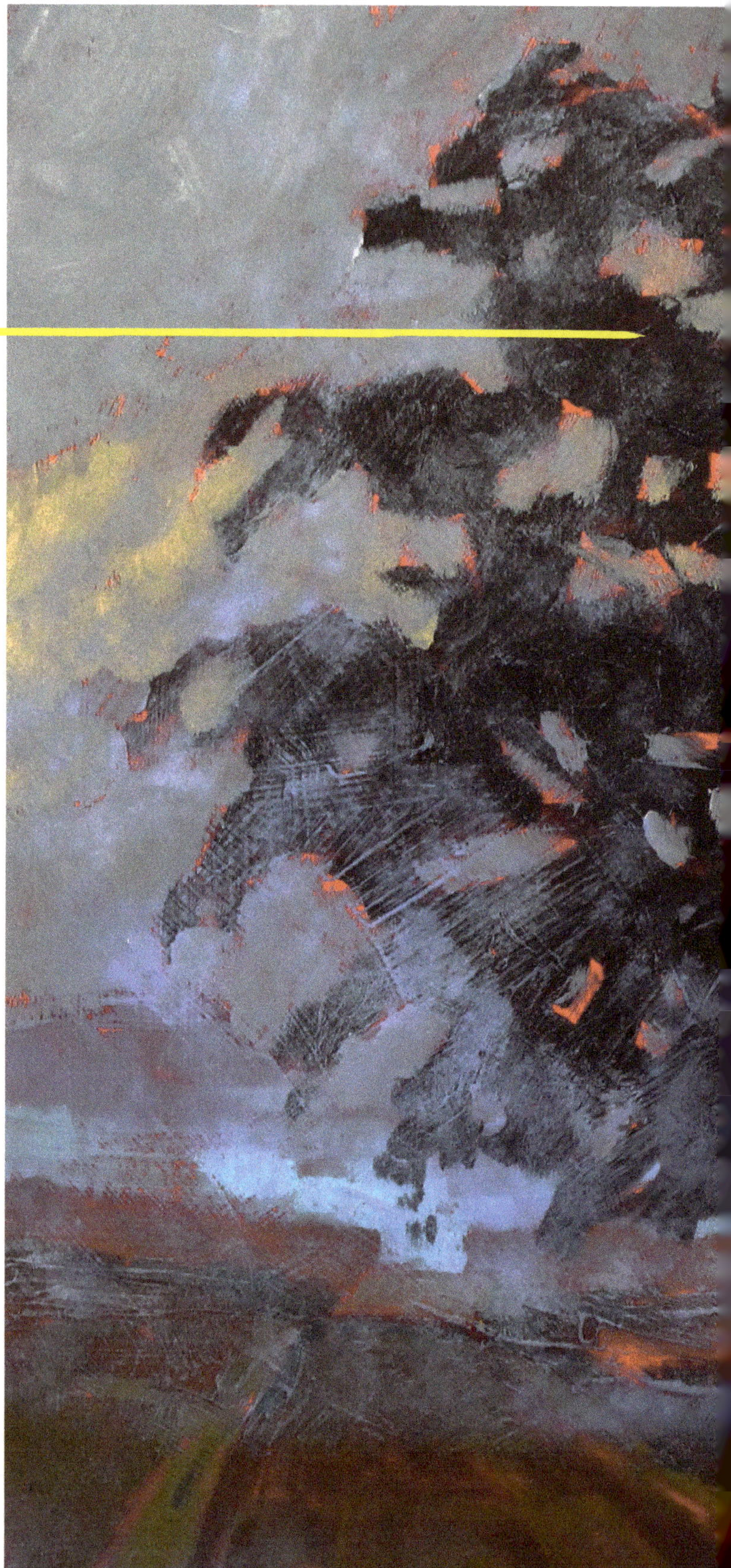

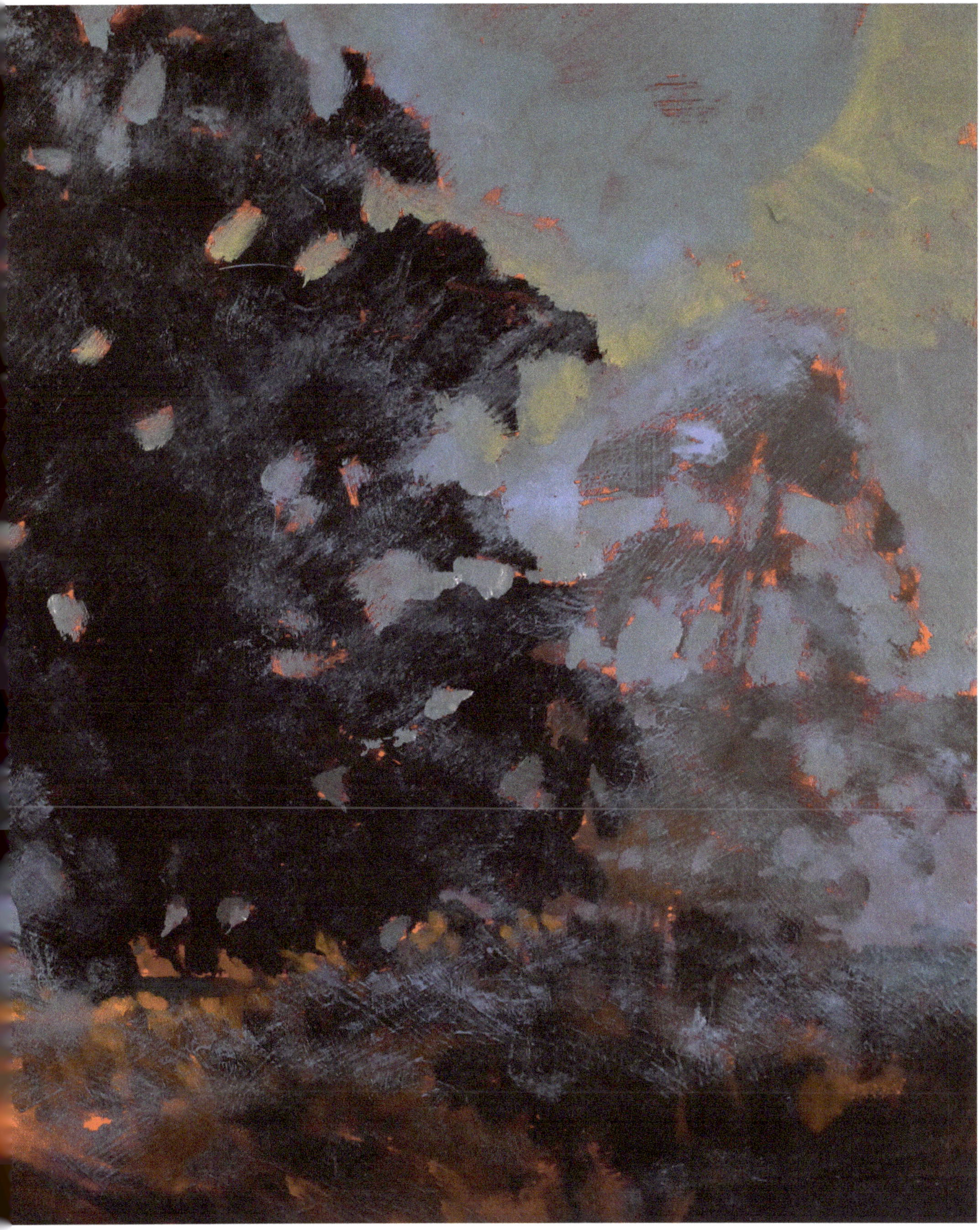

Slowing the Drying Time

As you've learned, acrylic dries quickly. Adding water is the easiest way to slow the drying time of acrylic paint. Matte and gloss medium can also be added to slow the drying time, as well. But all of these options change the appearance of the paint as it comes from the tube. The following examples demonstrate the three ways I use acrylic paint most often in the field.

Straight from the tube: The first example depicts one heavy brushstroke made with cadmium red light straight from the tube.

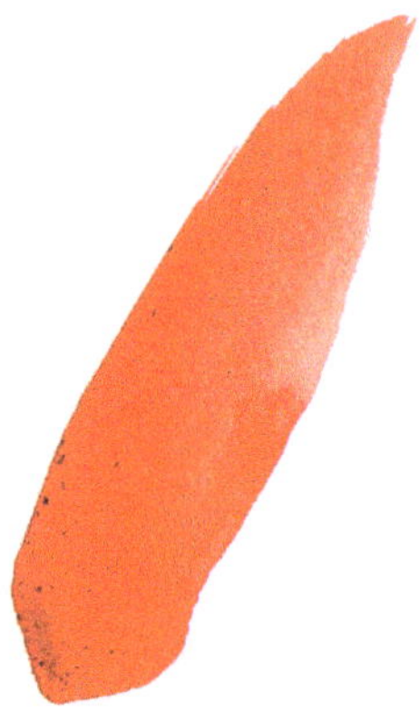

Thinned with water: I dilute the paint by half with water. Notice that the value gets lighter and the paper shows through a little. Some artists like to start this way with an acrylic wash (similar to watercolor), or complete their entire painting with diluted acrylic. Experiment to find out what you like and what gives you the look and control you want.

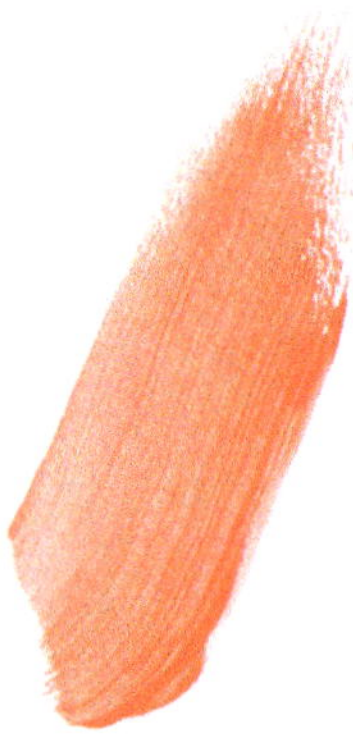

Mixed with matte medium: I mixed cadmium red light with matte medium at about a 50-50 ratio. This substantially extends the pigment and, like water, makes the passage more transparent. Some painters mix matte or gloss medium into their paint and "glaze" with the mixture. This step takes extra time and is not always practical in the field.

I prefer to use heavy-bodied paint directly from the tube. I rarely add matte or gloss medium. However, you may find it helpful to add a bit of water to get the paint to slide off your brush more easily or to dilute the paint for small details. Experiment to see what works for you. Just remember that any time you dilute the pigment you also reduce its saturation and intensity (brightness).

Blending Colors

Because acrylic dries faster than oil, there are technical issues to address in terms of blending. I usually employ three or four different methods for blending one value or color into another.

Because oil paint dries so slowly, there is more time to make adjustments to the work. This can be done in the field or in the studio after a *plein air* session. This extra drying time allows oil painters to infinitely adjust where one shape meets another.

We can give clues about what's important in our painting by how we handle these "edges." The harder the edge is, the more it will be noticed. I usually reserve the hardest edges for my center of interest or focal point. The viewer's eye is led right to the area of highest interest.

As I write this, my coffee mug filled with pencils and pens sits close to me. If I stare at that mug, everything behind it is a little out of focus. Those edges are "softer" compared to the distinct hard edges of the mug and its contents. Everything outside the window behind it is nothing more than a blur. No distant edges at all; the edges are lost. This is the way we see.

As painters, we can use blending to alter the edges of adjoining colors to create this effect. My three go-to blending options are shown on the following pages.

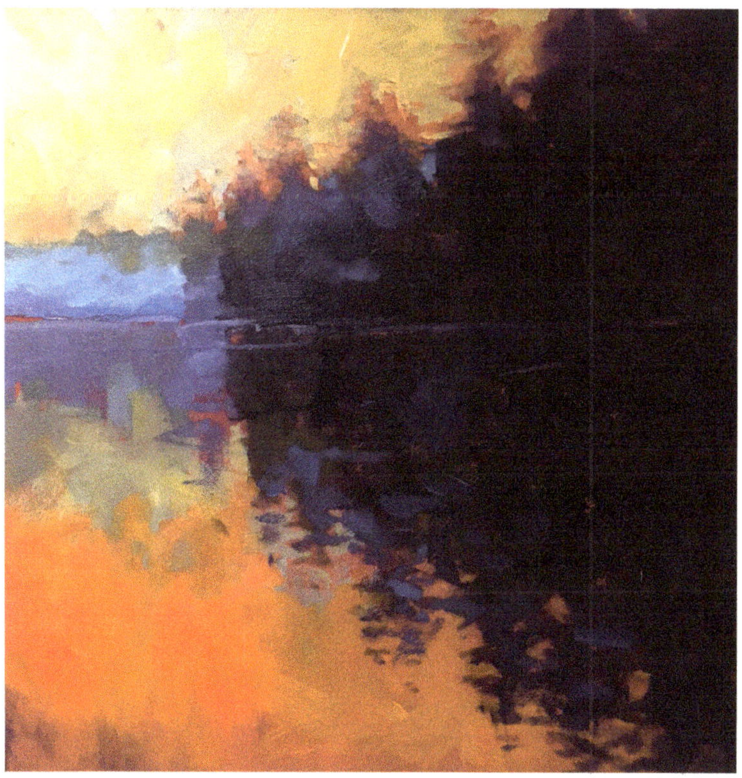

I painted the large sky shape in *Morning Reflections* using the wet blending method (see page 48). From left to right on my panel, I applied cadmium yellow light mixed with white, cadmium yellow with no white, and cadmium yellow deep. While the paint was still wet, I blended all three together. How you handle transitions between differing values and different colors is part of the challenge.

Hard edges between shapes are not a problem with acrylic paint because the paint dries fast. However, soft edges and lost edges are more difficult to obtain. This is when wet blending or scumbling come in handy.

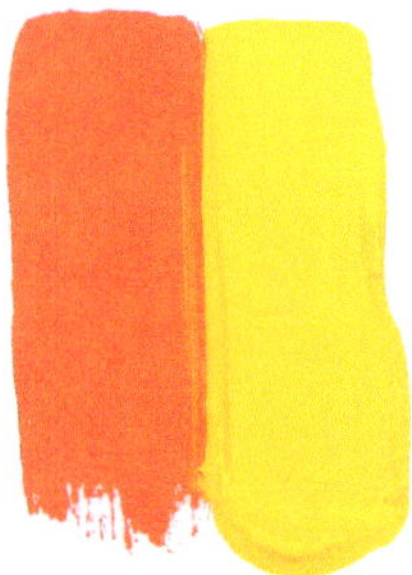

Side by side: Placing one strong color next to another makes a good, clear delineation. Usually the viewer can make that visual transition as they work their way through the painting.

Broken color: I often use broken color in the sky and cloud shapes of my landscapes. The good thing about blending this way is one or both of the colors can be dry. Place smaller strokes of one color over the other where the two shapes meet. If both colors are still wet (as in my example), use small strokes of both colors, one over the other.

Wet blending: For this technique, all strokes, or passages, need to be wet. Place strokes side by side; while they are still wet, blend the two passages together. Sometimes it takes multiple blends to get the look you are trying to achieve.

One work around for softer edges is to place similar values next to each other. If the value is the same or close, that edge will appear to be visually blended, especially when compared to the hard edge of dissimilar values. (See the example on the right.) In the example on the left, I placed the secondary colors green and orange next to each other. Their values are close, and the edge between the stokes appears softer when compared to the very dark blue and very light orange of the other example.

Landscape painters use hard, soft, and lost edges to convey distance, particularly when painting vistas. Generally, the farthest elements are the softest, so the edges between the shapes are more indistinct. As you move toward the foreground, the edges become more distinct. Usually, items in the foreground will have the hardest edges.

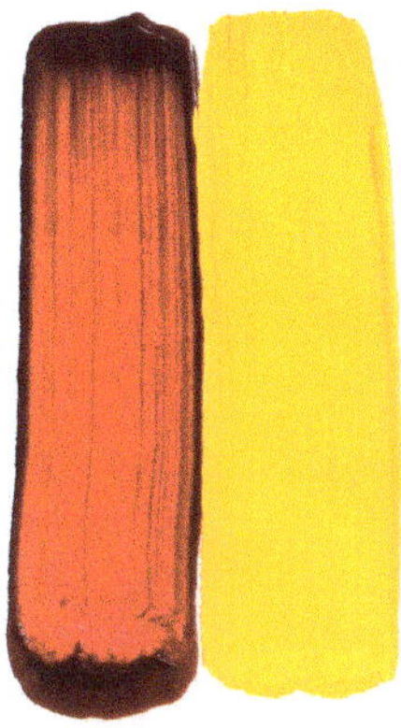

Hard

Hard: This example shows a hard edge between the alizarin crimson and the cadmium dark. This draws the eye in a painting and tells the viewer that this is an important area.

Soft

Soft: We can still see the difference between the shapes, but the junction is softer and less distinct. This tells the viewer this area is less important.

Lost

Lost: Here the edge between the red and yellow has been completely lost. Lost edges no longer form separate shapes. This tells the viewer that other areas of the paintings are more important.

Page 50, *Fall Reflections*

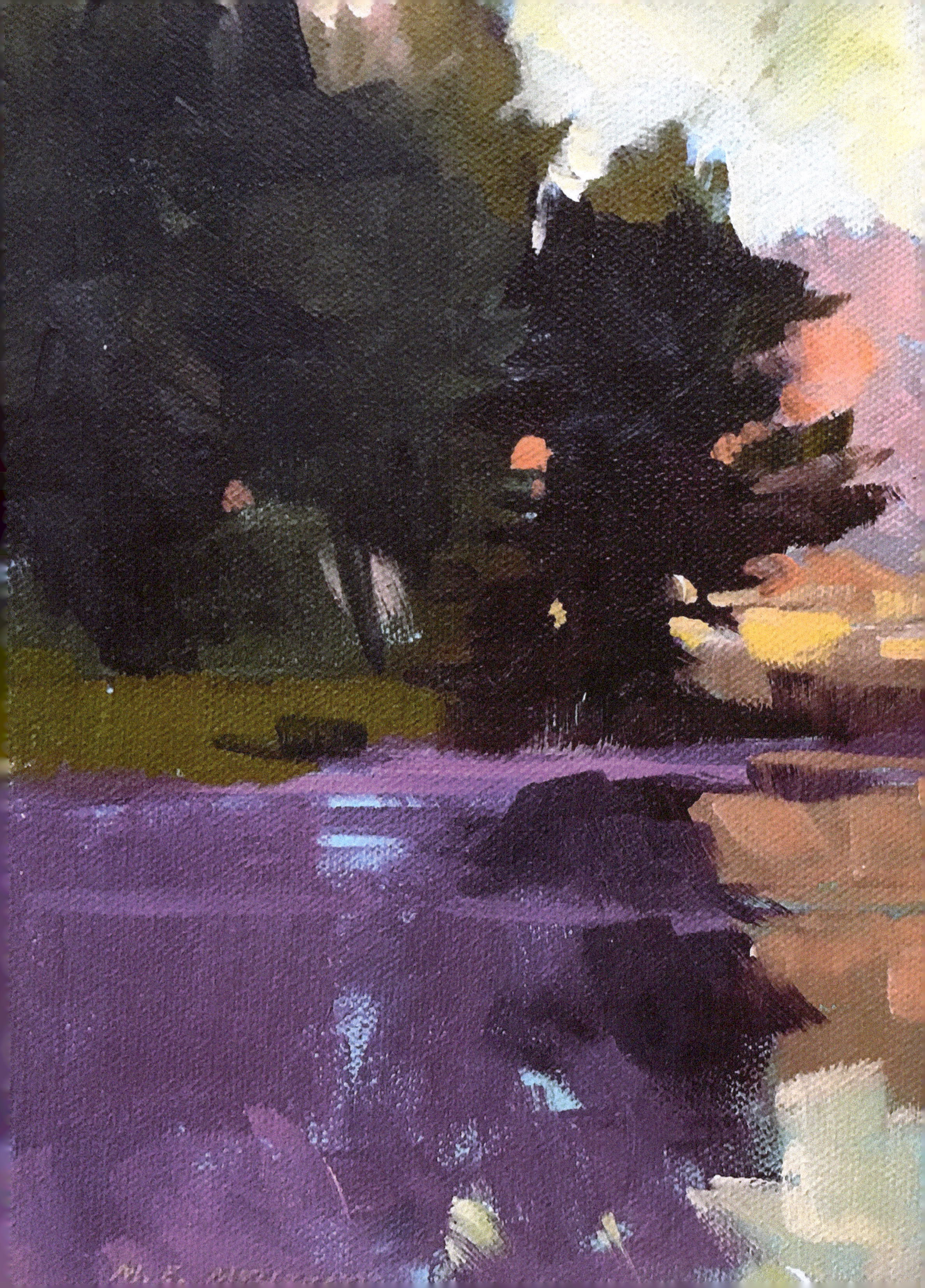

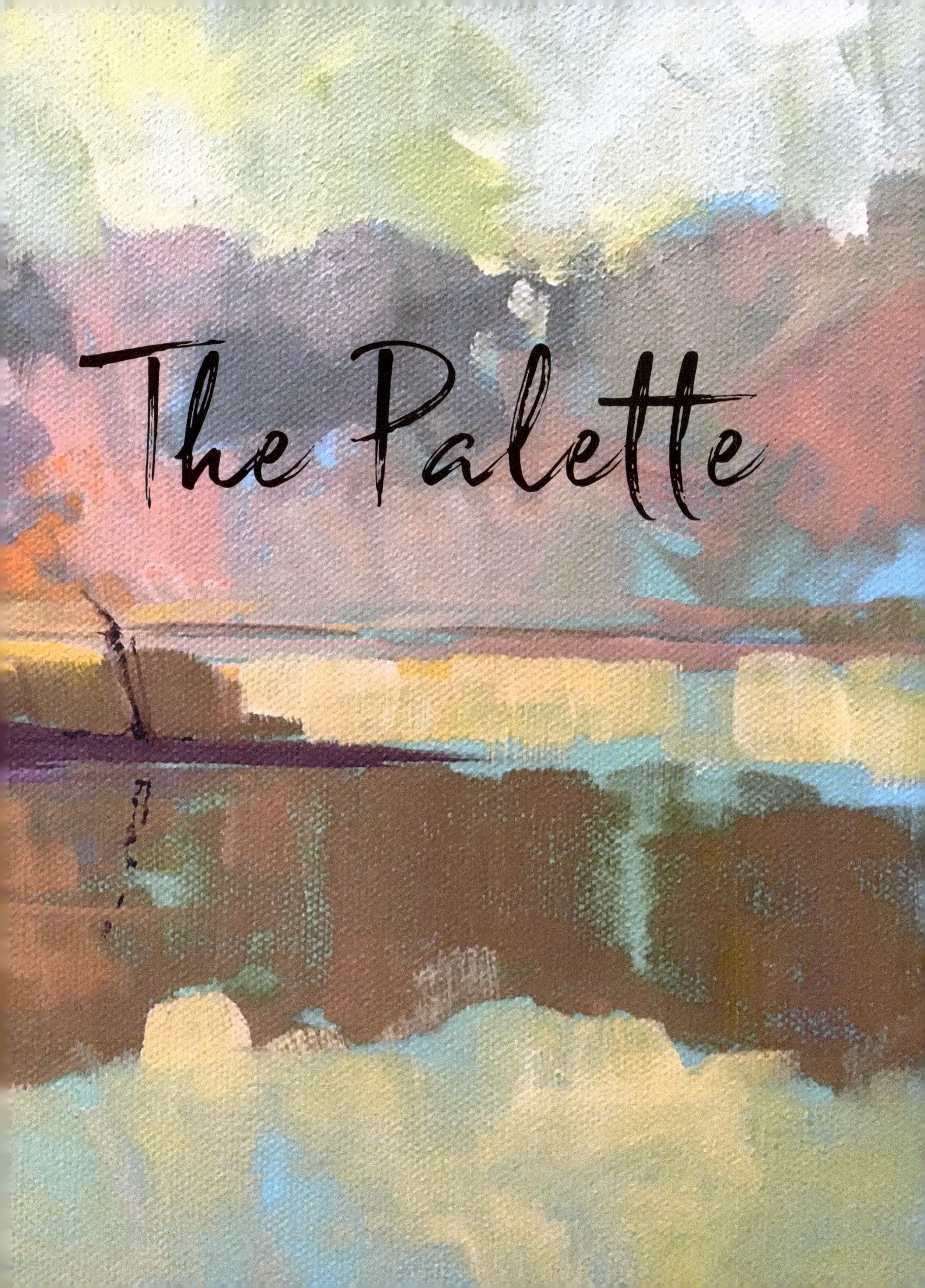
The Palette

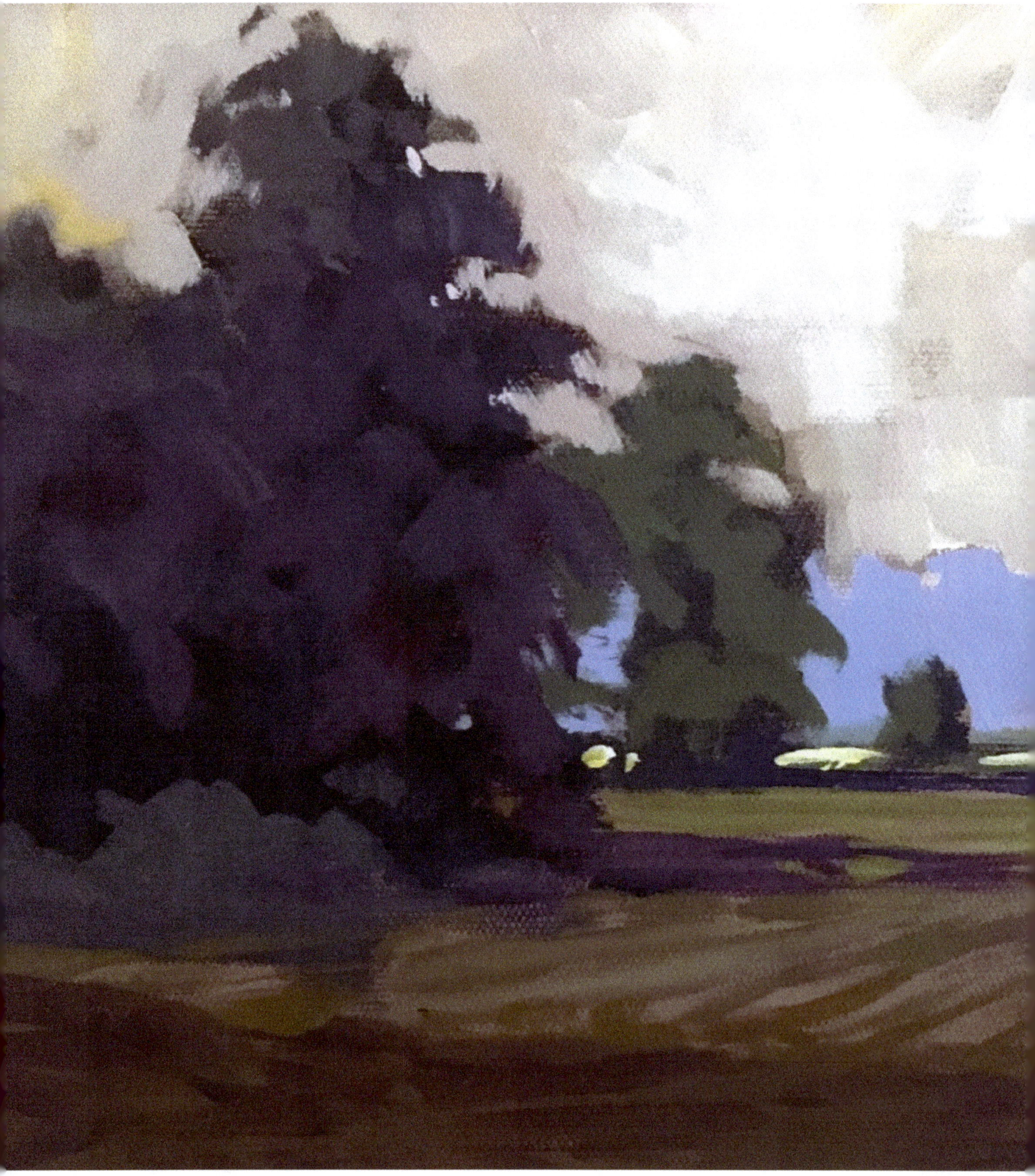

Choosing Colors

There are many different acrylic color options, but packing too many tubes of paint gets heavy. I'm always looking for ways to reduce the weight of my supplies in the field; this is why I carry a split primary palette.

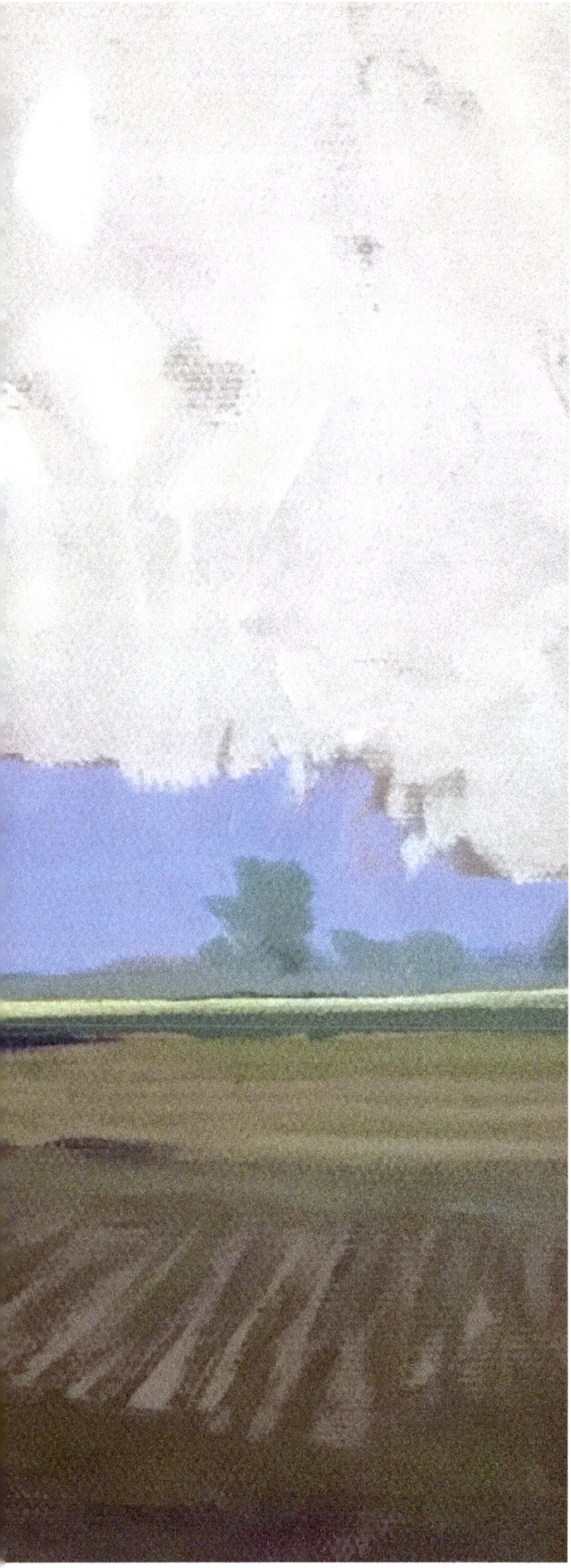

1. The natural palette

This palette includes alizarin crimson, cadmium red, yellow ochre, cadmium yellow, ultramarine blue, and white. These colors will produce the secondary colors—violet, green, and orange—but not always intense mixtures. There are those who prefer this more subdued palette. They feel that these colors produce tones that most represent what they see in the field. I sometimes find this palette useful on cloudy days or when depicting fields or forests that have subdued color.

***Summer's Beginning* is an example of this more subdued natural palette.**

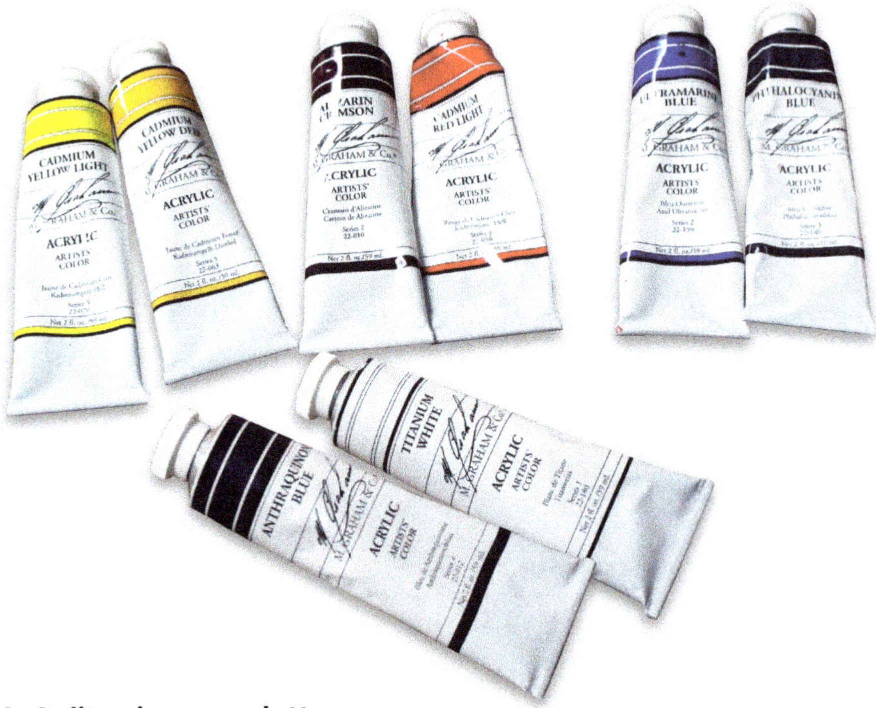

Cadmium yellow light, cadmium yellow deep, alizarin crimson, cadmium red light, ultramarine blue, phthalo blue, titanium white, and anthraquinone blue are the usual colors I carry with me in the field. Sometimes as a personal challenge, I throw in an odd color and try to build a painting around it. It's always good to keep things interesting.

2. Split primary palette

The split primary system is the palette I use for the majority of my *plein air* work. In fact, this is the palette I use for ninety percent of my work. It includes a warm and a cool version of all three primaries, plus white. I will occasionally add anthraquinone blue (a very dark, cool blue—warmer than phthalo but cooler than ultramarine) to my phthalo and ultramarine. Sometimes I'll just carry the anthraquinone alone. The six colors are: alizarin crimson (cool red), cadmium red light, (warm red), cadmium yellow light (cool yellow), cadmium yellow deep (warm yellow), phthalo blue (cool blue), and ultramarine blue (warm blue), plus titanium white. Sometimes I use ivory black, but if I can mix a dark hue without the use of black, I do so.

Notice there are no secondary colors (green, violet, or orange) included. I know there are some *plein air* painters who carry many tubes of paint, and by taking along green, violet, and orange, you can save some mixing time. However, I prefer controlling the saturation (intensity) of my secondary mixtures and reducing the amount of supplies I carry.

As you know, complementary colors are opposite each other on the color wheel. Each primary color has a secondary complement. Blue is the complement of orange; red is the complement of green; yellow is the complement of violet. If you mix complements (the secondary colors), the resulting mixture will be a neutralized color, such as neutral brown or gray. This phenomenon is something I take full advantage of with my split primary palette.

Split Primaries

I like to use a split primary system for a few reasons. For one, with the addition of black and white, I can match and mix just about any hue or value I want. I can also control the saturation (intensity or brightness) of my secondary (orange, green, and violet) mixtures.

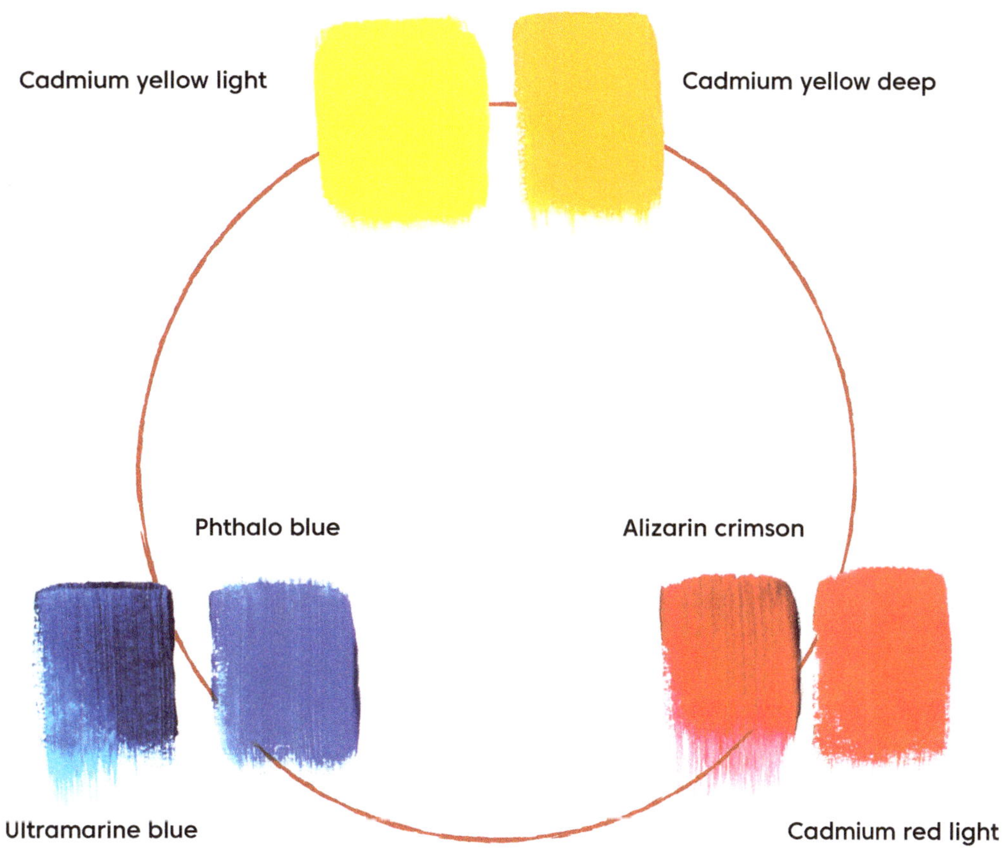

Think about the greens of early spring. As those first buds open into new leaves, the green is bright and fresh. As we move into midsummer, the leaves become slightly less intense, and the greens get warmer. By late summer and early fall, the leaves become much warmer, sometimes approaching brown. With my warm and cool yellows and my two blues, matching this annual progression is easy.

Mixing Greens

If you mix a cool yellow (cadmium yellow light) with phthalo blue, both of which tend toward green, the resulting mixture is a very intense green. The opposite of green on the color wheel is red. If you mix opposites, they neutralize (dull) each other.

Cadmium yellow deep leans toward orange. It has some red in it compared to cadmium yellow light. Ultramarine blue leans toward the violet; it also has some red in it. If you mix a green from these two colors, you are getting red from two sources. Red, being the complement (opposite) of green, neutralizes the resulting mixture, which produces a warmer, less saturated green. The same phenomenon occurs when mixing the secondaries orange and violet.

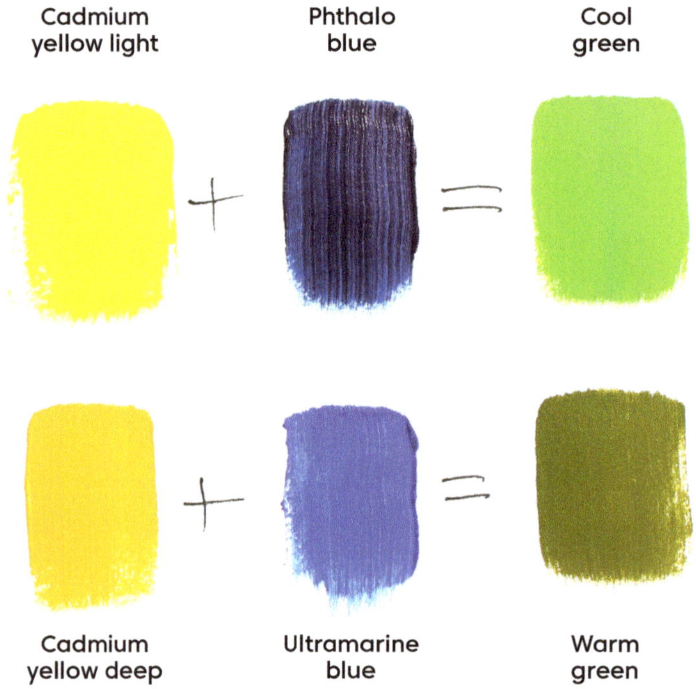

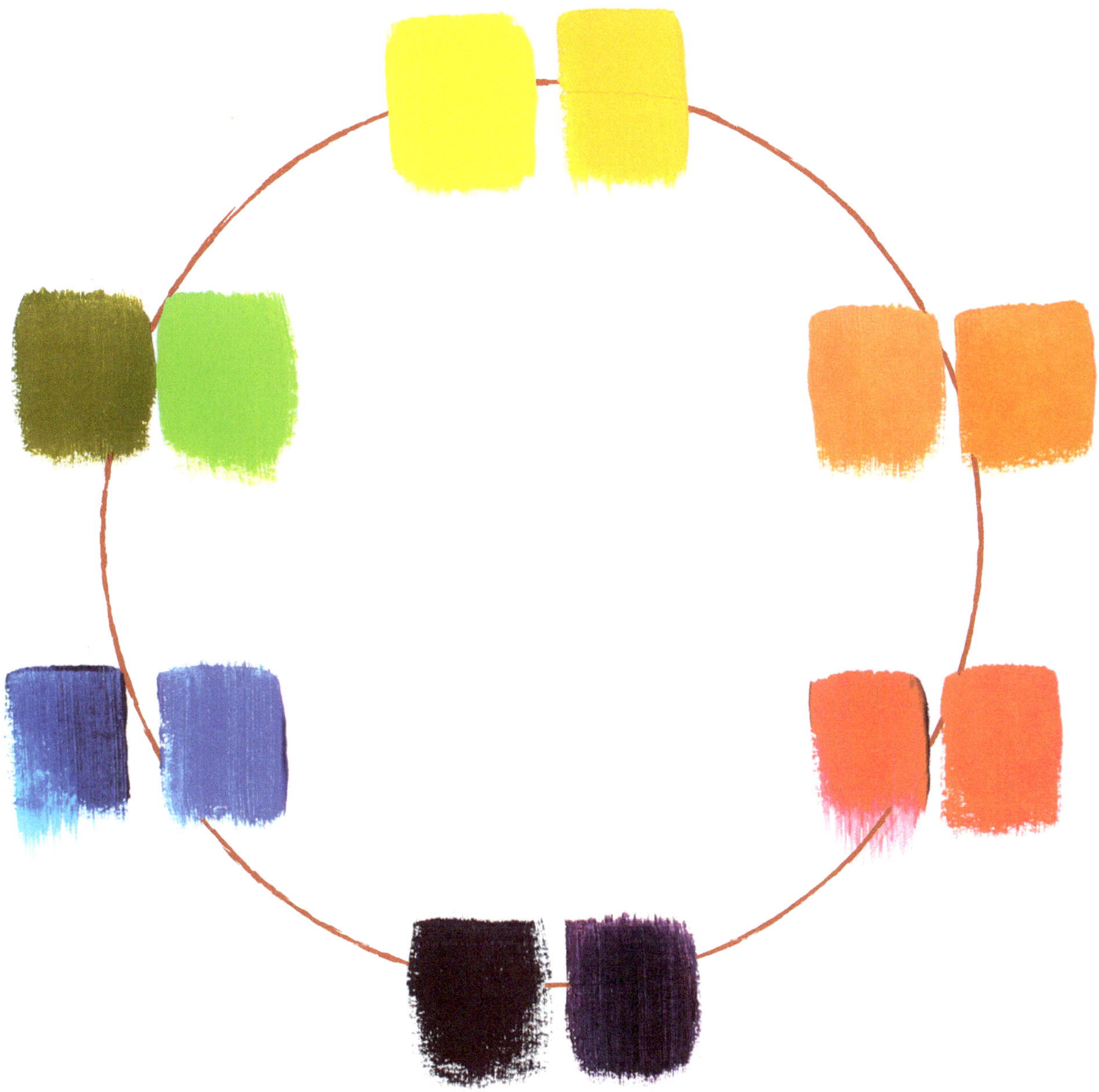

When you take into consideration all the possible mixtures of two blues and two yellows, plus black and white—not to mention the addition of their complements—you begin to see that a split primary palette is not limiting at all.

Mother Color

A "mother" color refers to a premixed color that will form the basis for all other mixtures. Using this base color in all or most other mixtures provides unity of tone or temperature in the finished work.

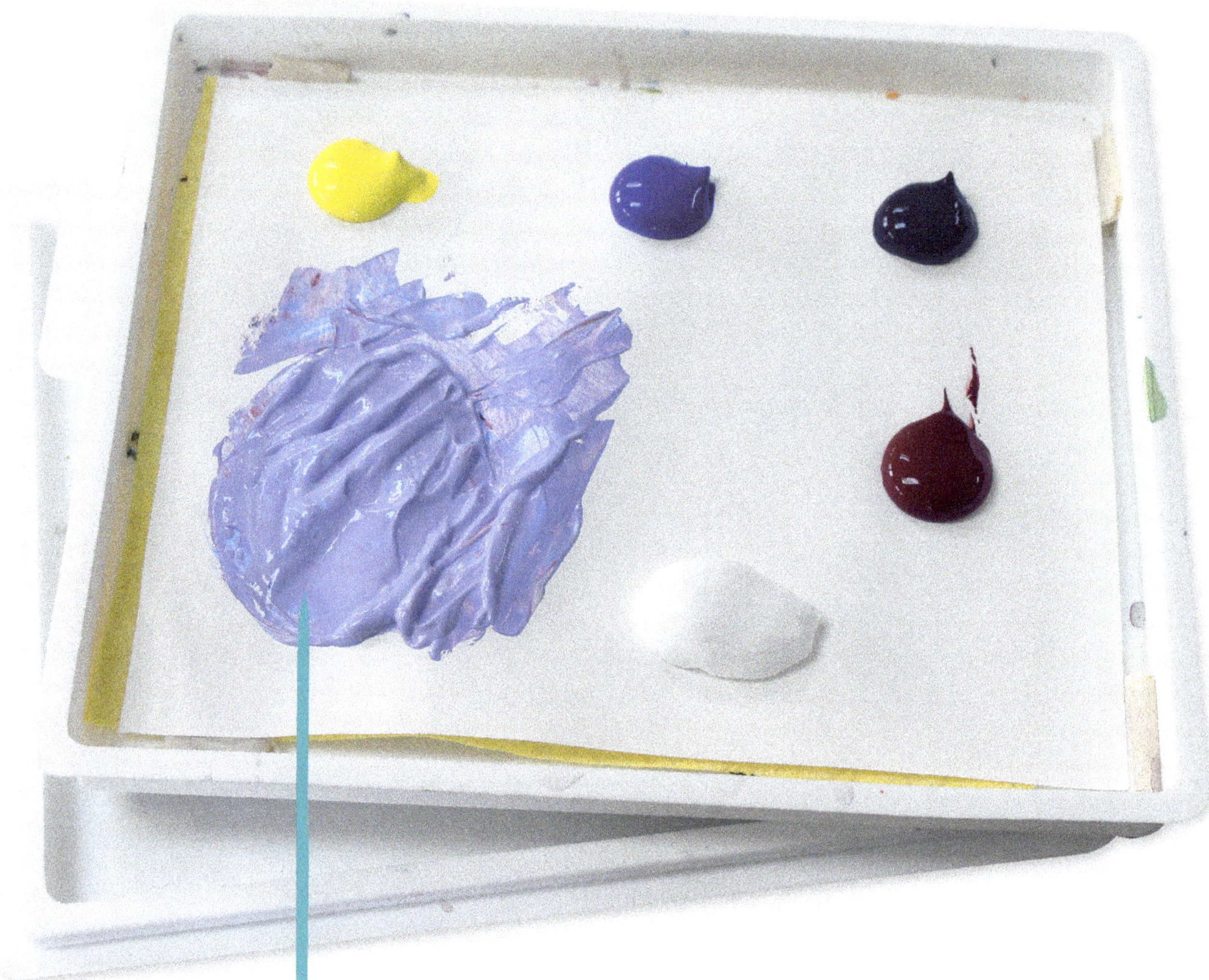

My mother color is a mixture of ultramarine blue, alizarin crimson, and white. For this painting, I also add a small amount of cadmium yellow light to this violet mixture to slightly reduce the saturation level. My palette setup includes a large mixture of my base color, along with cadmium yellow light, ultramarine blue, anthraquinone blue, alizarin crimson, and white.

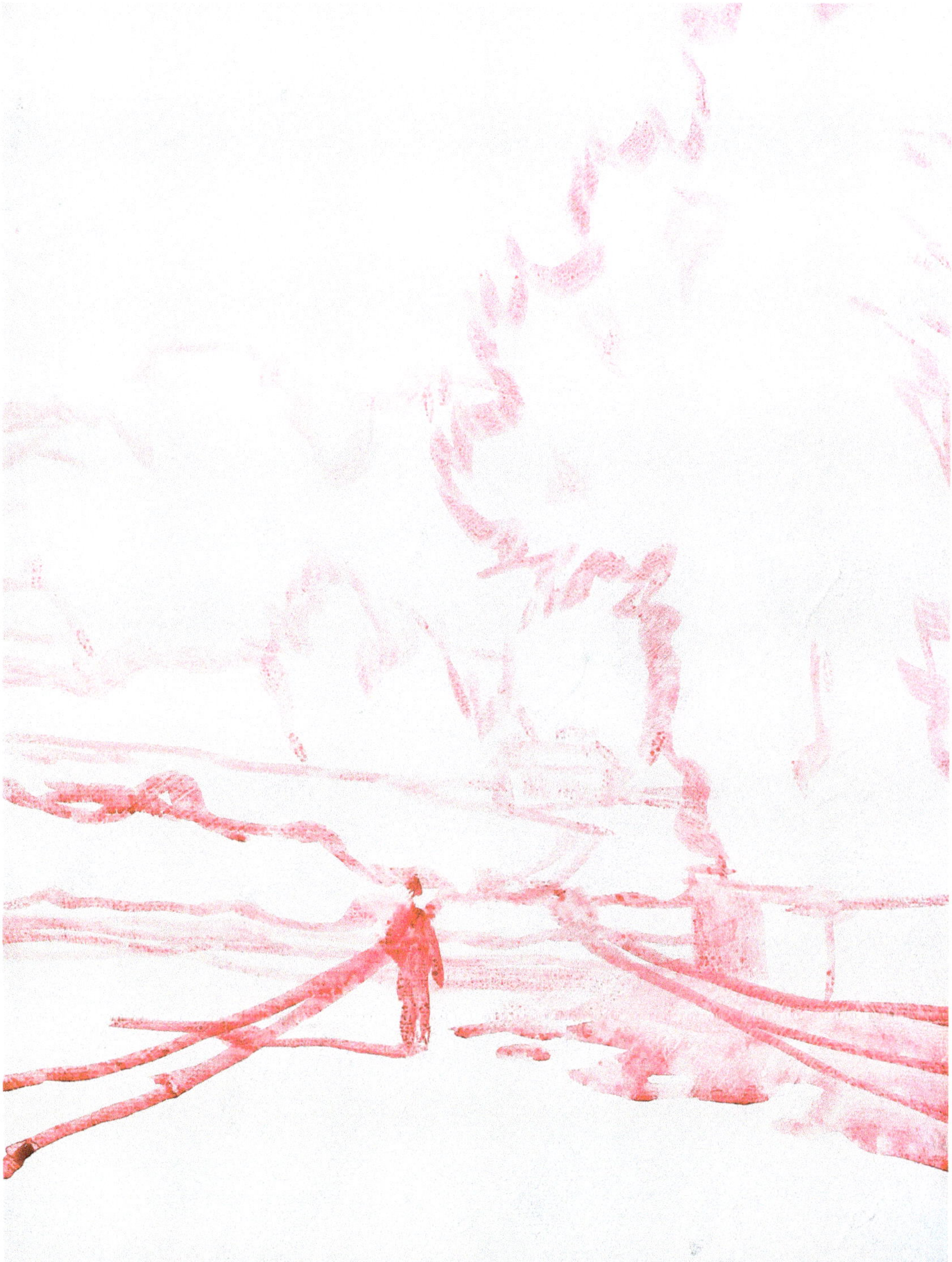

This vista is directly from my sketchbook. This scene is from just outside the village of Arley, in Cheshire. My friend John was walking ahead of me when I sketched this quick shot of the path that leads to the village. The lone figure became the focal point and allowed me to surround it with the beautiful countryside.

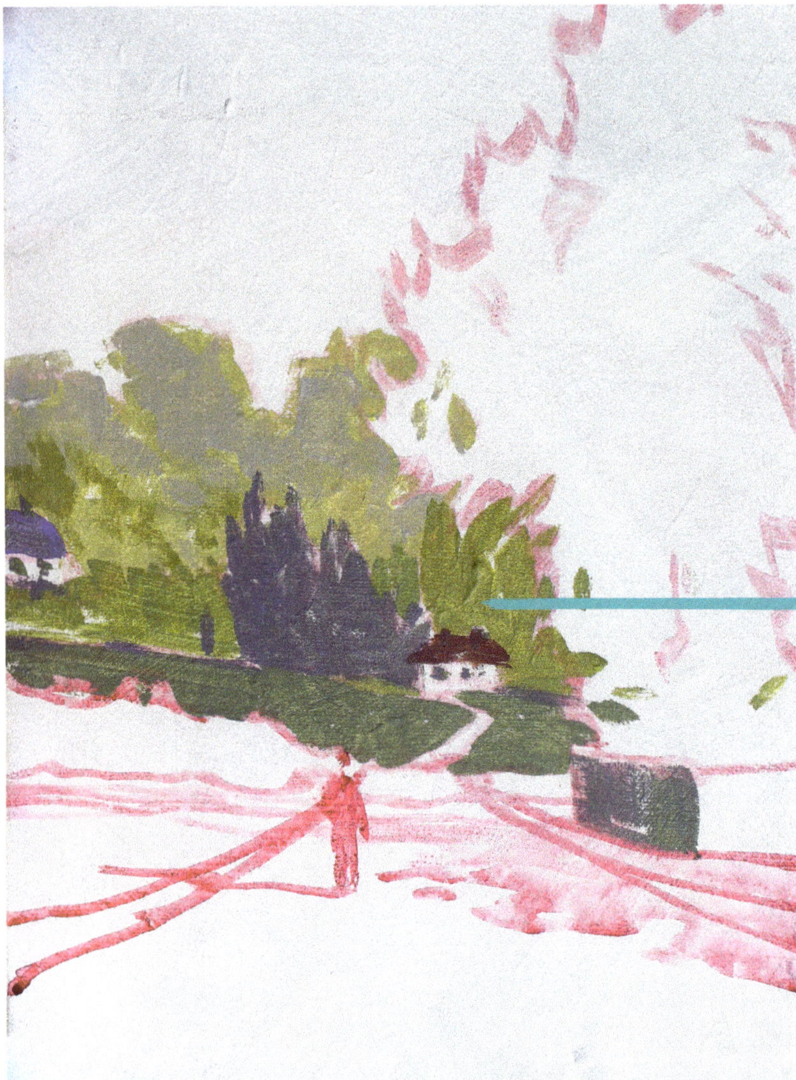

The first pass includes all the muted greens and violets mixed with my mother color. I keep the background lighter and more subdued with the addition of white and my violet base.

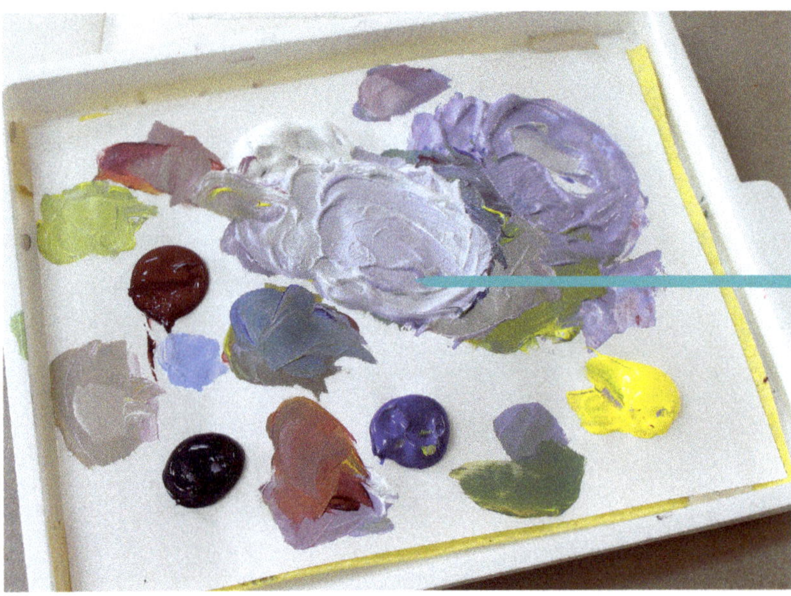

Every single mixture in the completed painting (opposite) includes some of my violet mother color. This provides a cohesive tonal "glue" that helps hold the finished painting together.

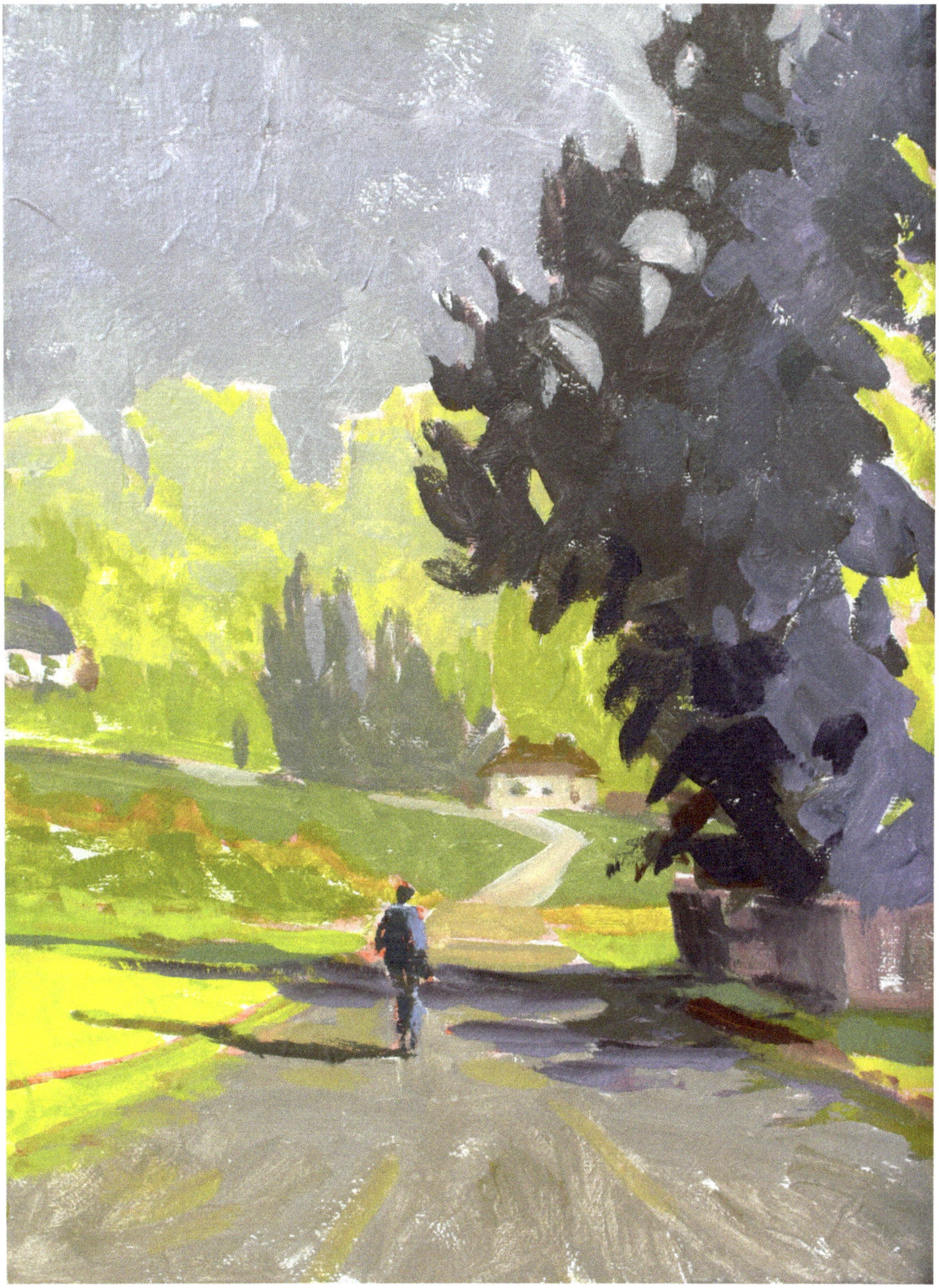

Rural England
(acrylic on canvas)

The completed painting features the near complement (yellow-green) to my violet mother color. Every mixture in this painting has some of my premixed mother color included. Try this if you feel your color choices are too many or if you think your paintings could use some "mothering."

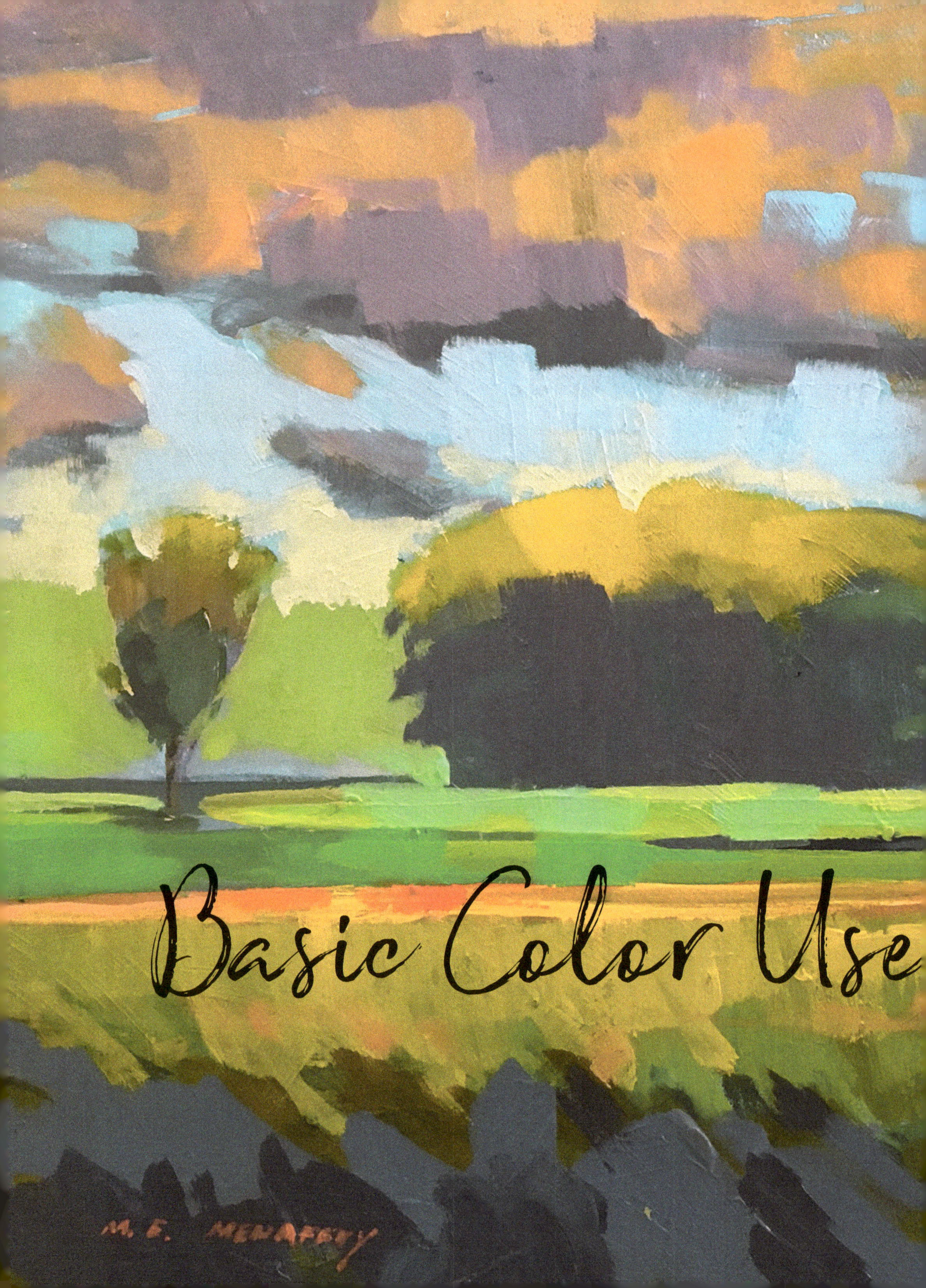

Basic Color Use

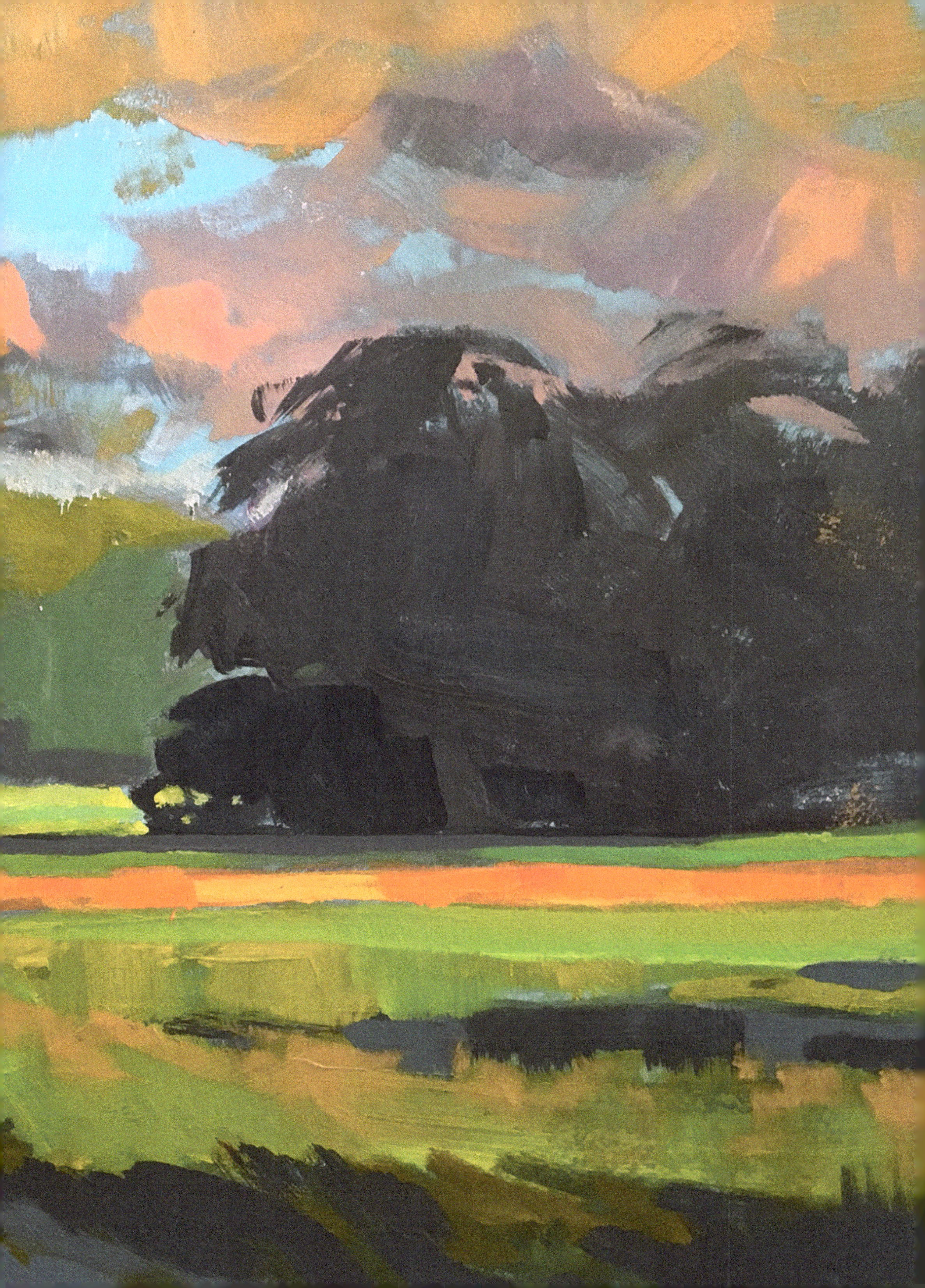

The Principles of Design

The principles of design are unity, harmony, balance, rhythm, repetition, variety, dominance, and contrast. There are variations to this list, but these are the main principles that govern our use of the elements of line, shape, color, value, texture, form, and space. For me, however, it is impossible to keep all of this in mind while painting. There is just too much to think about. So I select the principles that most often inform my work in *plein air* and concentrate primarily on those, namely dominance, unity, and contrast. I use the principle of dominance (color, temperature, value) to supply unity. I use contrast (size, shape, value, hue) to imply importance.

In the previous chapter, I discussed using a mother color to use and mix with all or most other colors. This method of working helps to supply unity to the work. Also covered was using a dominant temperature (warm or cool), which also helps hold our painting together. Another way to create unity is by illustrating dominance of hue (a lot of one color) and dominance of value (a lot of one value). Using color and value in this way works as the "glue" to help hold everything together.

The photograph at right was also used as the basis for the painting on page 61. For the paintings on the following pages, I've taken the liberty of greatly simplifying the scene by outlining only the biggest shapes. Sometimes it's more important to leave out extraneous elements so you can get to the heart of your visual story. I wanted the figure and the shadows that move from right to left to be the stars of this show.

Page 62, *Summer Fields*

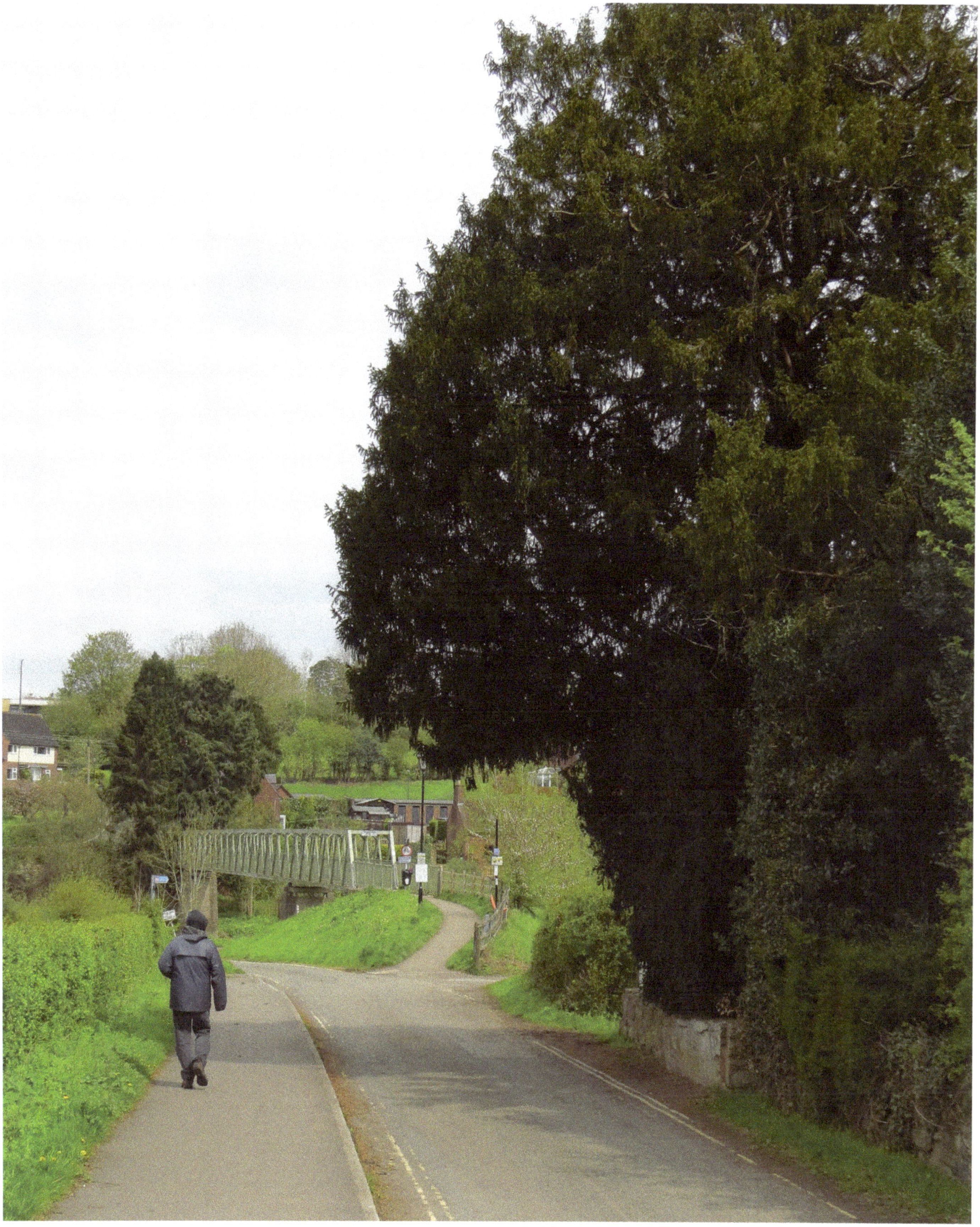

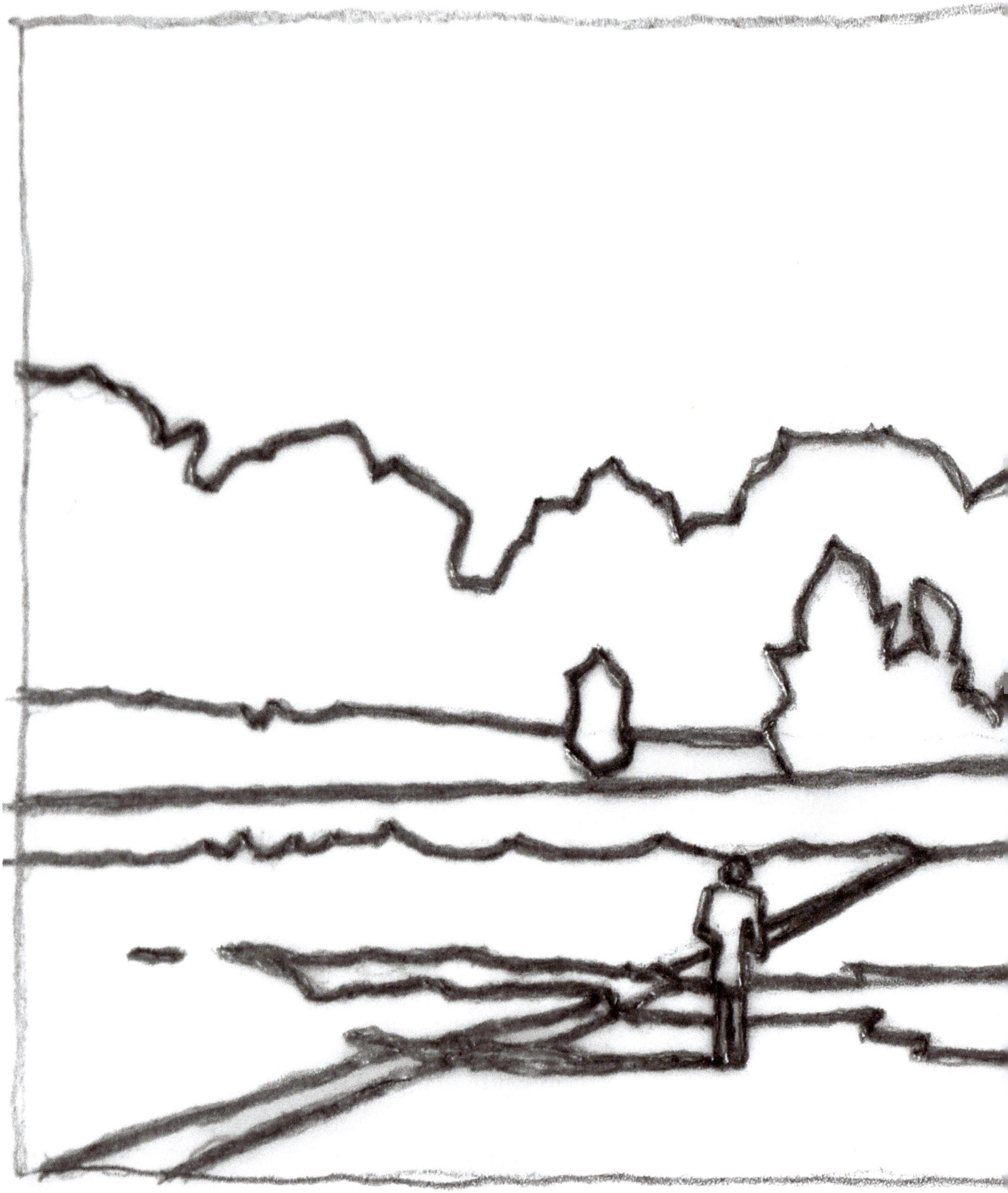

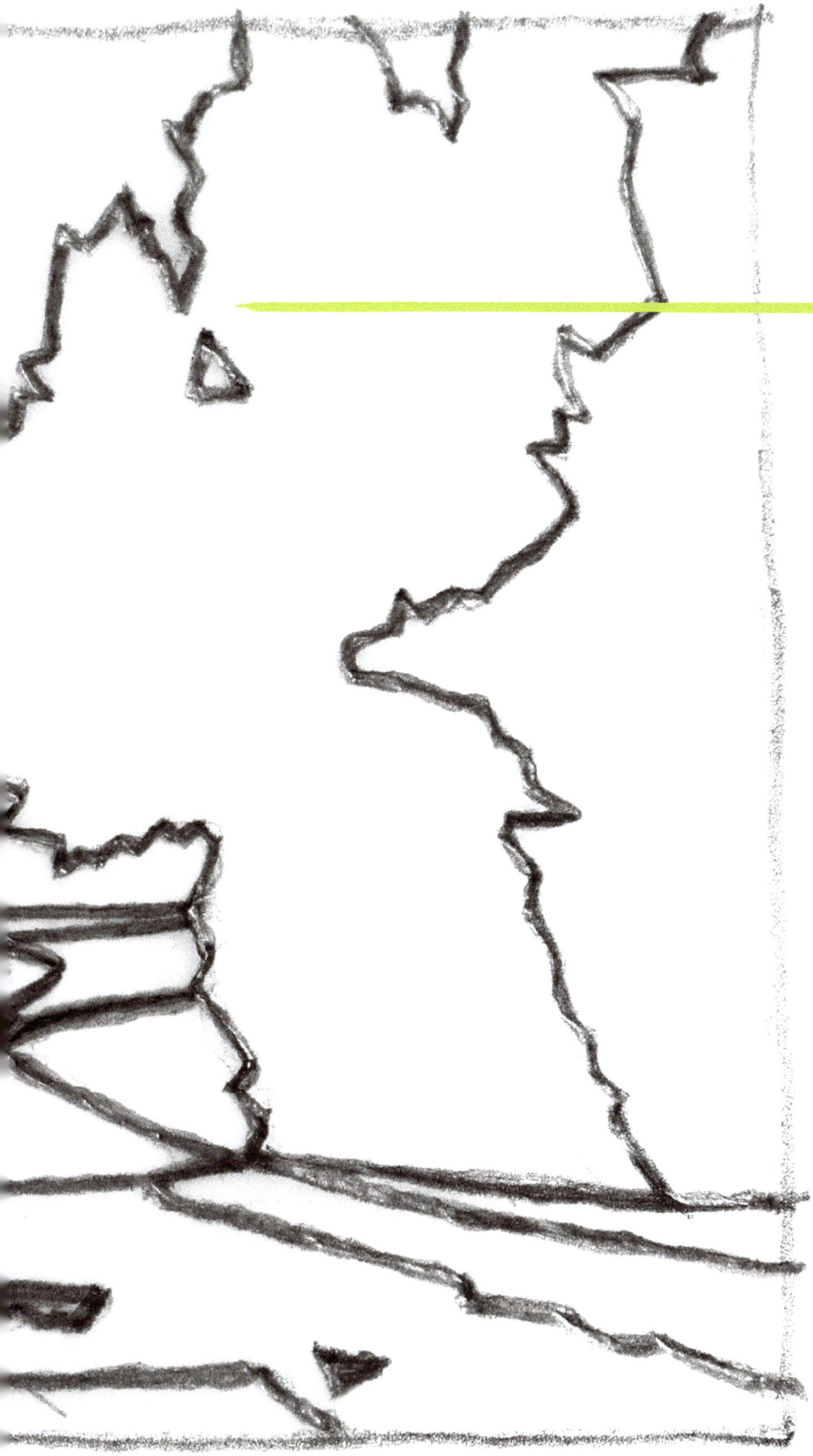

In this contour drawing, I left out the clouds, the buildings, and the bridge. I simplified and outlined the other larger shapes; then transferred the drawing to six pieces of watercolor paper for the following demonstration paintings.

Rural England
(graphite on tracing vellum)

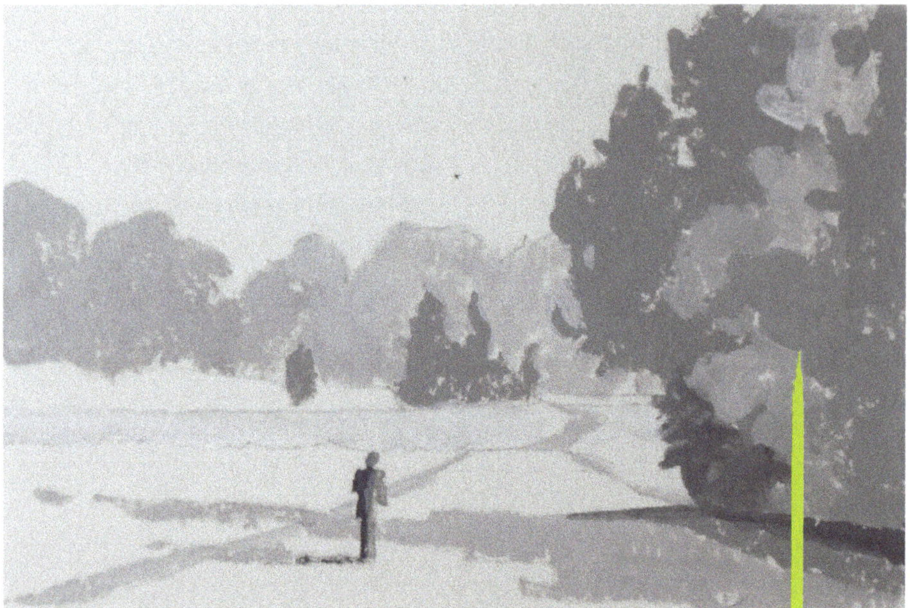

Light-value dominant grayscale painting
(acrylic on paper)

This value painting (above) features a simplified design with all the largest shapes well-defined. There is contrast in value (very light next to very dark) in the focal area (the figure), and there is also a variety in the size of shapes used in the focal area—some large, some medium, and the smallest shape, the lone figure.

Using white or very light for the big sky shape, part of the distant hills, some of the middle and foreground, and the road itself guarantees that the light value is dominant. This acts as the glue that holds it all together.

Train yourself to see color as value (black, white, grays); this will help you use color more effectively.

In this color sketch, I followed the values in my grayscale painting. The most-used and dominant value is light. These light areas help hold together the secondary palette of orange and violet.

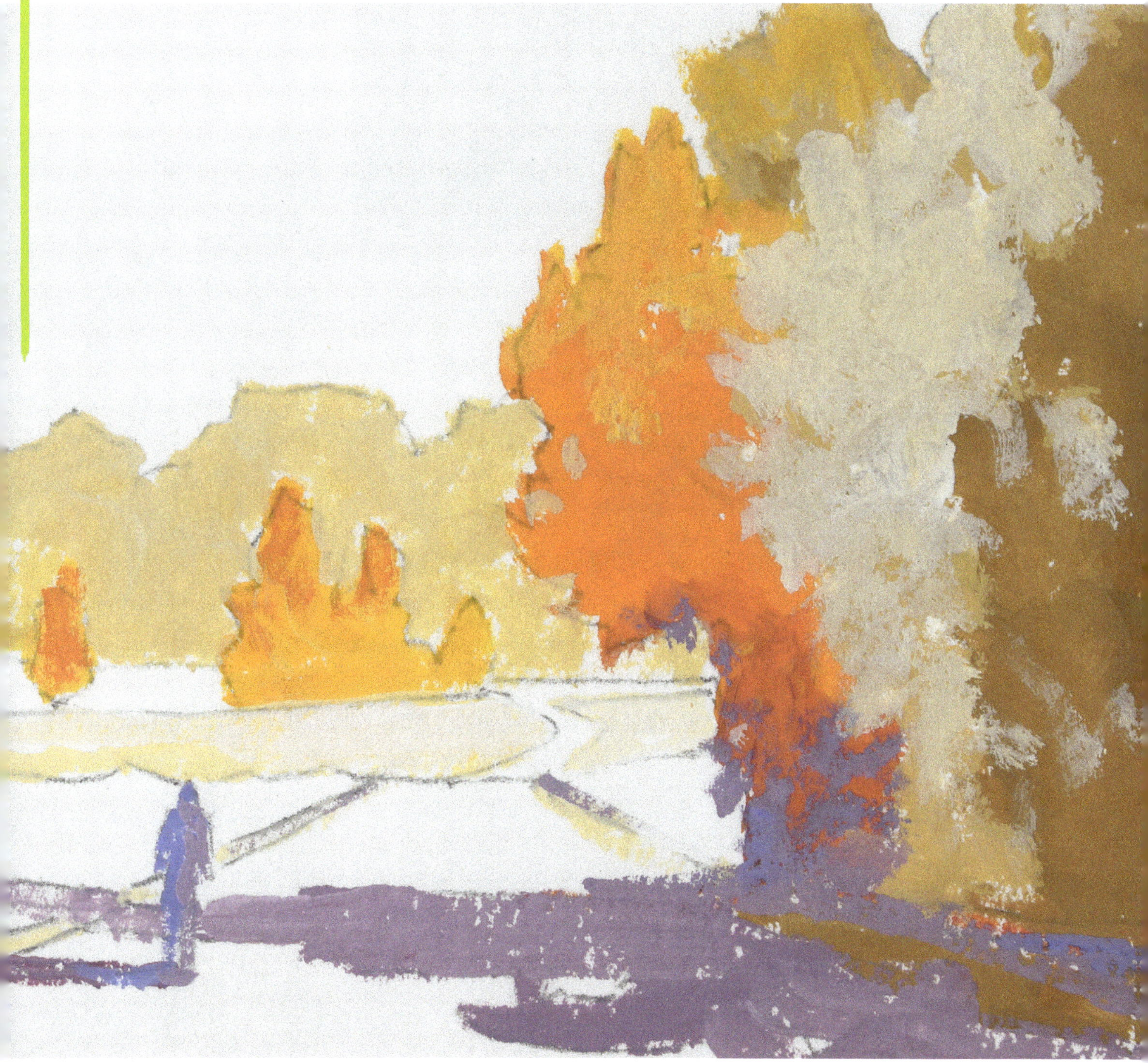

Light-value dominant in color (acrylic on paper)

Middle-value dominant grayscale painting
(acrylic on paper)

In the grayscale painting above, I've used a mid-tone value for all of the shapes in the distance and most of the ground and path in the foreground. I've saved the darkest dark for the edge of the tree on the right, which leads the viewer to the darkest dark and lightest light in that lone figure. Again the dominance of the middle value helps hold it all together.

I've used both a dominant color (ultramarine blue) and a dominant value (mid-tone) to act as strong features to hold my sketch together. Sometimes it's necessary to change the relative value of the shapes we use in our paintings—something most painters do when working in the field. Our goal is to make good paintings, not necessarily reproduce what we see. This value sketch features the middle values. Everything except the figure is a mid-tone or darker. I've placed light and dark together to bring attention to the figure. The light right side indicates the direction of the sunlight, as do the shadows from the trees on the right side of the sketch.

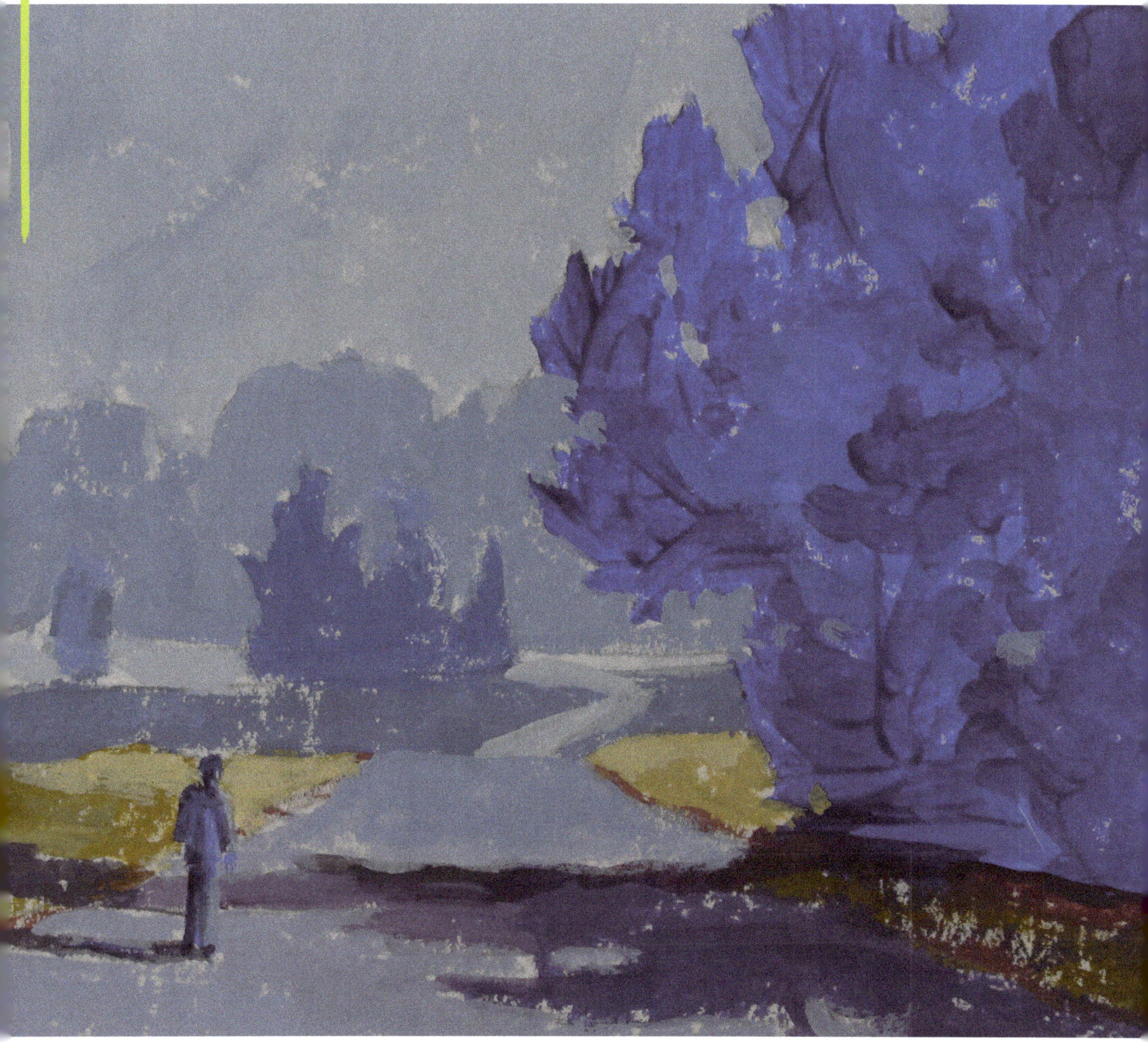

Middle-value dominant painting in color (acrylic on paper)

Dark-value dominant grayscale painting
(acrylic on paper)

In this final example, I've used both a dominant color (alizarin crimson and cadmium red light mixed with black) and a dominant dark value. Again, this could very well be a nocturnal scene with dramatic shadows formed from moonlight. Feel free to alter where shapes go and their relationship, value, and color. Your goal as a *plein air* painter should be to make the best painting you can at that moment and have fun!

Page 74, *Red Dog Wood*

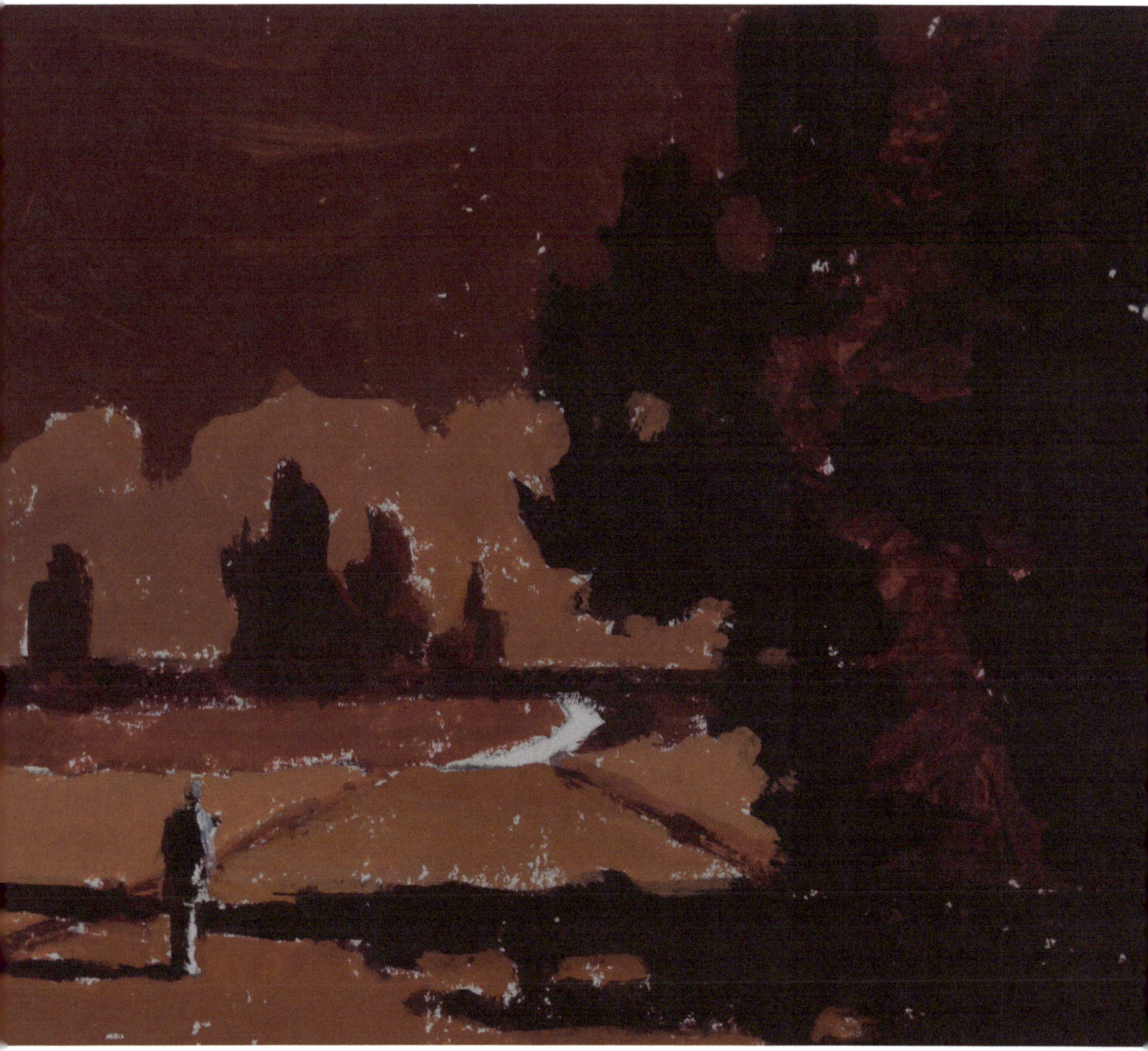

Dominant dark and dominant color (acrylic on paper)

Planning a Painting

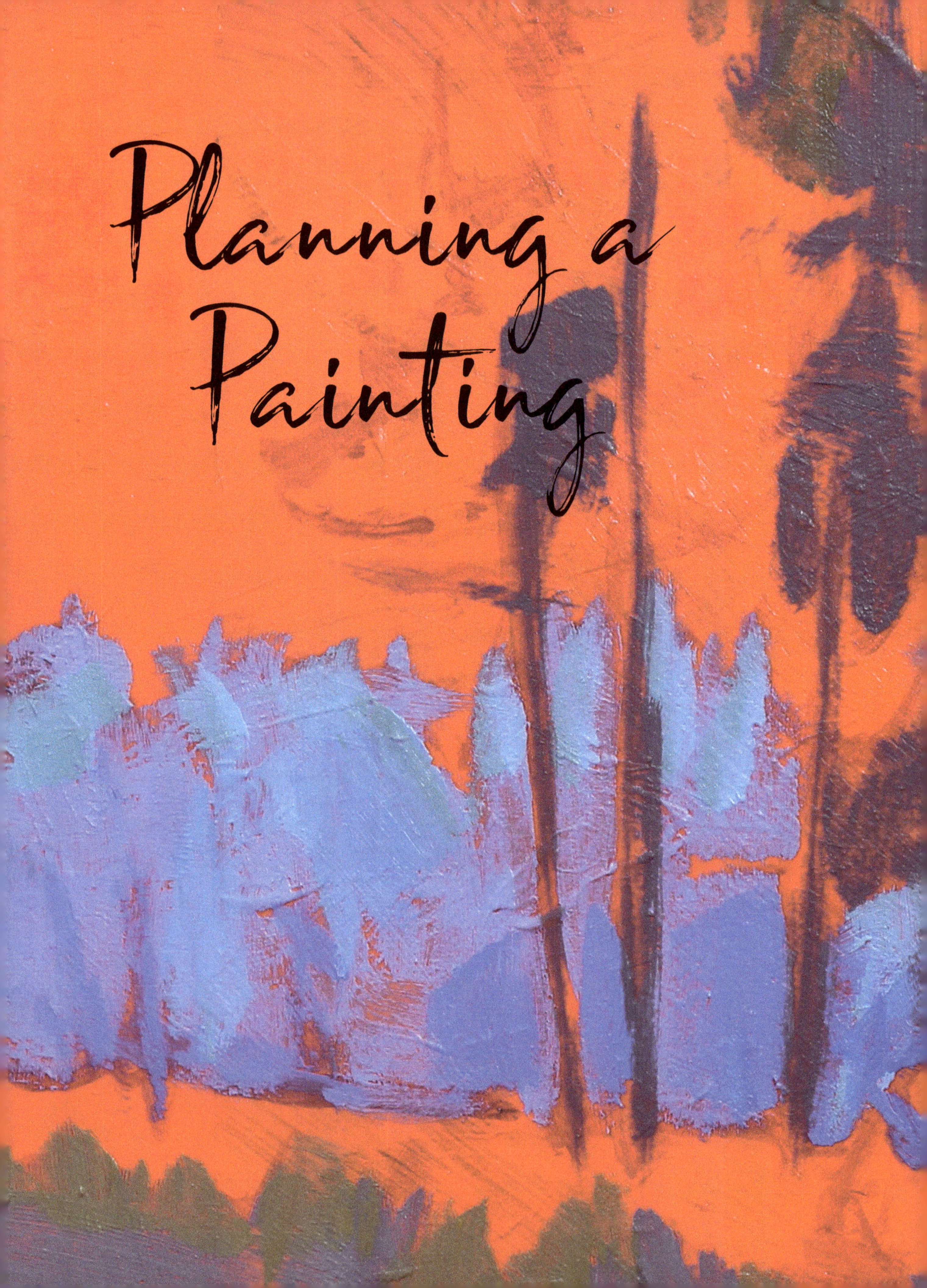

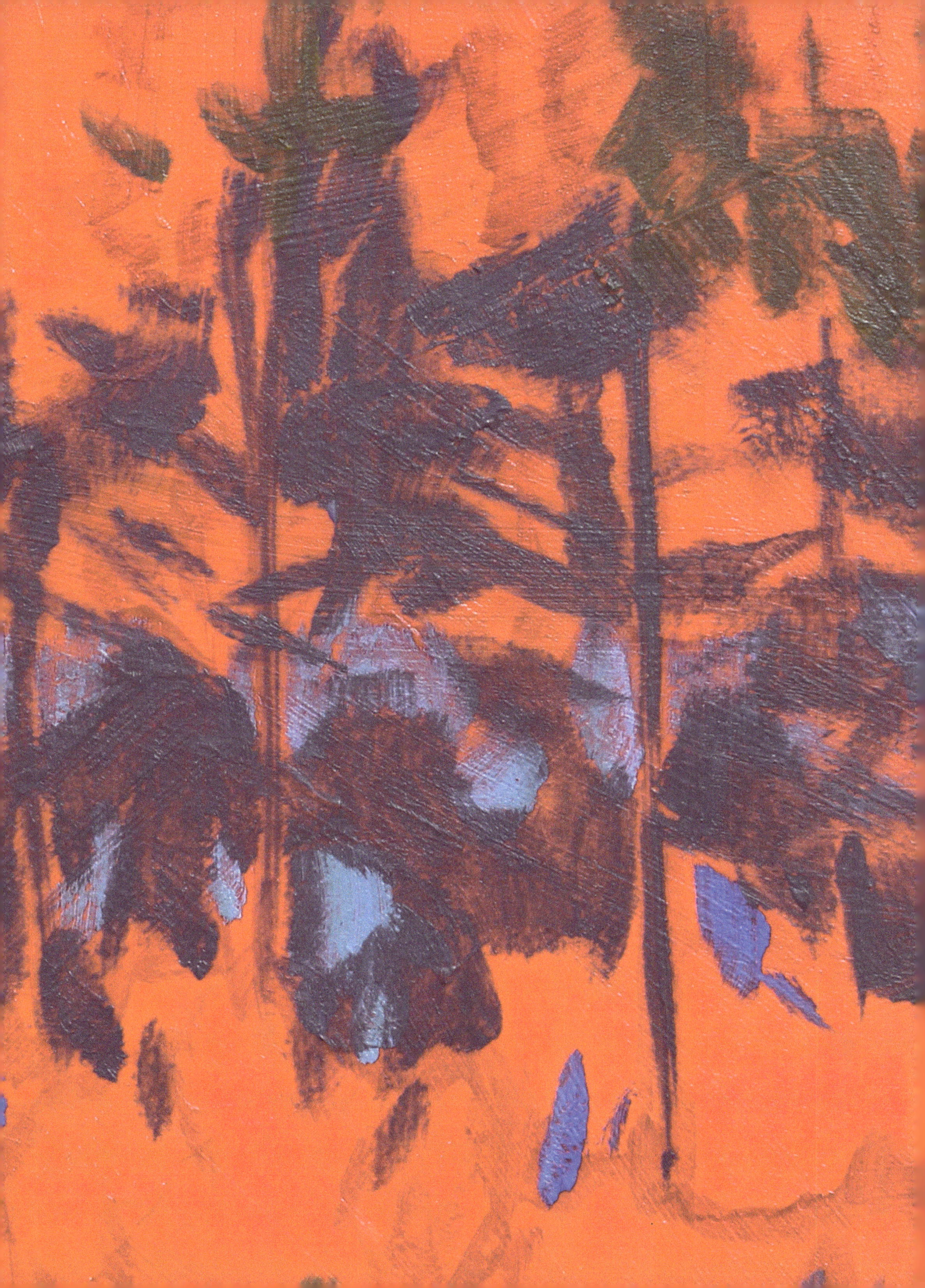

Painting as You Perceive

I prefer sunny mornings and foggy days to paint *en plein air*. I love the long shadows of early morning light—the quality of the light close to dawn. I also love the mood of a foggy day. Fog causes the light and the dark ends of the value scale to drop out, pushing all the values toward the middle. What is uninteresting on a sunny or cloudy day becomes mysterious and subtle on a foggy day. The easiest way to build interest in an otherwise ordinary scene is to plan it out.

About half the time, once I settle on a painting location, I take a quick photo, and then I draw a small 2-by-3-inch or 3-by-4-inch compositional value plan in pencil. These little sketches provide the relationship of the big shapes (how they fit together) and the value of each shape (how light or dark those shapes will be). This plan is especially important when the light is changing rapidly.

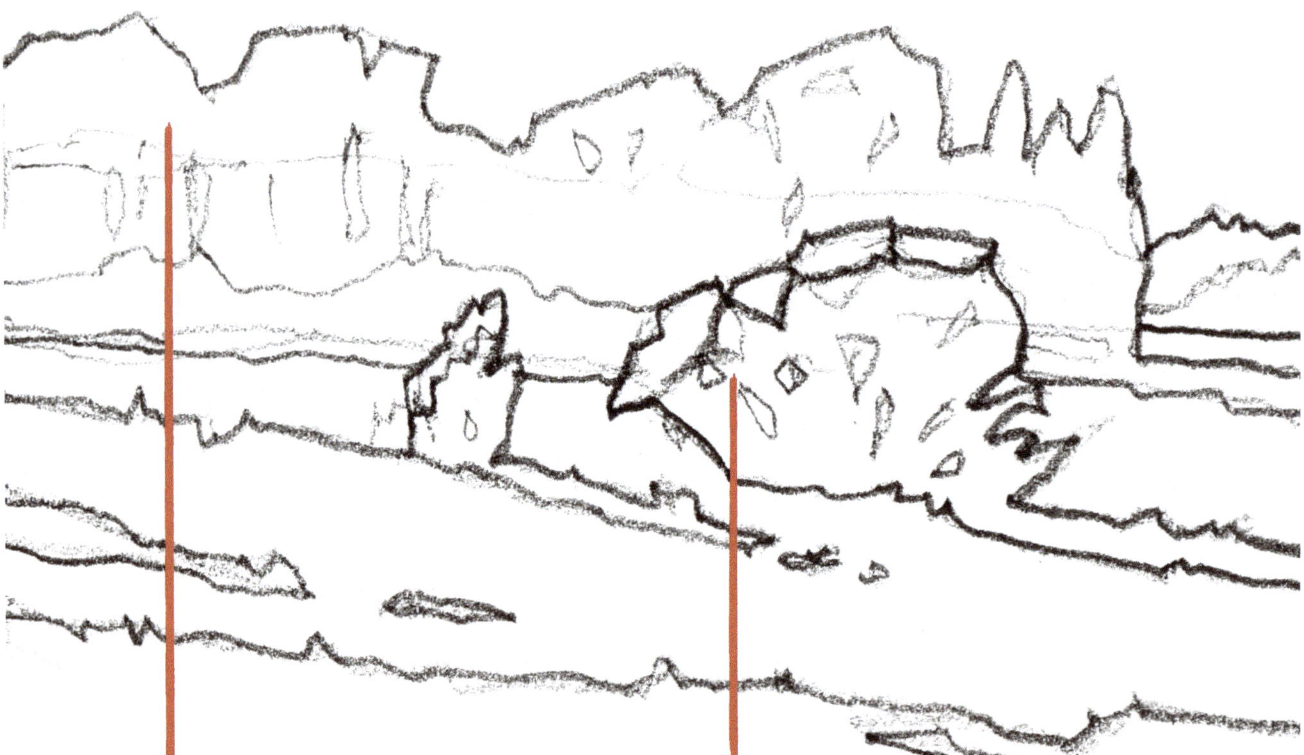

The first step in a contour (outline) drawing is to establish where the big shapes go.

Next add the values to those shapes. This tells me how light or dark each shape should be. This is my plan, but I am not locked into this outline. If I think deviating from this will make a better painting, I do so.

When I'm satisfied with my outline, I add the values. I generally use five values: white, light, medium, medium dark, and very dark or black. These five are enough for me to execute the painting, knowing that I may slide from one to the other or even add an in-between value. Once I'm satisfied with my plan, the fun begins!

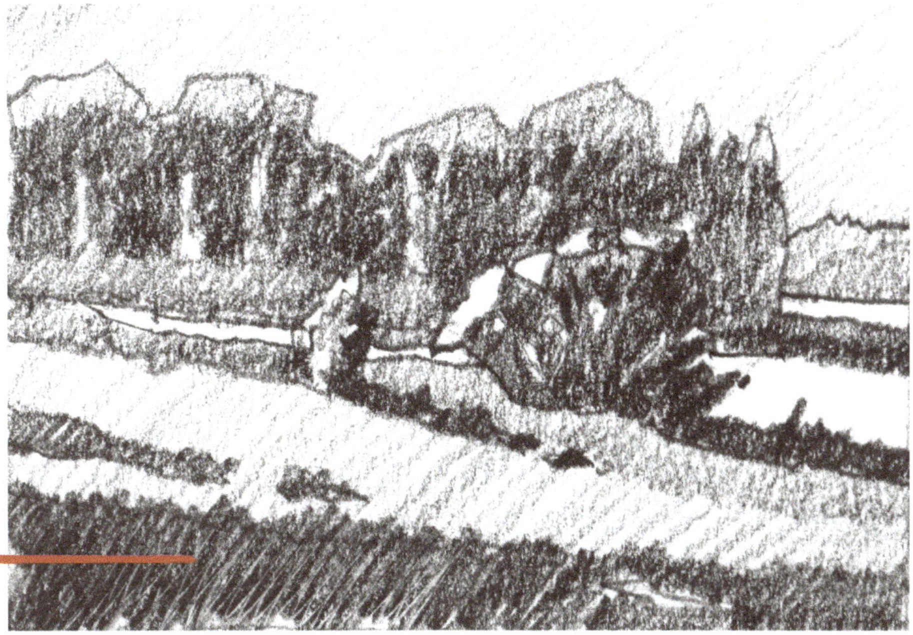

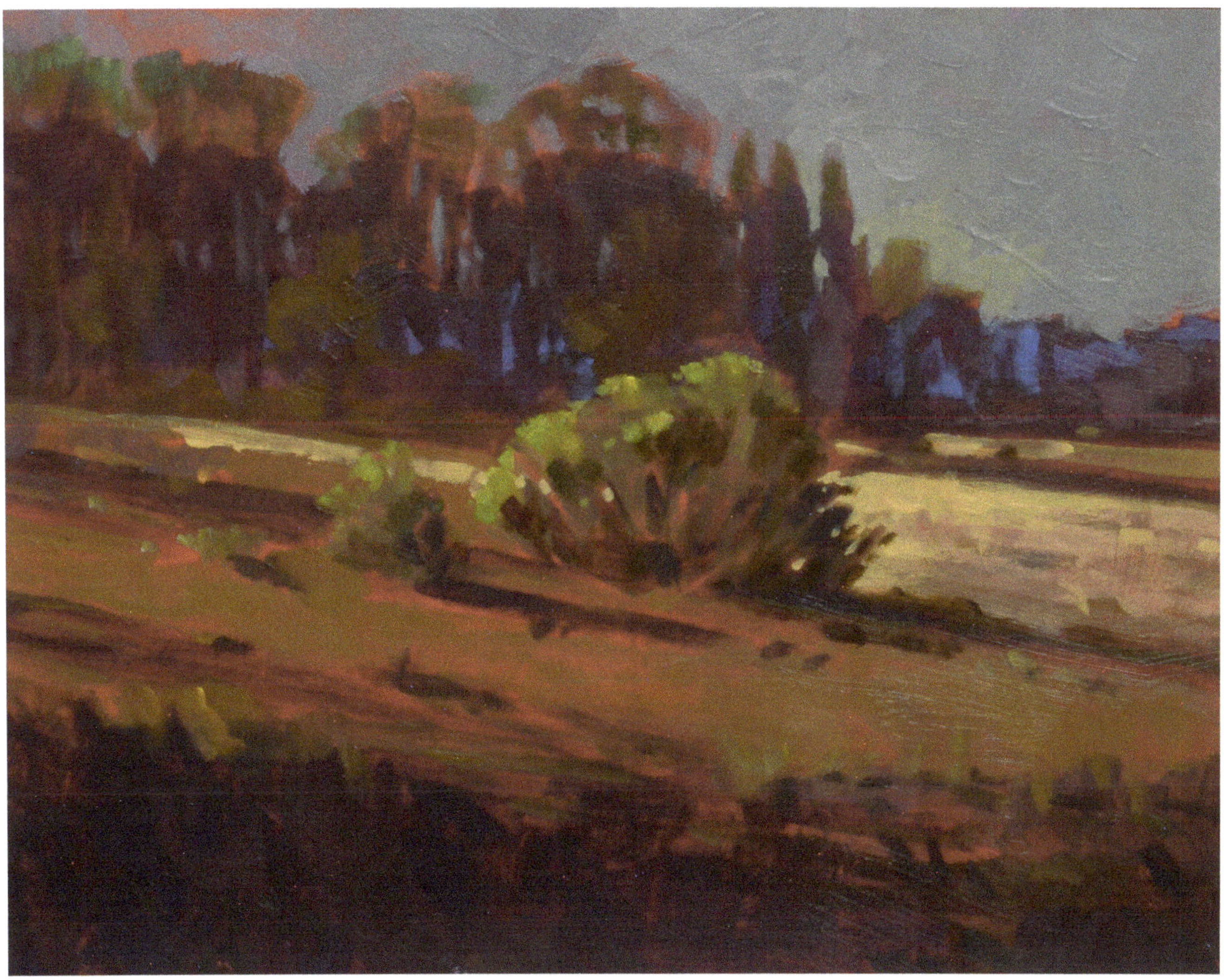

Planning a Painting

When the natural scene is fairly average, it becomes your job as the artist to make the painting interesting. For example, it is most difficult to make a painting on a cloudy day. The light is scattered evenly, there are no dramatic shadows, and everything is bathed in an overall sameness. Perhaps try to find an unusual viewpoint or a different color combination for the composition. The use of interesting, interlocking shapes offers many design possibilities. Improvise, experiment, and remember your goal is to make a good painting.

This drawing is from my sketchbook. It illustrates the "bones" of the composition—where the shapes go and how those shapes relate to one another. Next I need to add the lights and darks—my values.

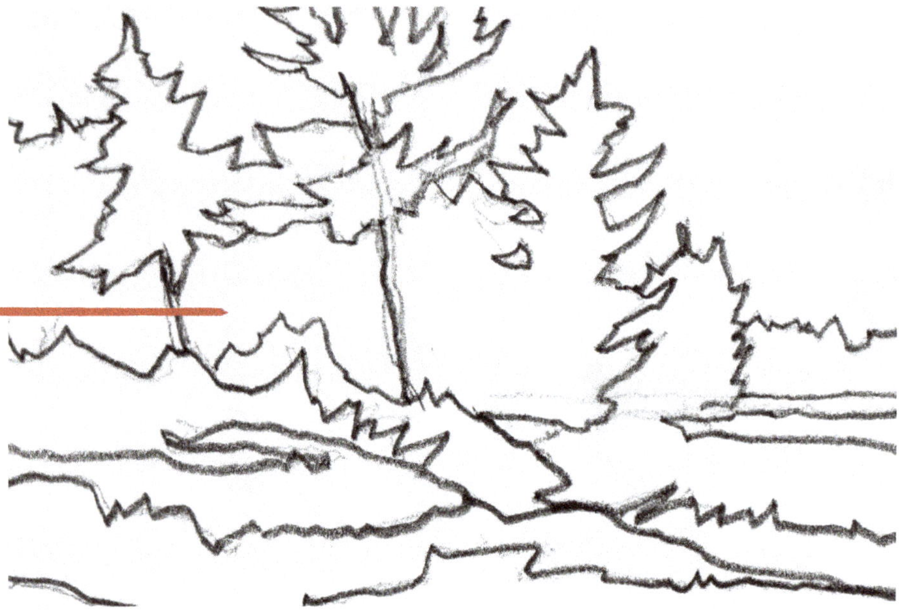

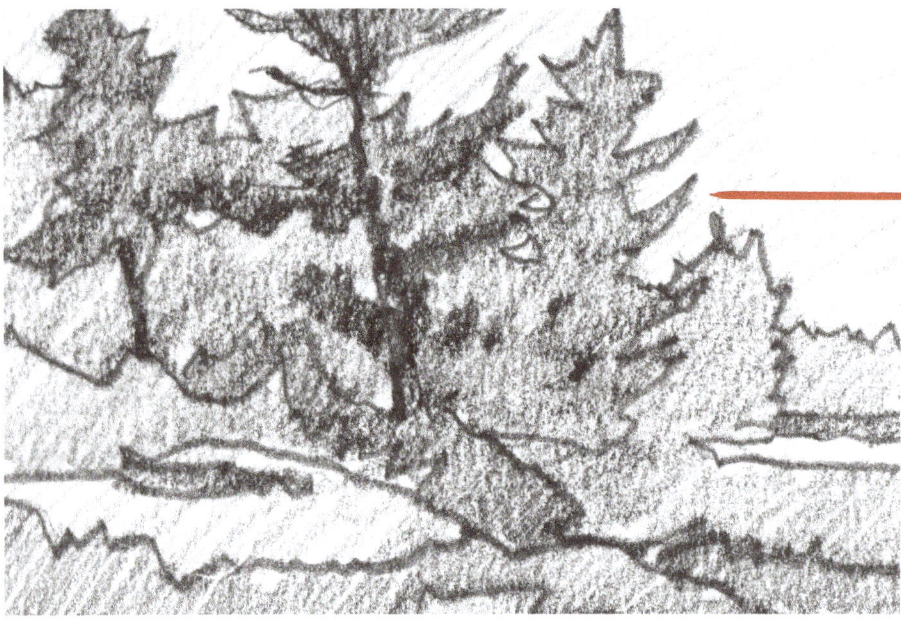

The lights and darks are now all in place. There's neither value contrast nor cast shadows to play with.

It's a gray day, but I did my best to make the interlocking shapes that form the foreground—especially the sky and tops of the pine trees—as interesting as possible.

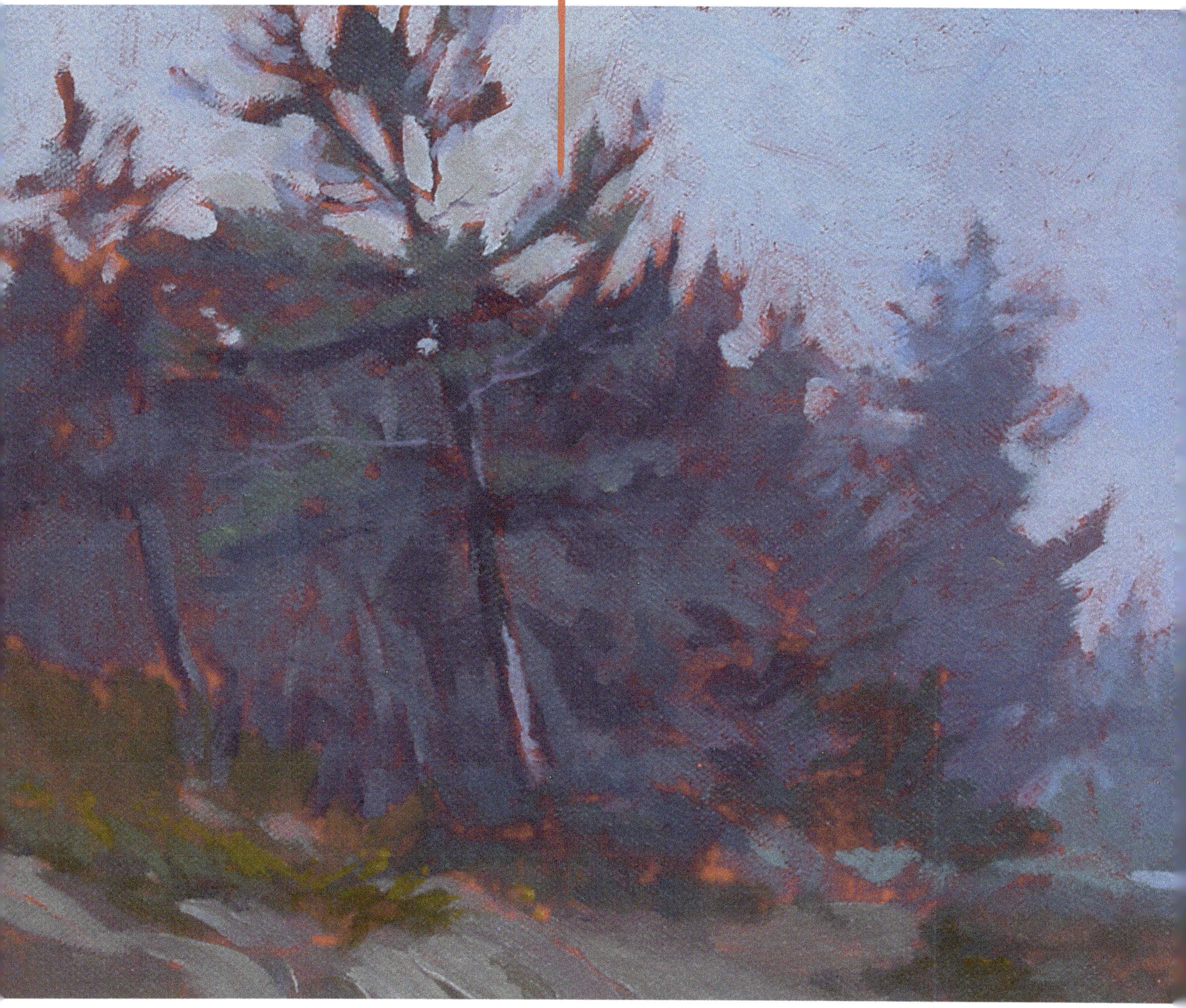

The Focal Point

Once we decide where and what to paint, the work really begins. Something we see causes us to say, “I’d like to paint that!” That becomes the focus of our work. Sometimes it’s referred to as the focal area, the focal point, or the center of interest. Whatever the name, it’s the star of our visual show.

Our eyes take in everything they see. If we had unlimited time, we could probably do a good job of painting “everything.” However, our viewers would rather see what’s important; not necessarily everything. We need to edit what we see, which means to simplify and leave extraneous items out of our paintings. The more we leave out, the more the viewers will fill in. Usually, the more involved the viewer, the more he or she likes our work.

The Process

1. Choose the focal area of the scene.
2. Contour the shapes (outlines).
3. Assign values to every shape using value contrast for important areas and close-value relationships for supporting areas.
4. Re-organize the arrangement, if you want to change the focal area. (You can also do this before step 3.)

1. Find the focal area.

My sister lives beside a beautiful lake in northern Michigan. I love visiting, as there is an endless amount of beautiful scenery to paint. For this painting, I chose a view from the water. At this time of day (late afternoon/early evening), the light hit the two large pines on the right side of the composition. Those light shapes were surrounded and framed by dark pine boughs. This strong value contrast (the difference between a light shape and a dark one) was what initially captured my interest. I decided this would be the “star of my show”—my center of interest.

2. Contour the shapes.

I created a contour (outline) drawing in my sketchbook of the shapes as I wanted them arranged in the painting. This is where the simplification and process of omission starts. Try it—you will be surprised by how much information you can leave out and still have the viewer "get it."

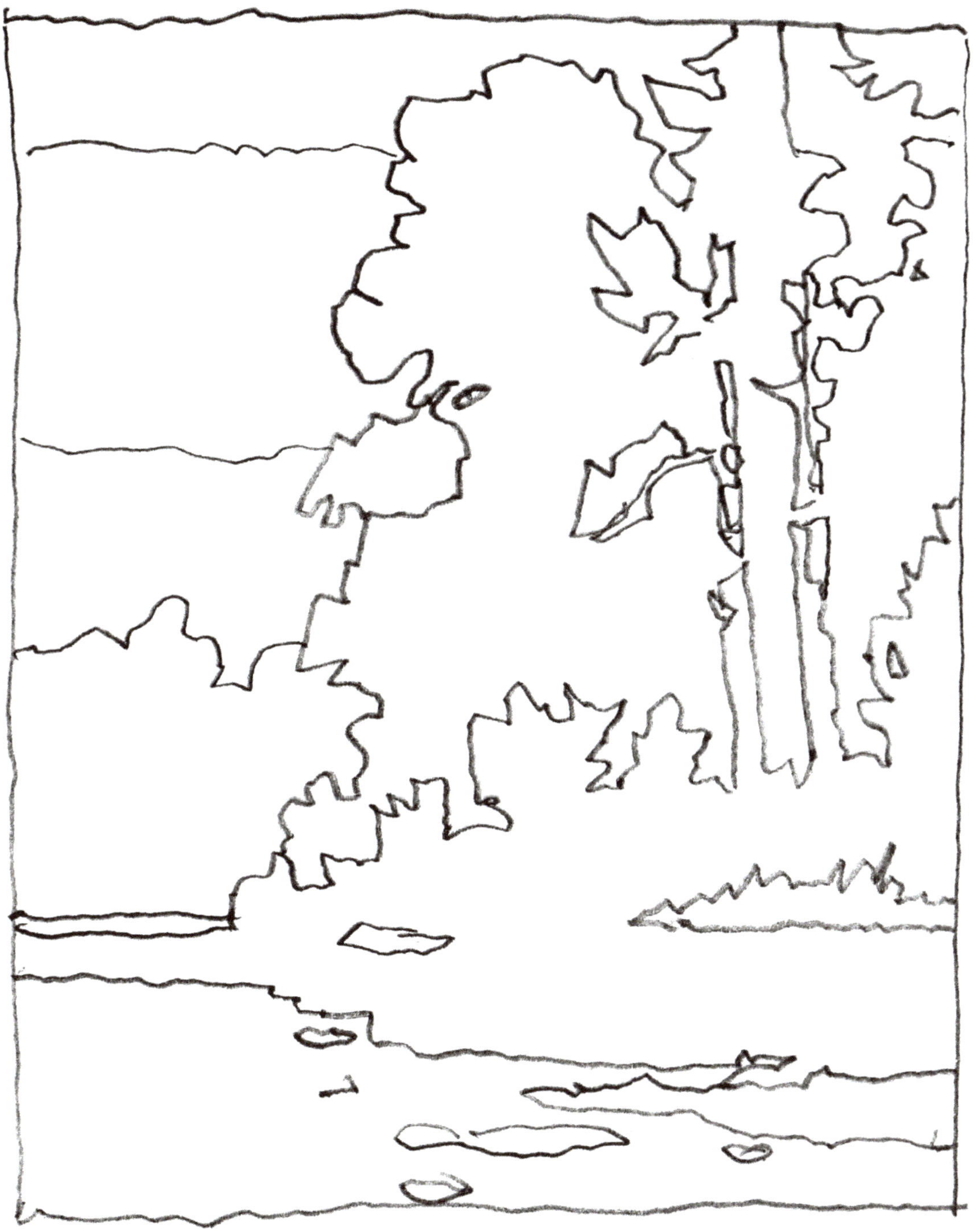

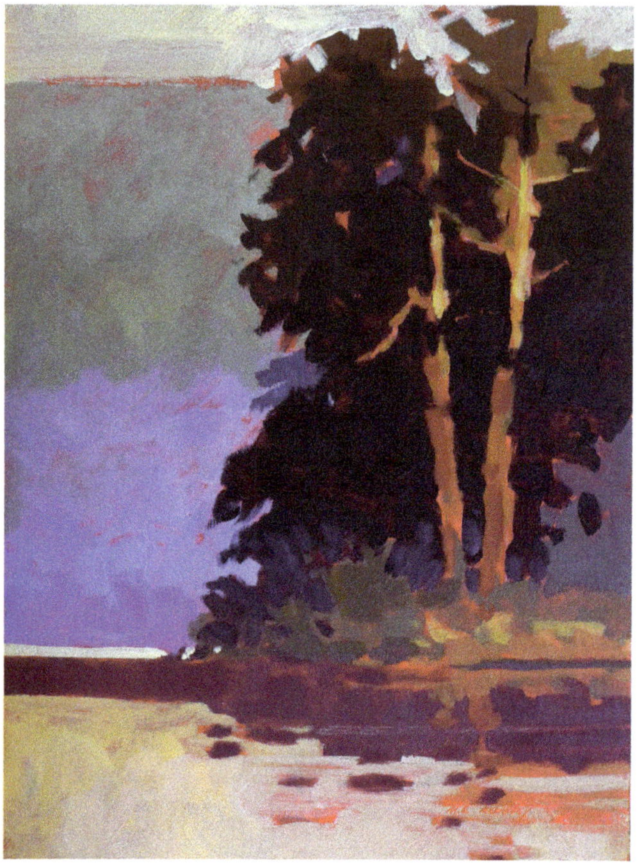

3. Assign values to every shape.

Here the center of interest is clearly defined. My darkest dark and my lightest light draw the viewer's eye to those sunlit tree trunks. In addition, I used smaller shapes surrounded by larger shapes in this area. The contrast in size also emphasizes the focal point: the upper right where the light hits the tree trunks. This light is nicely framed and contrasted by the darks behind it. I use a 5B pencil, which is soft and can easily make darks, to shade in the values as I want them to appear in the final painting.

4. Redesign to change the focal area.

But what if I decide to change the focal area? It is possible to completely change where the viewer looks by emphasizing different elements. I decide to add a small, dark sailboat. But if I leave it at that, there would be a visual conflict between the small shape of the sailboat and the light and dark shapes on the tree trunks. To solve this visual dilemma, I reduce the value contrast in the tree trunks so that my gaze is drawn more to the small sailboat in the lower left part of the composition. Remember, you can change anything that you think might result in a good painting!

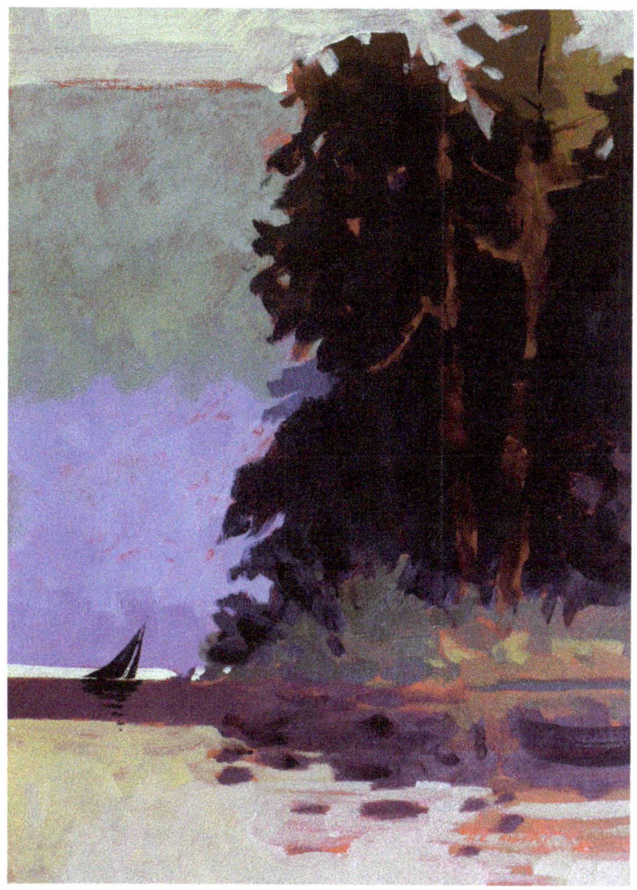

Step-by-Step Project: *Early Spring*

I start this project with a 2-by-3-inch sketch, introducing the big shapes.

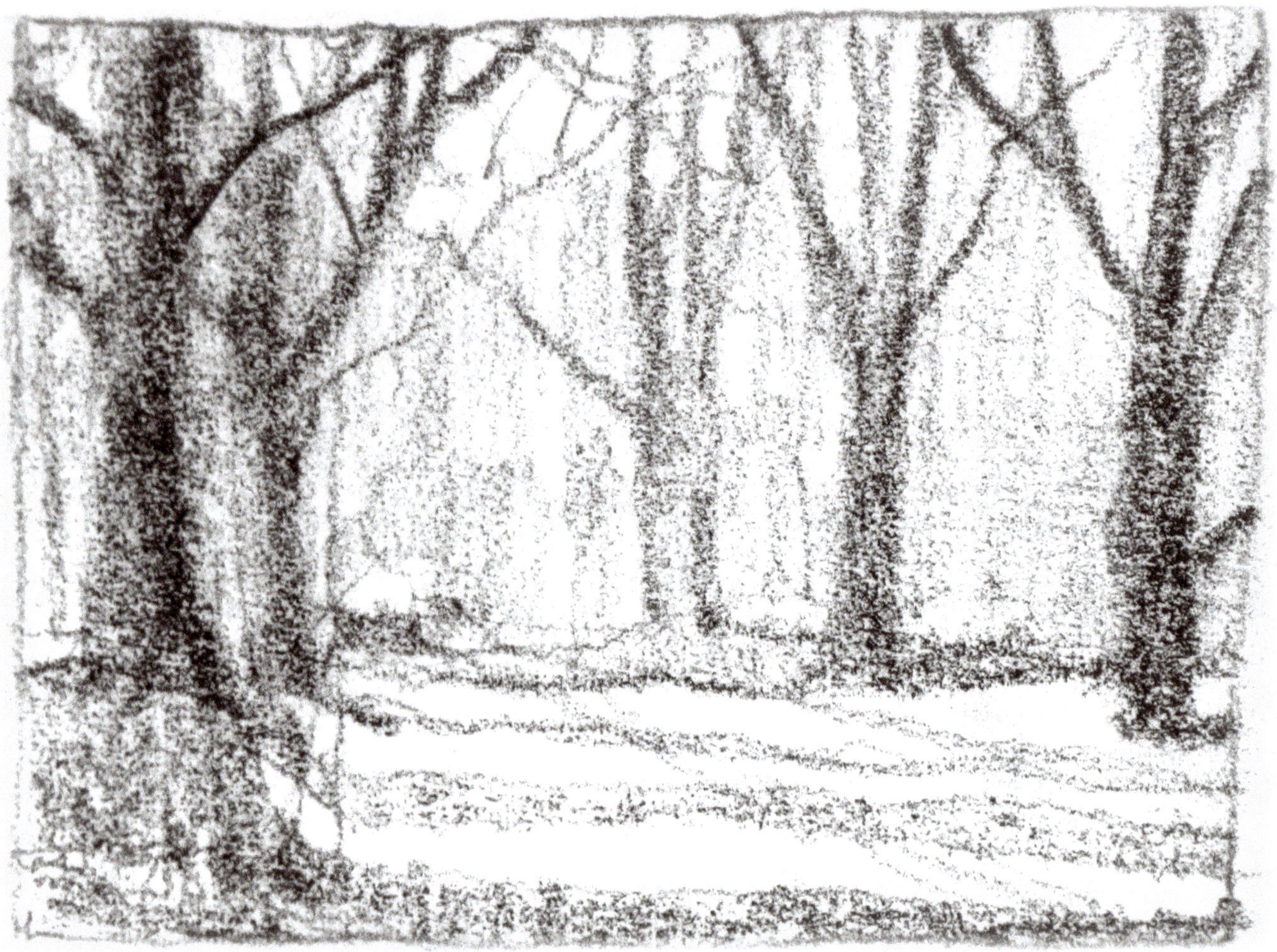

Step 1

I start with a background mixture of ultramarine blue and alizarin crimson with enough titanium white to create a middle value of violet. I paint the entire panel, including the edges. Alizarin crimson is slightly darker than a mid-tone, so I use that to draw all the big shapes on the panel. I also decide that a square format will tighten my design considerably.

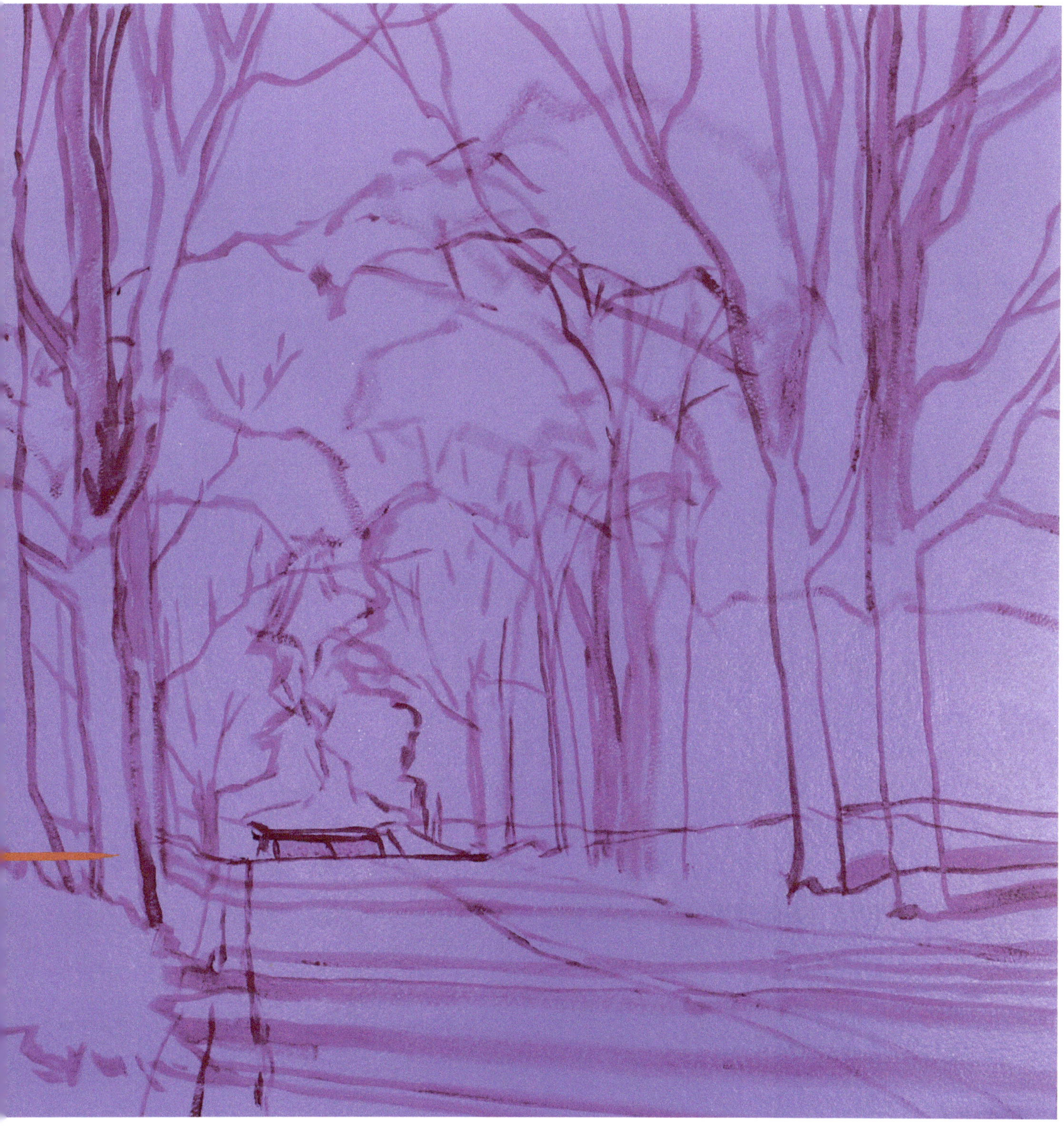

Step 2

The converging lines that form the side of the country road lead the eye into the distance. To give the viewer a bit of a destination, I use mixtures of cadmium yellow deep, a bit of alizarin crimson, a small amount of ultramarine blue, and white in the area shown. I paint the trees along the horizon line on both sides of the road using a mixture of ultramarine blue, a small amount of cadmium yellow light, and plenty of white. I keep this distant tree line cool in temperature to help it recede into the distance.

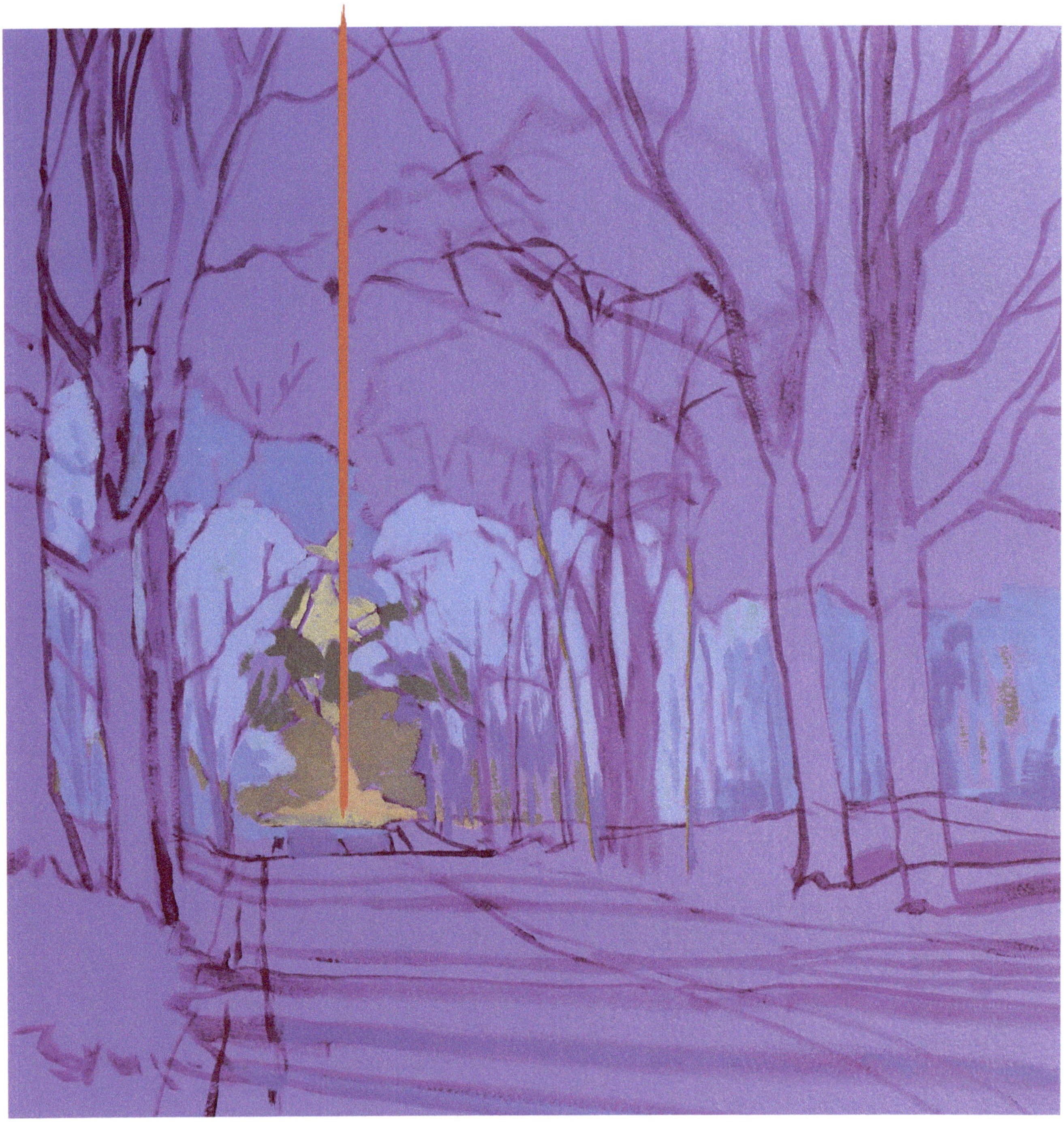

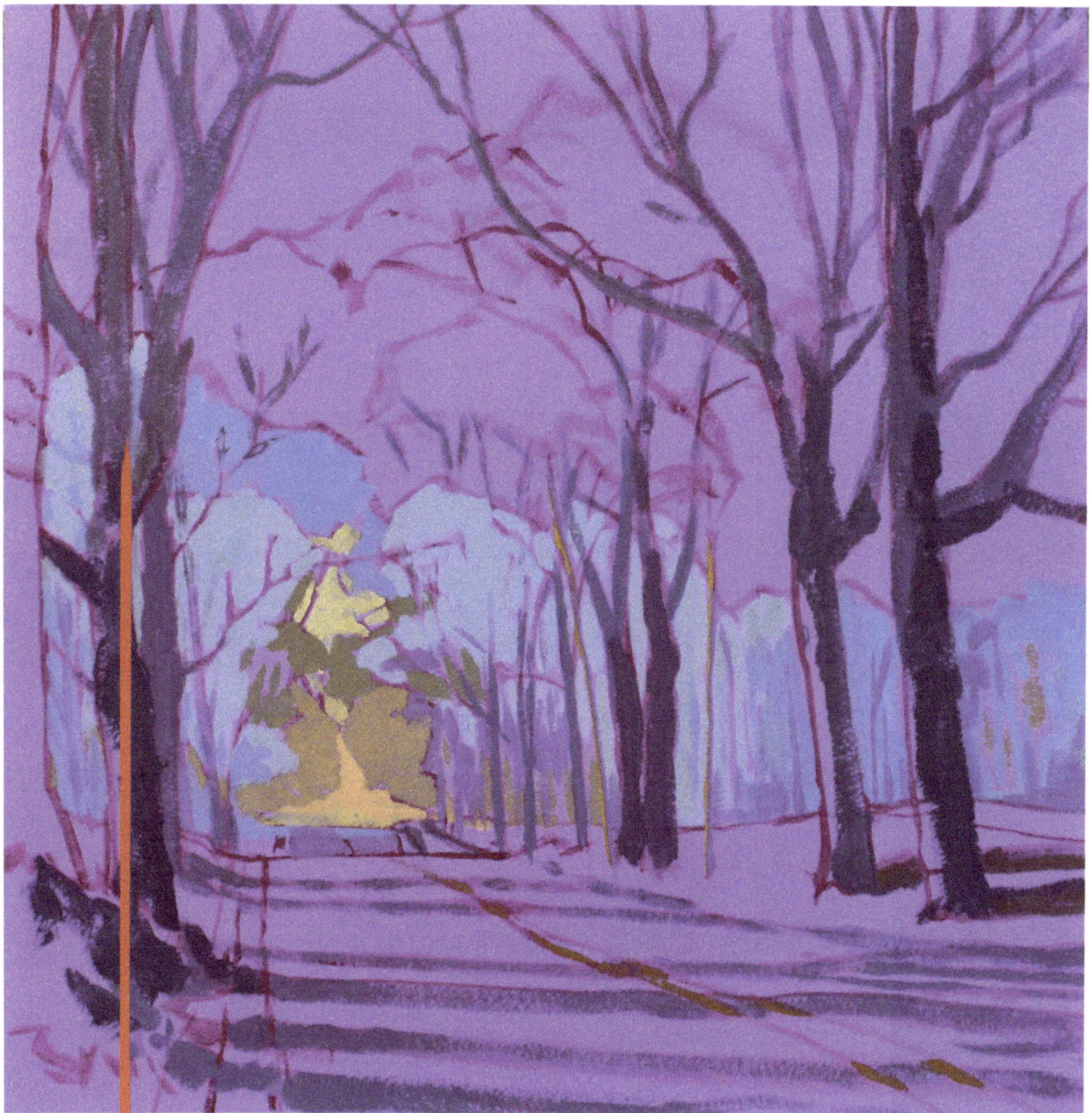

Step 3

I paint all the trees and their shadows with a neutralized violet. Complementary colors when mixed together neutralize each other. First, I make a medium dark mixture of ultramarine blue and alizarin crimson. To this mixture I add a small amount of cadmium yellow deep. Yellow is opposite violet on the color wheel. Opposites, when mixed together, will tend to dull or neutralize that color. I add some white to this subdued violet. I paint all the trees (except where the light hits on the left side), and I extend this color into all the tree shadows. This has the effect of simplifying those shapes. As the trees recede into the distance (and get smaller), I add a bit more white to slightly lighten those areas. I also use this lighter mix to paint the branches up in the sky.

Step 4

In early spring, the tops of the trees show new growth. I indicate this with a saturated bright green. To give the viewer a sense of increased saturation or intensity for those shapes, I switch from ultramarine blue to phthalo blue. Phthalo blue is cooler and tends toward green. When mixed with cadmium yellow light, it makes a saturated green. I add a bit more yellow and white to lighten the tops as an indication of extra light hitting those shapes.

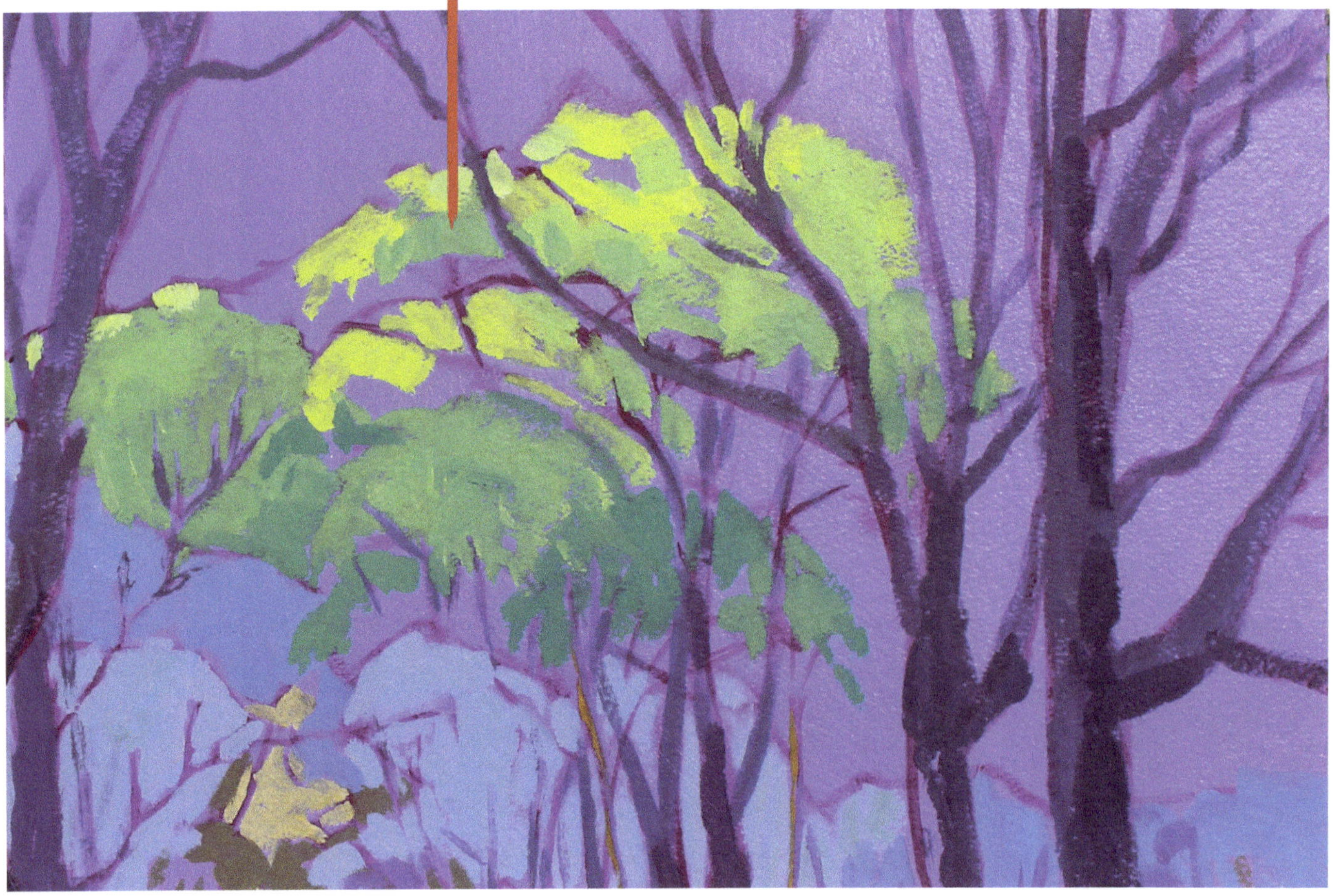

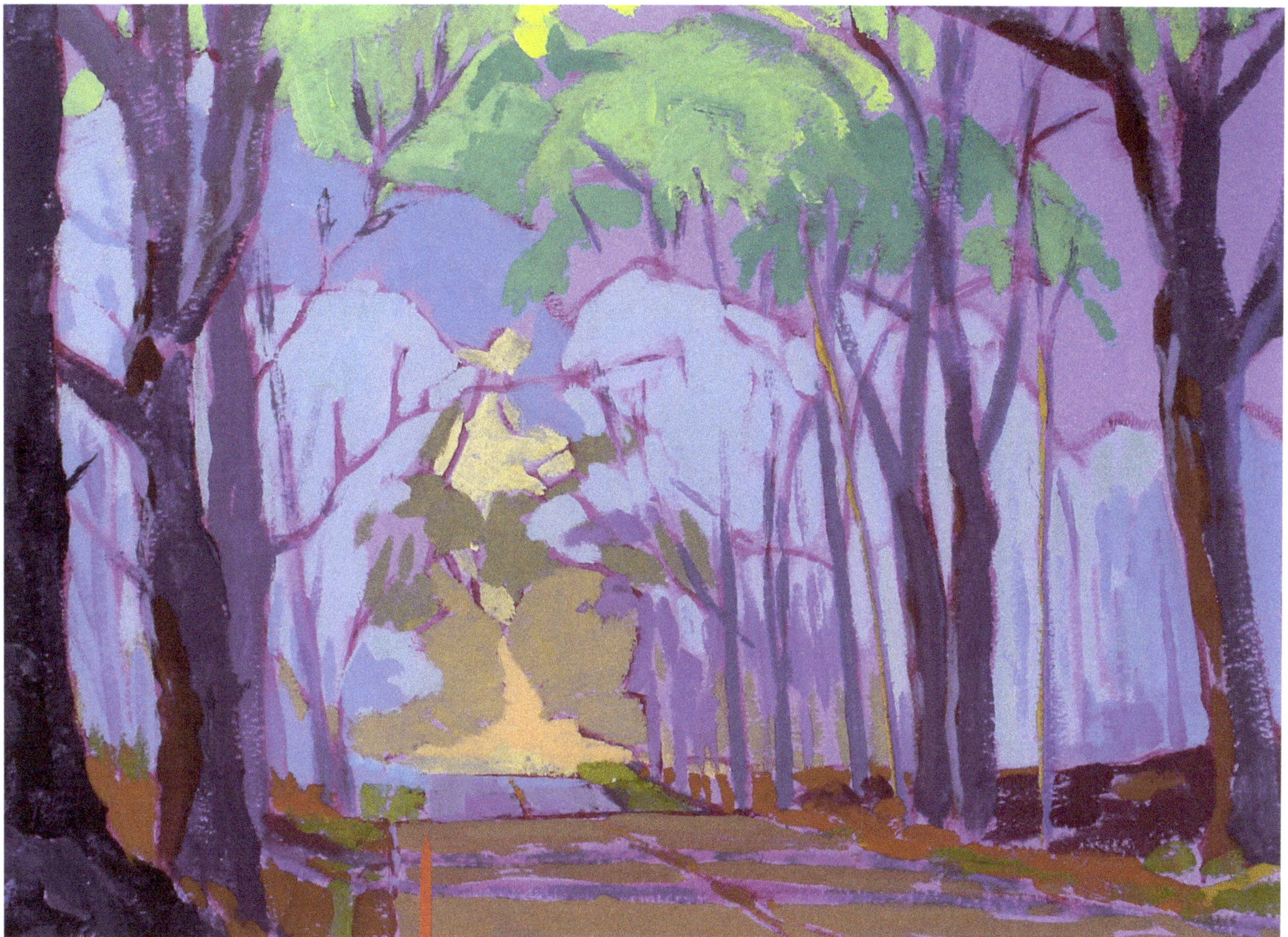

Step 5

The shapes that make up both the ground and the road between the shadows are decidedly warm in color temperature. I again "push" that relationship by using a mixture of cadmium yellow deep with a bit of alizarin. On the sides of the road, I reduce the amount of alizarin and add more ultramarine blue to produce green for the new grass.

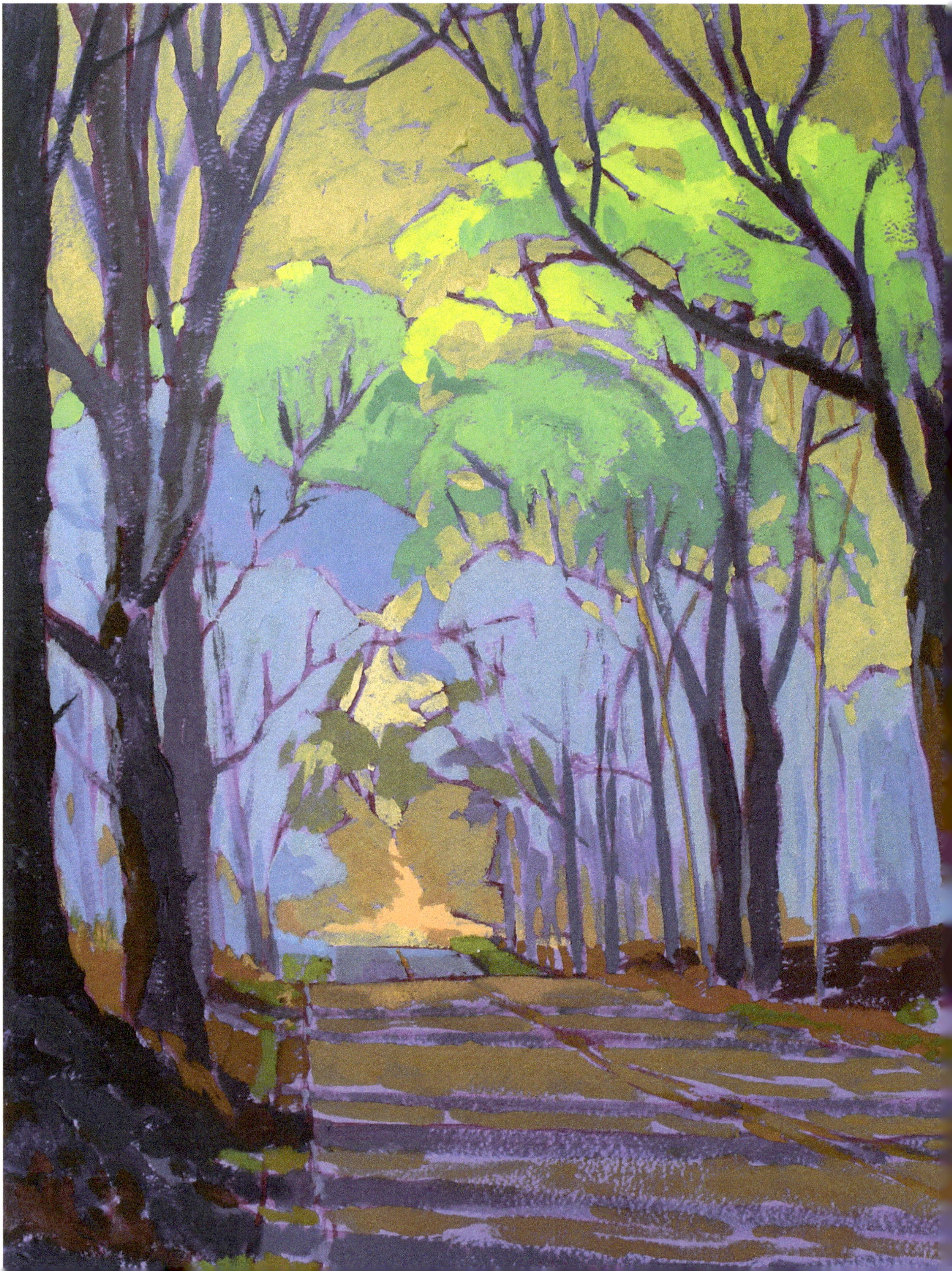

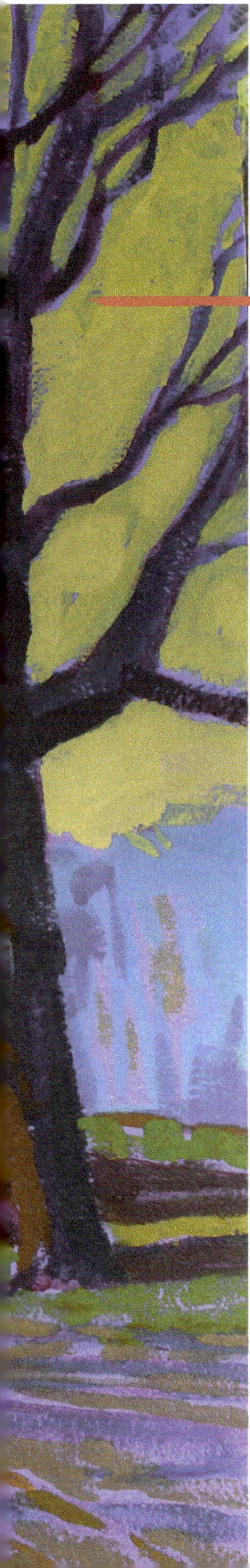

Step 6

I decide to go with a light, neutralized yellow (made by mixing cadmium yellow light, a bit of violet, and lots of white) for the sky area, hoping to contrast with the warmth of the orange around the distant road and the warmer color in the tree shapes just above where the road disappears. As always, as the shapes get smaller, the size of my brush gets smaller. For the larger negative shapes between the branches, I use a size 6 short flat. For the smaller shapes, I switch to a size 4 flat. I work quickly, allowing some of the violet to show throughout the entire painting. This provides some unity and, I hope, some sense of early spring.

Early Spring
(acrylic on paper, mounted on panel)

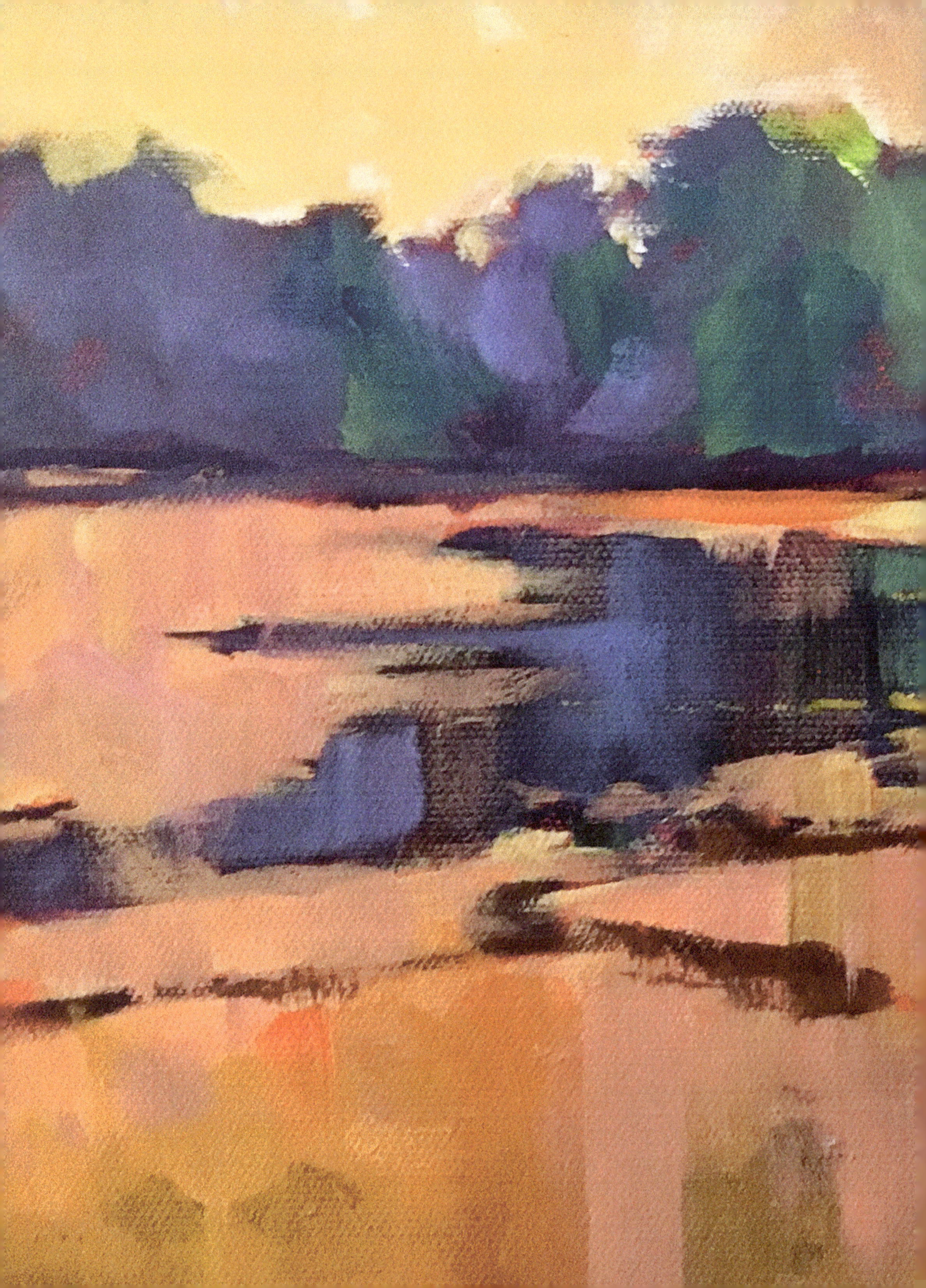

Different Approaches to Painting

Finding Your Style

There are many ways to approach painting outdoors. This chapter features some of the ways you might like to start, but it is by no means all-inclusive. There are days when I abandon all previous methods of beginning, so that I can explore something new or just make a big mess!

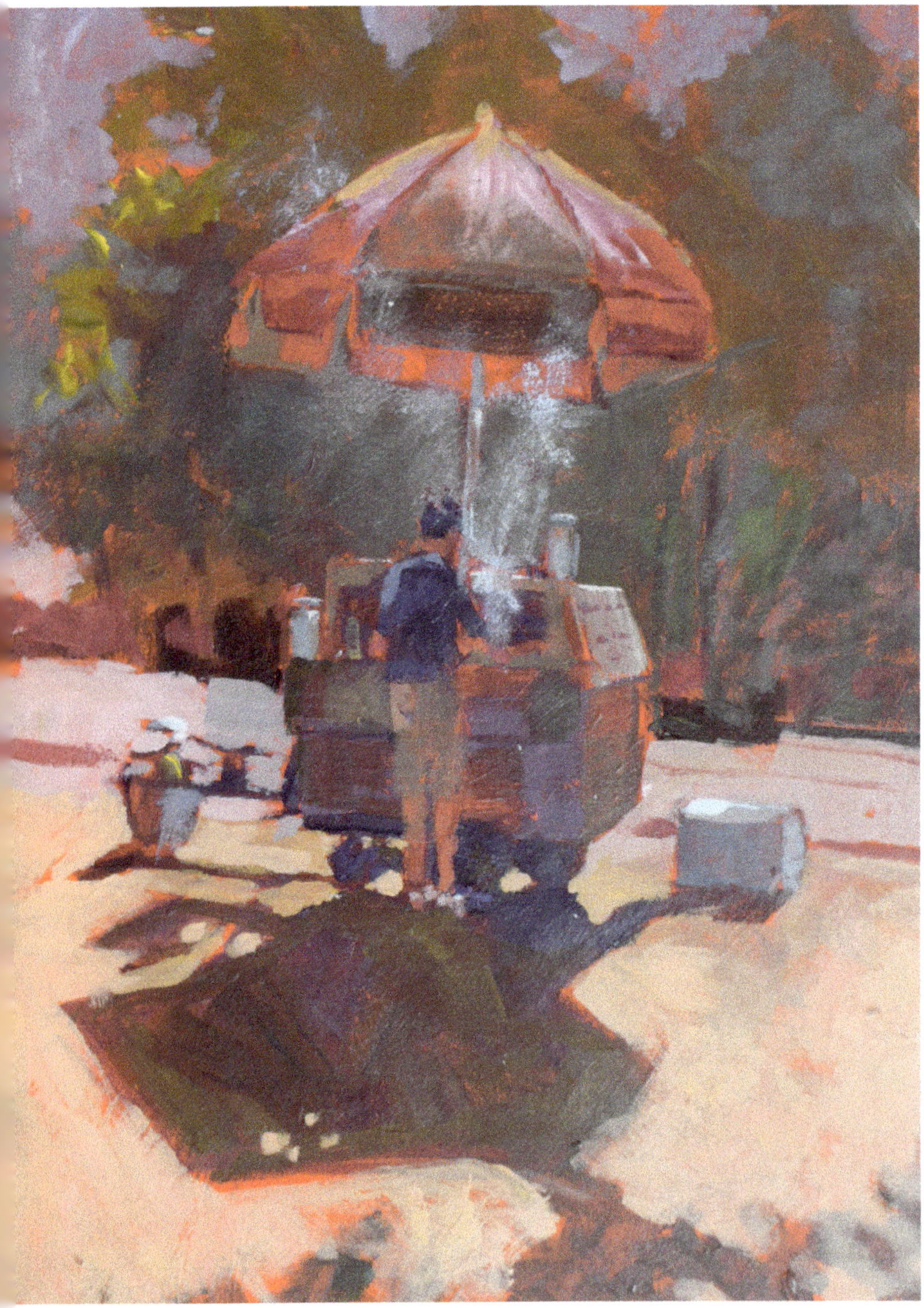

Hot Dog Vendor (acrylic on panel)

Starting with Basic Shapes

I created this 12-by-9-inch painting on-site in New York City. It was morning, and the guy who owned the hot dog cart was just getting started. The scene was backlit, throwing shadows toward me. That strong morning light negated some of the color, turning the local color into a warm neutral. I loved the steam that was rising up from that first batch of hot dogs, and I used dry-brush scumbling over an already dry passage to indicate it. I did not have much time that morning, so it was necessary to get the gist of the vision I had for the painting in a short amount of time.

First, I eliminated the buildings behind the trees. The buildings would help set the scene in the city, but the vendor's setup is my story. I also eliminated about a dozen other people. I felt that to include them would prove unnecessary distraction. I want the viewer to focus on the vendor, the setup, the shadows, and particularly that steam.

For the sake of this demonstration, I've reproduced my toned panel, including the outlines of all the basic shapes I needed. Notice that there are two lines: one dark line in pencil and another in white pencil on top of that. My cadmium red light-toned panel was too close in value to the graphite pencil lines, making the lines hard to see. I always carry a white water-soluble pencil for such occasions. White against the mid-value cadmium red light shows up much better.

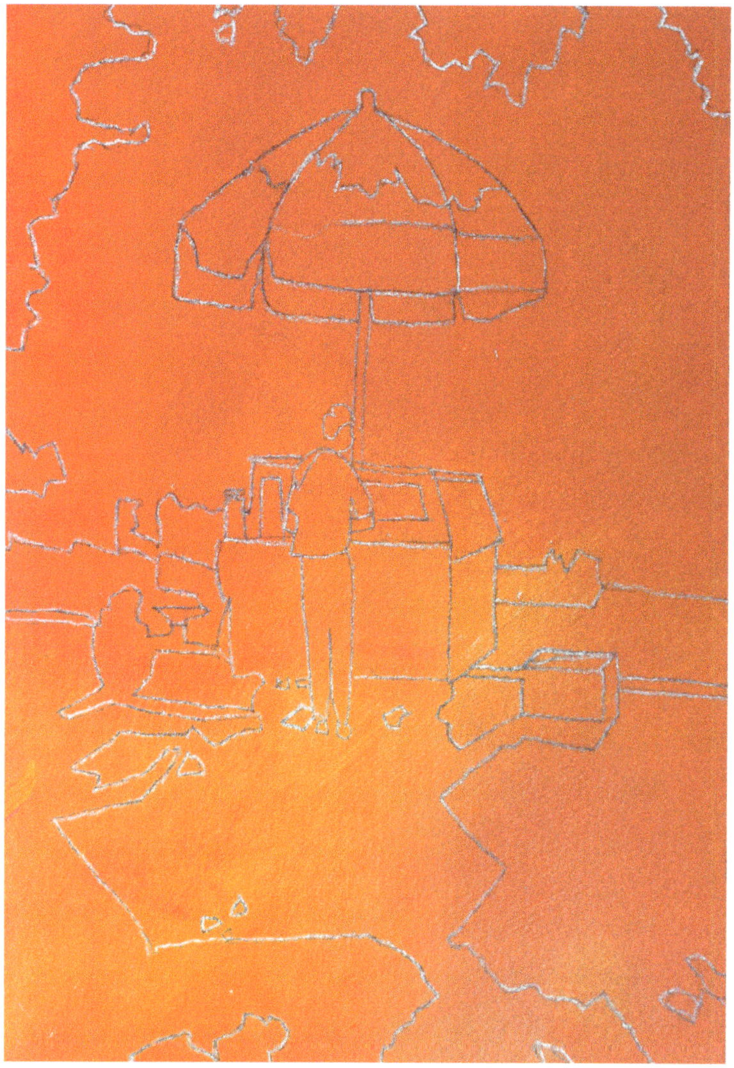

Page 92, *Wet Lands*

Starting in Grayscale

Many artists like to do a value study (black, white, and grays) before they begin the final painting. This is also called a *grisaille*. Most often this is done as a small version to help the artist better see their value plan, but this gray beginning can also be used as the first base layer. I skip this step when painting in the field. If I deem it necessary to have a value plan, I do it in pencil in my sketchbook.

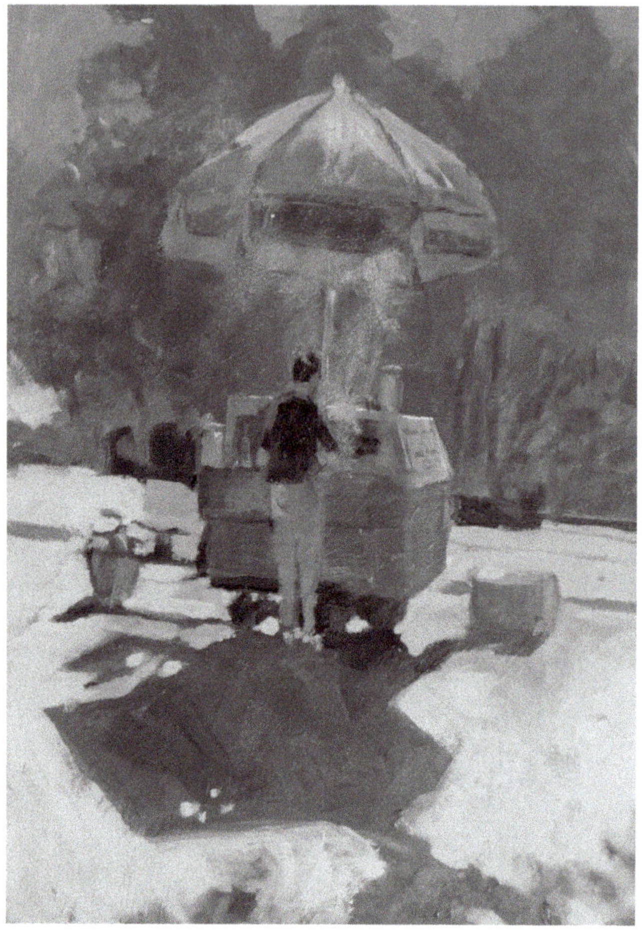

Let's take a look at my vendor painting in grayscale. This would be a fair approximation of an actual grisaille painting using values only. I like the way the middle values hold the lights and darks together. In this painting, there are lots of middle values: mostly light with a bit of dark. This is a good ratio of values, and this relationship also holds true for color temperature. It can be visually confusing to have fifty percent warm colors and fifty percent cool colors. With an equal balance of warm to cool, there is no clear dominance and your painting will lack unity. As I paint, I keep this idea close. I try to lean my paintings either warm or cool, with bits of the opposite also included. Take a look at the examples provided on page 97.

Temperature Dominance

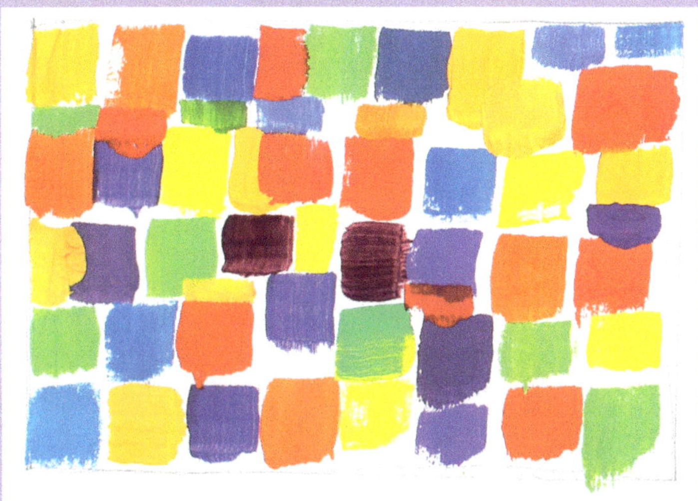

The example at left is equally split with warm and cool colors. There is no clear dominance of temperature. This makes for a confusing composition. The eye bounces all around with no place to rest. Outdoors this effect can happen if fifty percent is warm earth, and the other fifty percent is cool sky. If this is the way it actually looks, I always change it.

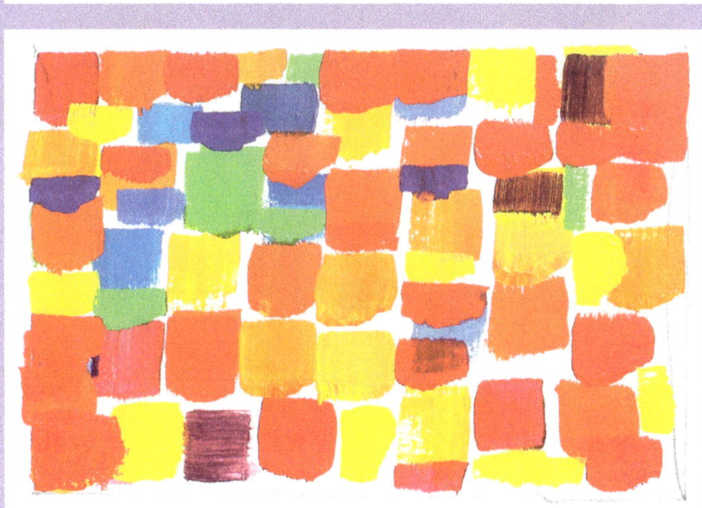

This example dominated with warm colors. The reds, yellows, and oranges fill most of the rectangle. There are enough cool shapes to counter all that warmth, and those cool shapes draw the eye because of temperature contrast.

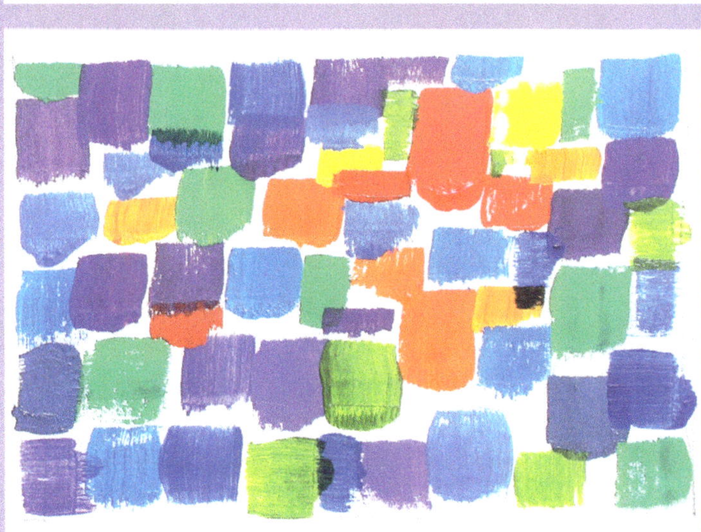

This example shows a dominance of cool colors contrasts with just a bit of warmth. Try warming up or cooling down areas of your painting to adjust the temperature dominance. This should provide unity and harmony in your work.

Color Temperature Unity

We want to avoid an even split of warm and cool colors. As soon as you get close to an even split in temperature, the visual vibration can be unsettling to the viewer. I believe it was Picasso who said something like, "You should be able to say, this is a 'blue' painting or this is a 'red' painting." He also believed that a dominance of hue (and therefore temperature) holds everything together. Let's take a look at two examples of a warm-dominant painting and a cool-dominant painting.

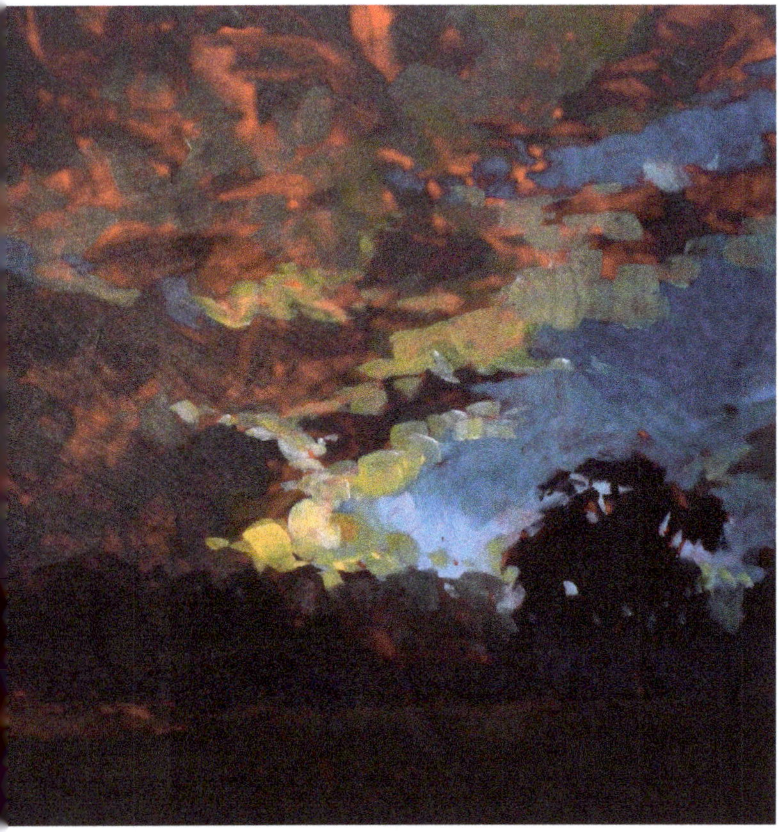

Dawn Sky (acrylic on panel, *plein air*)
Warm clouds; warm hints of the sun; warm, dark foreground; and trees—that warm temperature dominance sets off the hint of blue (cool) sky peeking through the clouds. I always try to avoid a 50-50, 60-40 split of temperature. A 70-30 or, better yet, an 80-20 split between your warm and cool colors is a better balance for your painting and for the viewer.

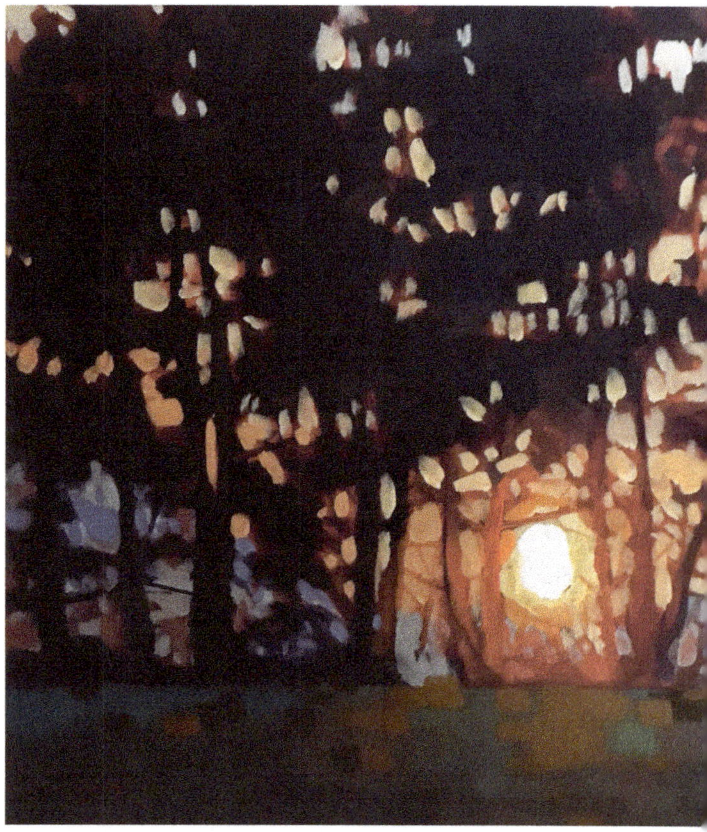

Morning Glow (acrylic on panel, studio)
The greens are warm, pushing toward a neutralized orange. The sky is warm and gets even warmer as you move toward the light where red and red-orange enter the picture. All this warmth holds together that strip of blue that runs along the horizon. This blue is the complement to all that orange and red-orange and acts as a foil to set off that beautiful sunrise.

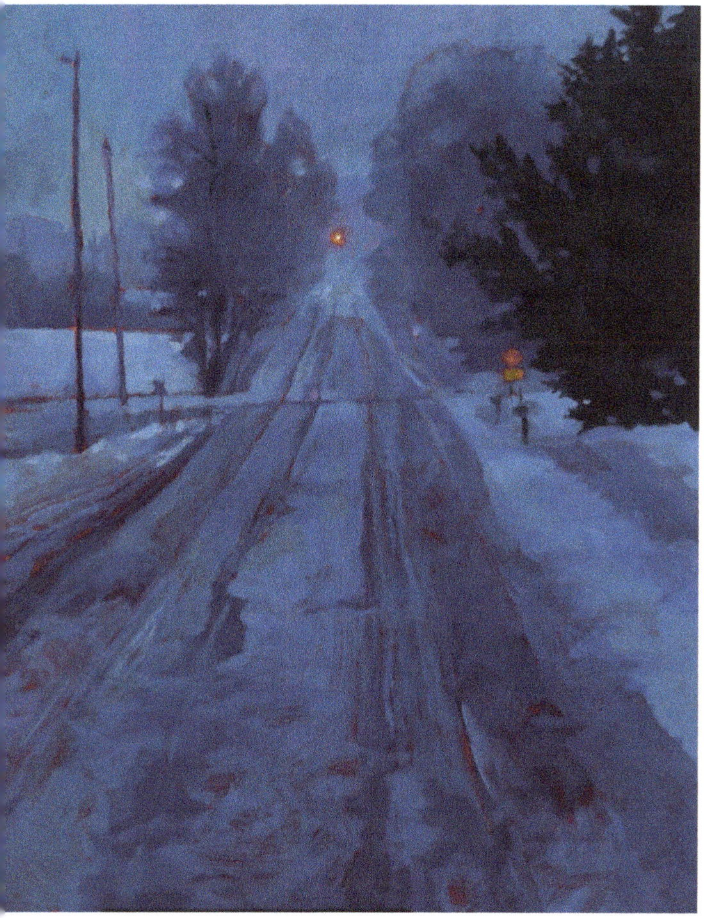

Corner in Winter (acrylic on panel, studio)
This is a corner about three miles from my house. It had just snowed, and the sunlight was starting to lighten the eastern sky. Everything had that blue, pre-dawn glow to it. You can see a hint of green in the pine tree on the right. The blinking light at the intersection, the stop sign, and very small amounts of my red ground are the only hints of warmth in the entire painting. This is a blue painting. That cool dominance holds the composition together and forms a nice foil for those tiny amounts of red and red-orange.

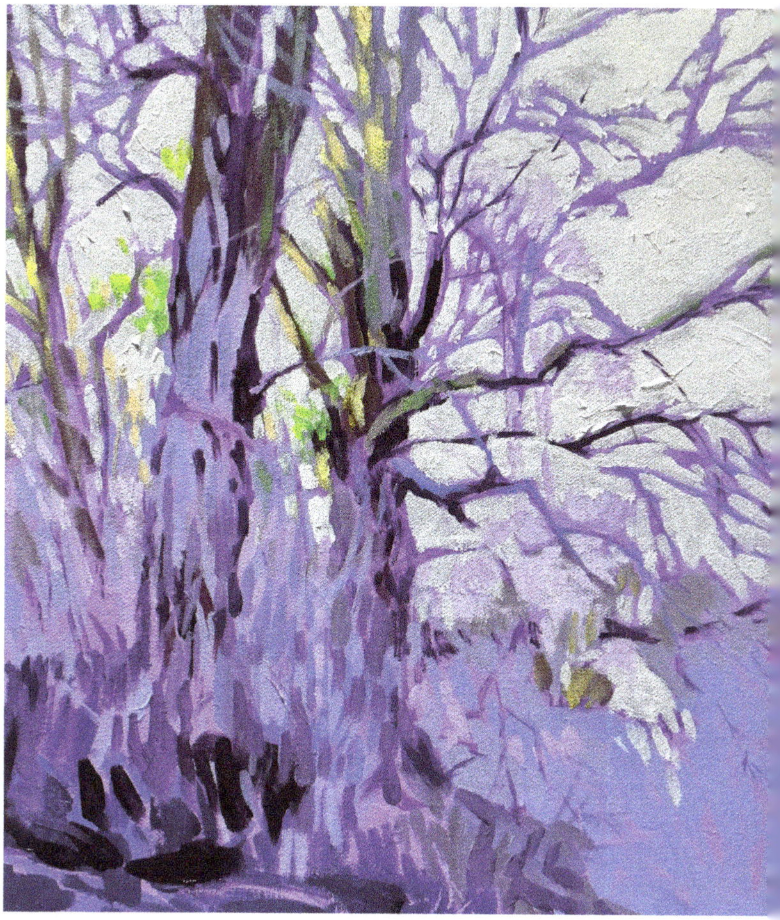

Deep Woods Violets (acrylic on panel, studio)
This is a violet painting, and the cool dominance was chosen to help say "deep woods" (to myself and the viewer). The complement to violet is yellow, and the near complement is yellow-green. I used both of those as hints of light on the tree trunks in the upper left. Using complements sets up a vibration that draws attention to that juxtaposition. Add the most value and color contrast to the focal area of the painting.

Step-by-Step Project: *Red Dogwood*

Occasionally, I may skip creating the pencil sketch and go directly to painting because I'm anxious to capture the scene and light before it changes. If I make a mistake in terms of value (how light or dark one shape is compared to another), hue (the actual color used), or temperature (how warm or cool the selected color is), I can correct it because I know how fast acrylics dry.

It was a rare January day in Michigan with temperatures in the high forties. The accumulated snow had melted. The afternoon light was coming in at a low angle from left to right, and the red dogwood bush seemed to glow. I set up in my front yard to capture the evening light hitting the pine trees, the field grass, and the red dogwood. I had to work fast, so I got right to work. No preliminary value plan this time. My easel was loaded with my usual eight or nine colors: cobalt blue, phthalo blue, ultramarine blue, alizarin crimson, cadmium red light, cadmium yellow deep, cadmium yellow light, and titanium white.

This photograph shows my equipment with the scene directly behind. My setup includes my easel, brushes, paint tubes, and prepared painting panel. I also have with me water, a paint palette, a collapsible water container, and paper towels. It is not my lightest setup, but it is my most self-contained easel.

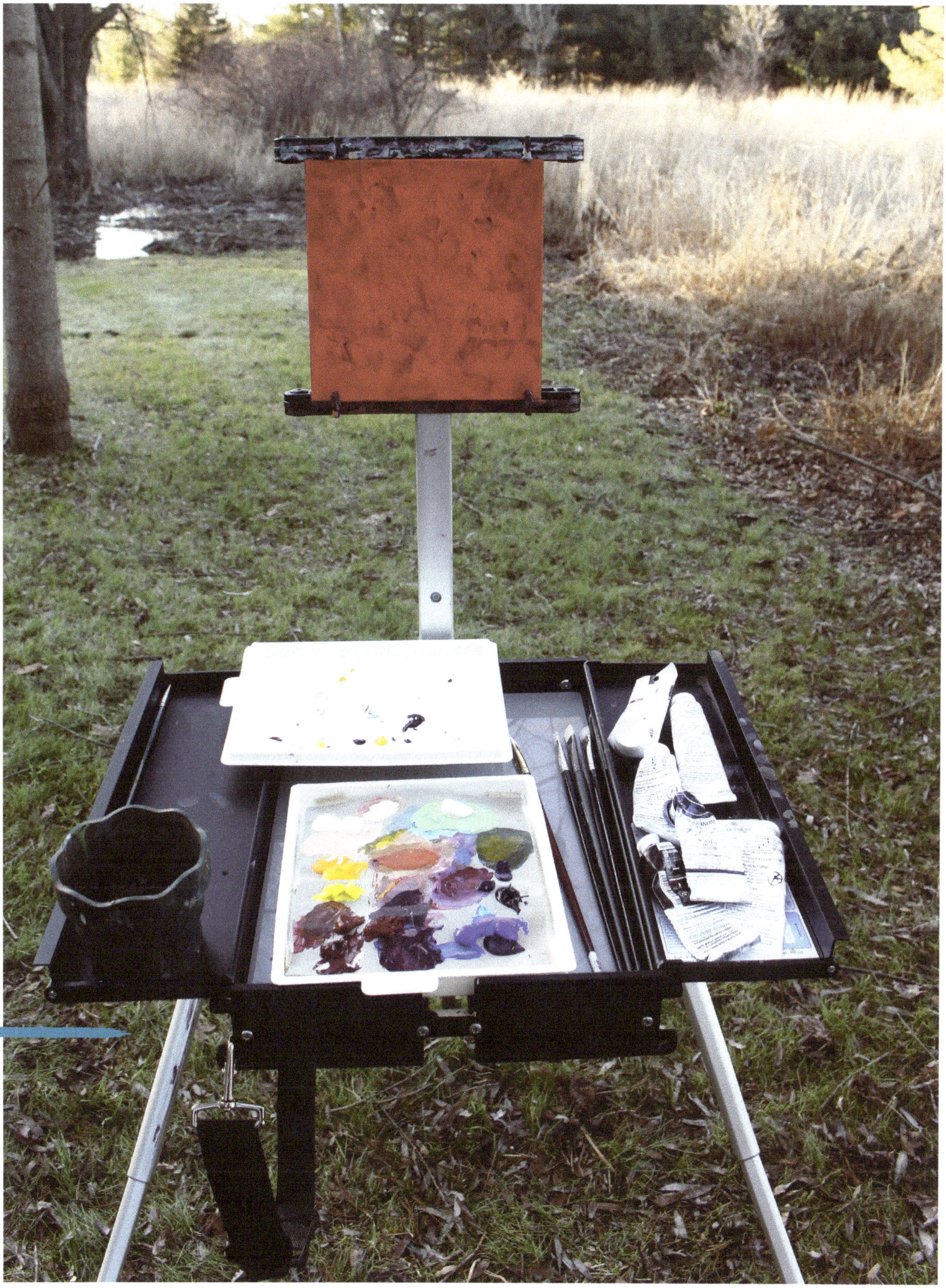

Step 1

I previously applied cadmium red light to an 8-inch square birchwood painting panel. I often use this color, as cadmium red light is a middle value straight out of the tube. This means that when I apply a stroke of another color, I can tell if that passage is lighter or darker than a mid-tone. It helps me determine my values. Another advantage is allowing some of the warm red to peek out as I paint. If I want my painting to have a warm dominance, I allow more of the cadmium red light to show. If I want my painting to have a cool dominance, I let less cadmium red light show. It acts as a warm accent to my cool colors.

I sometimes tone my canvases or panels with other colors, either to create the sky before I begin or to create a color scheme more fitting to the scene. I also sometimes begin on a white, gessoed surface that comes from a commercially prepared canvas or panel. Similar to an oil painting, my first pass is sometimes a wash of a warm neutral color to knock down the white.

Using my smaller size 4 short flat brush, alizarin crimson, and a bit of water, I outline the big shapes to set my composition on my 8-by-8-inch panel.

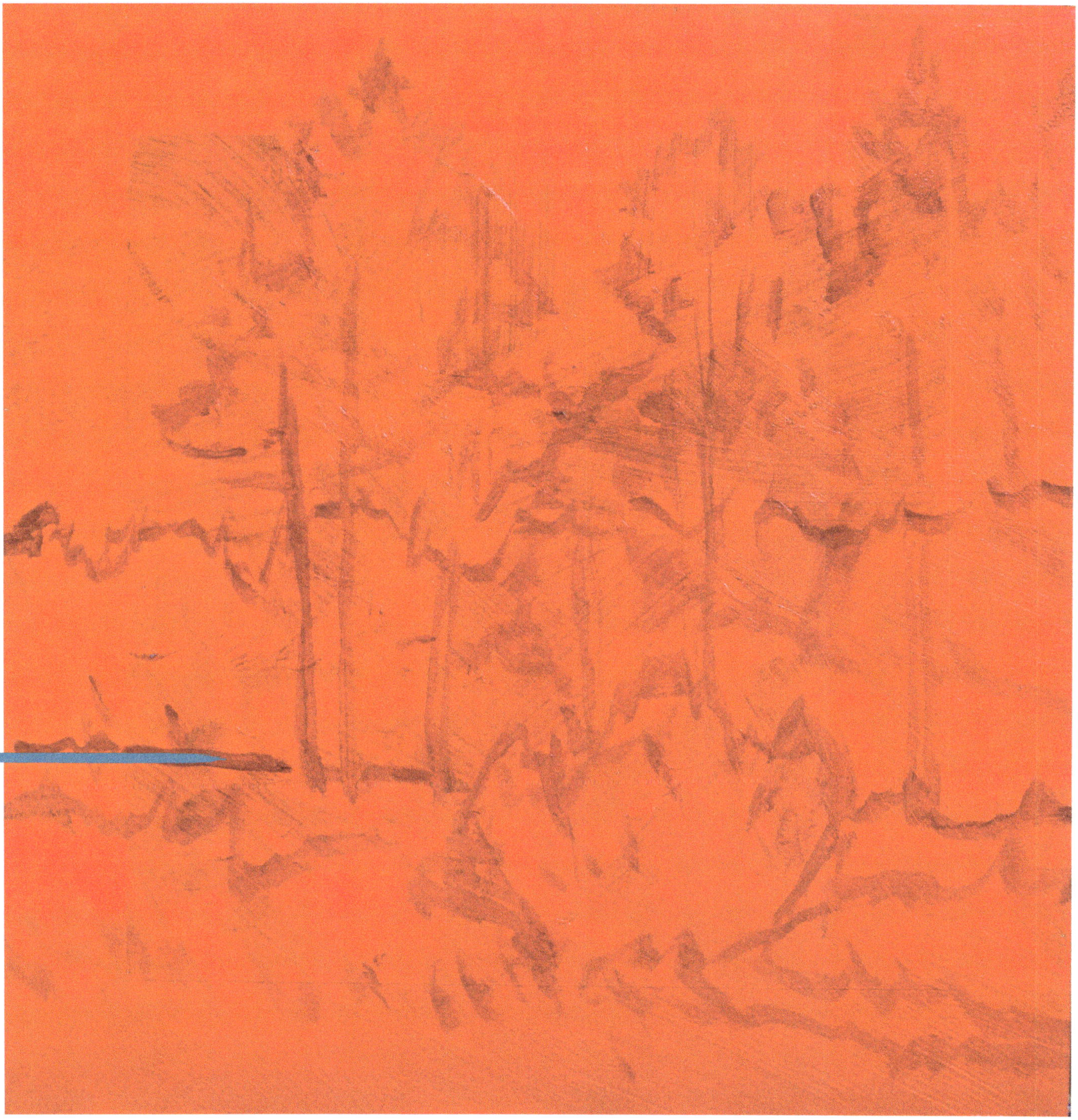

Step 2

The atmosphere changes the way we see color; as colors recede into the distance, they get both cooler and grayer. I almost always exaggerate atmospheric, or aerial, perspective. This painting will have a warm dominance, and I want the tree line to act as a foil to those warm colors.

Using a size 6 short brush, I combine a mixture of cobalt blue, a small amount of alizarin crimson, cadmium yellow light, and titanium white on my palette. I use this mixture (mostly blue) to paint the distant tree line at the horizon.

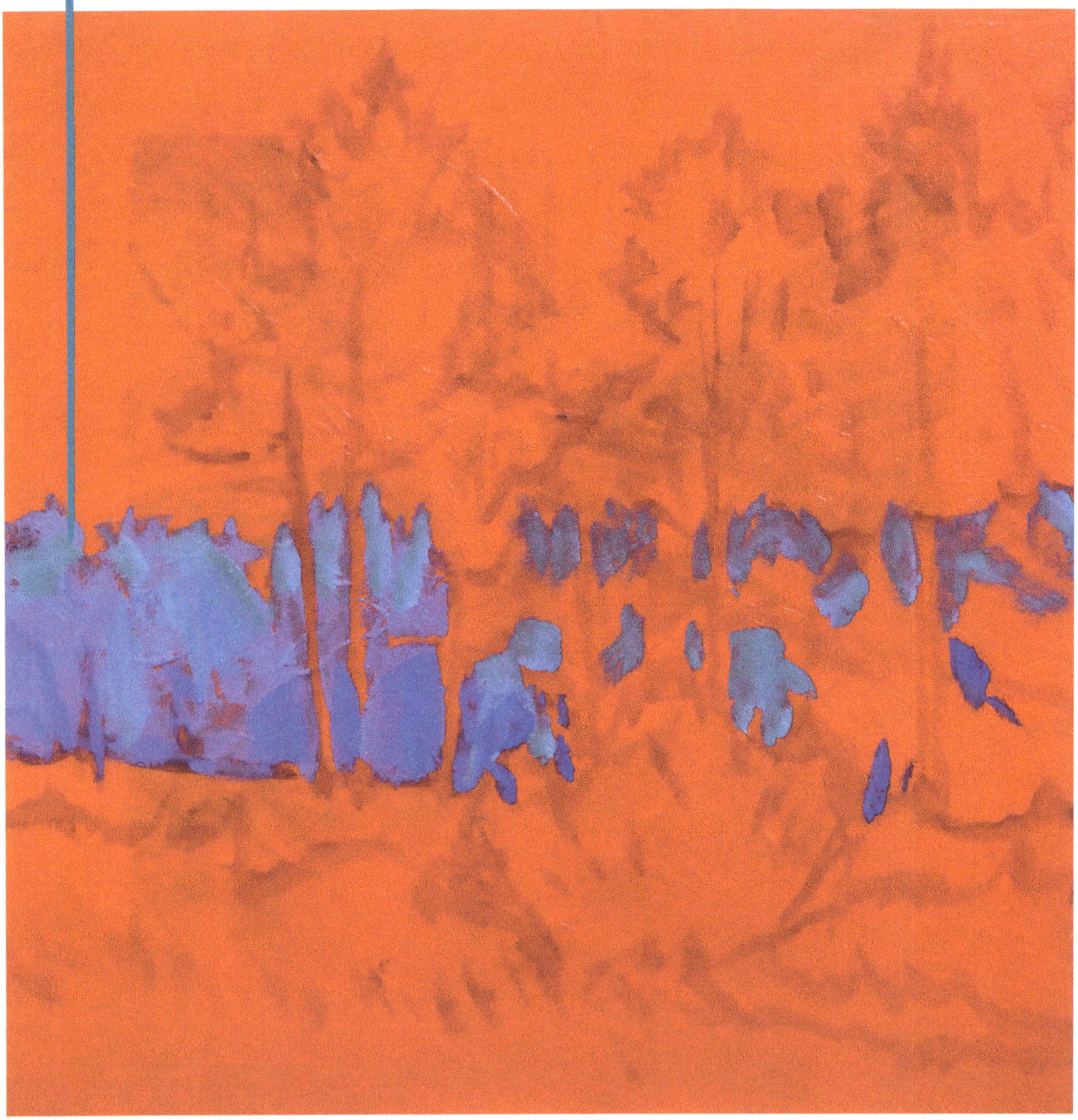

Step 3

I wipe my brush off with a paper towel. I don't always clean my brush between color changes because it saves both water and time. When the brush has a little bit of the previous mixture on the bristles, it blends with the next mixture and provides a bit of unity to the whole painting. Some of everything is everywhere!

Using a mixture of cobalt blue, alizarin crimson, a bit of cadmium yellow light, and white, I make a middle value of neutralized violet. I use this mixture to paint the shadow side of the pine trees, the shadow side of the tree trunks, and the top of the weeds in the foreground.

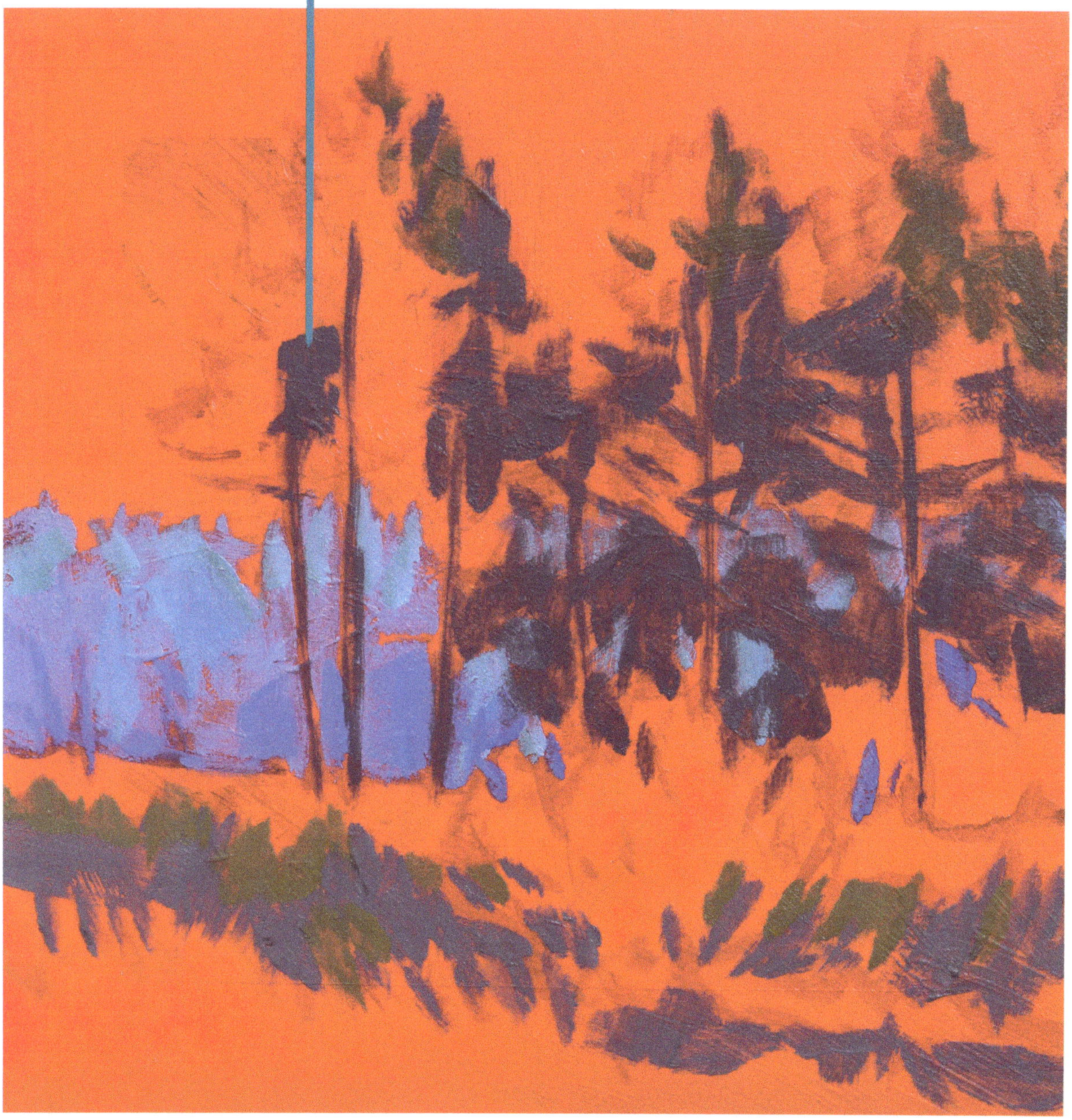

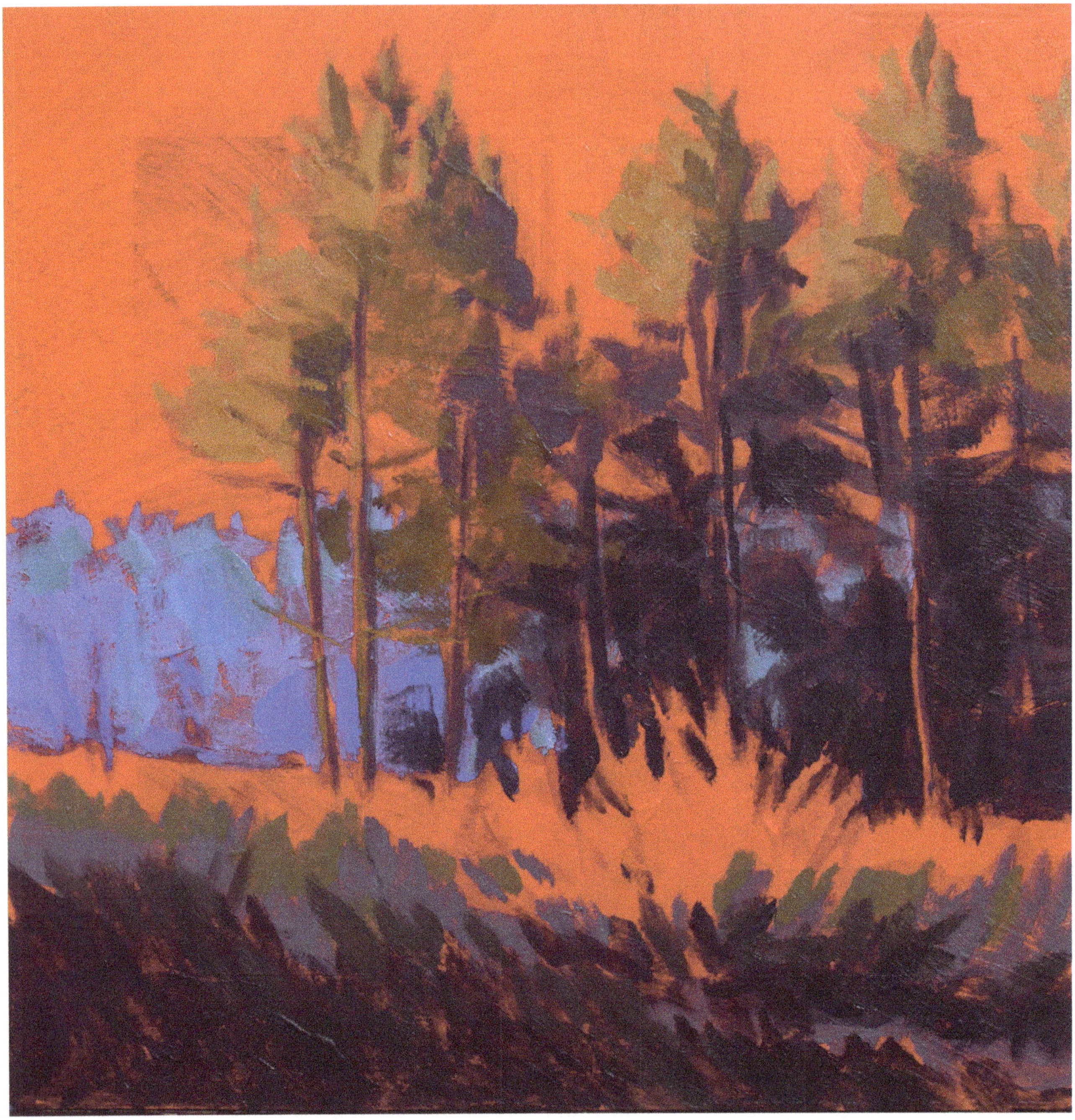

Step 4

I use cobalt blue, ultramarine blue, alizarin crimson, and a bit of cadmium yellow deep to create a dark, neutral violet. Still using my size 6 short flat, I paint this darker mixture (still one value lighter than black) on the lower part of the pines and in the foreground weeds. Both areas are in shadow.

Step 5

Time to add the light. For the red dogwood bush itself, I use a mixture of cadmium red light, alizarin crimson, a small amount of cadmium yellow deep, and white. I paint the sunlit side of the bush, and as I work my way around to the shadow side, I add more alizarin to the mixture. I use short, quick strokes to create an impression of the light hitting that bush.

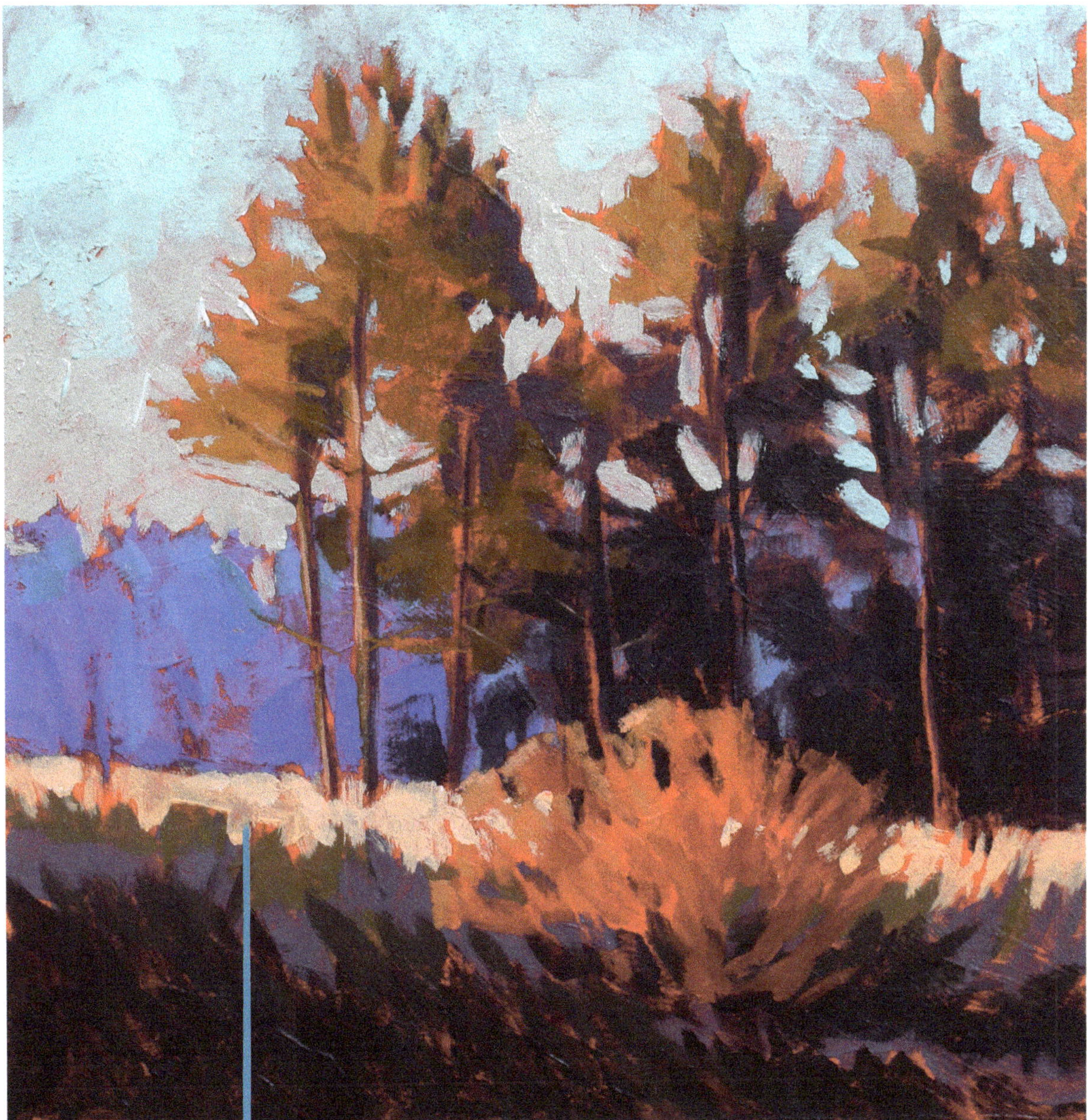

I wipe my brush and use a mixture of cadmium red light, cadmium yellow deep, and lots of white to make the color of the light weeds that rake across the entire composition. I paint this passage quickly, almost allowing my brush to skip across, just as the light did.

Step 6

I sometimes leave the sky for last. It helps me key the rest of the painting both in terms of value (the lighter the sky, the darker the other shapes appear) and in terms of the dominant temperature of the whole. In this case, I use lots of titanium white with some cadmium yellow light and just a touch of phthalo blue. I apply this mixture starting along the top of the distant tree shapes and in and around the middle ground pines. As I work my way up the panel (the sky usually gets darker as you approach the zenith), I add more phthalo blue into the mix.

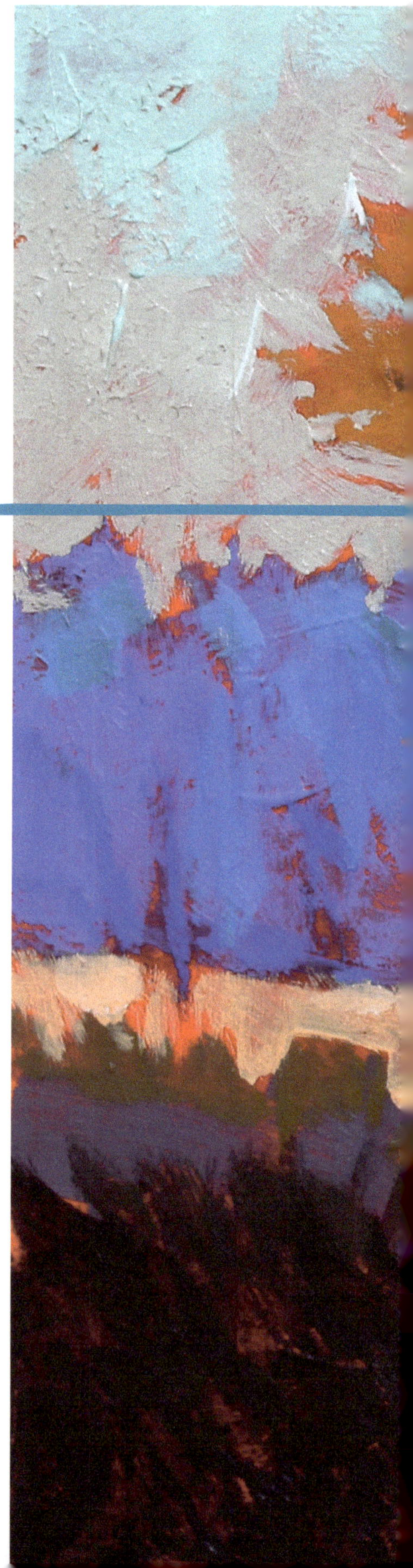

To finish, I switch to the smaller size 4 short flat and use that with the sky color to depict the gaps of sky in the pine trees. I'm always careful with those sky strokes; a few go a long way.

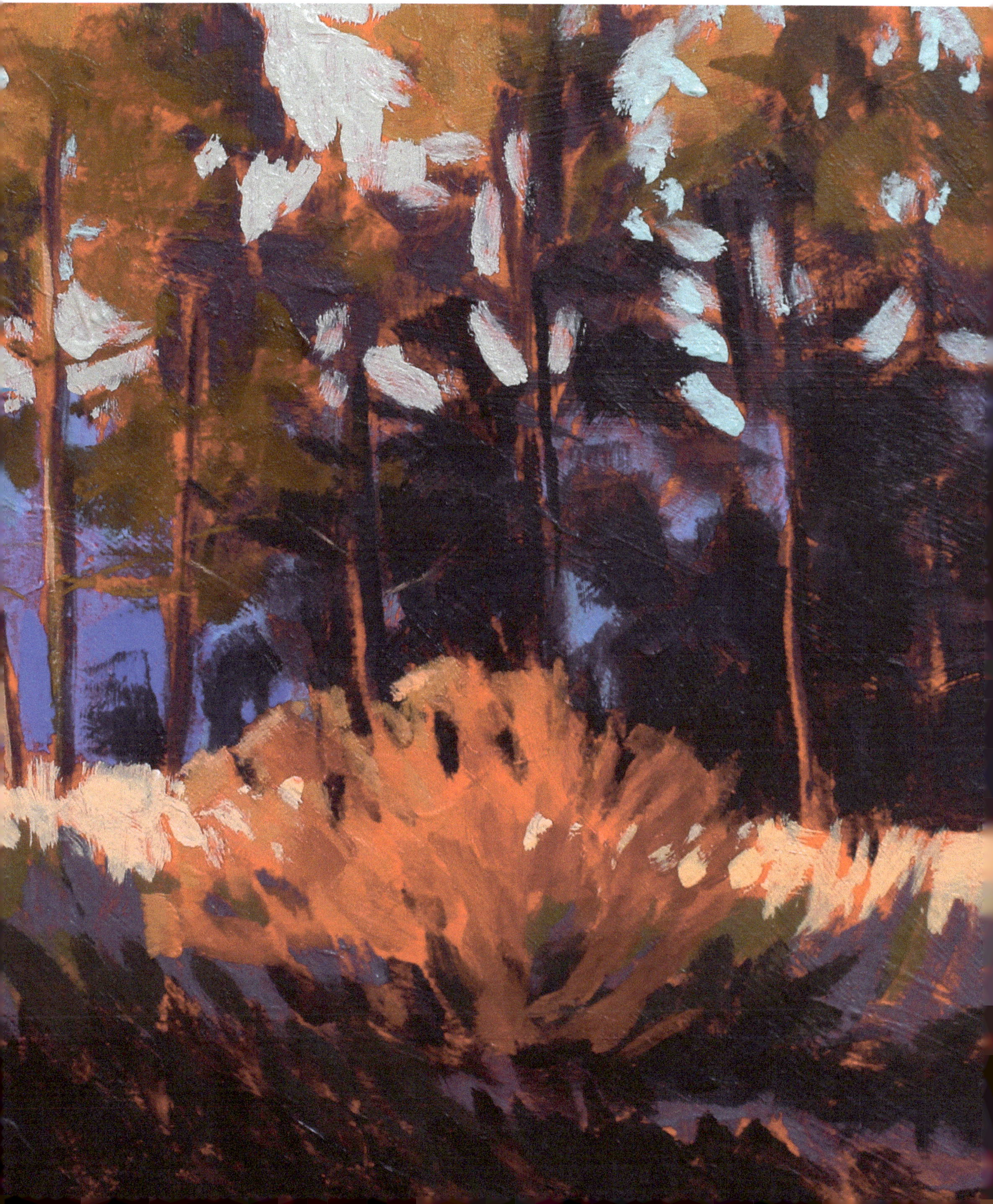

Finding Beauty

If I have to choose between finding a beautiful scene and painting it, and finding an acceptable scene and making the best painting I can, I almost always choose the latter.

Why? There is much beauty in the world. As I write this, I look out over the gardens that fill our backyard, and even though it is early spring, I can already see the flowers poking through. The grass is starting to green up, and the birds—back from their winter migration—are singing loudly. A beautiful scene for sure, but painted as is, I'm afraid it would be very boring. There's still a lot of brown, only one temperature of green, a cloudless blue sky, and small shadows (as it's close to noon).

Could I make a painting from what I'm seeing? Of course! But I'd have to get creative: change some of those browns to warm and cool grays; add variety to the greens; add clouds to an otherwise uninspiring sky; elongate the shadows; and connect foreground, middle ground, and background.

While I do sometimes paint exactly what I see, the excitement for me comes from rearranging what nature provides to make the best painting I can. This often means leaving out much of what I see. Like a camera, our eyes visually gather too much information. The problem with attempting to include everything in our paintings is that it becomes a confusing bundle of imagery.
What to do? There are two choices: Search until you find a scene that needs little in terms of adjustment, or paint the first thing that captures your eye and redesign what you see to make a good painting.

In *Morning Reflections with Pond* (opposite), I painted the scene almost exactly as I perceived it. The light was subdued, and the greens were varied. It was early in the morning so the sky appeared more yellow than blue, and the reflections in the pond were a close mirror to the grasses and trees from above.

Even the title is a "reflection" of what I was seeing. I felt I captured my sense of being there, and I was happy with that day's effort. There is a certain joy in painting things we find beautiful. And while I find that kind of effort to be fulfilling, sometimes I want to do much more.

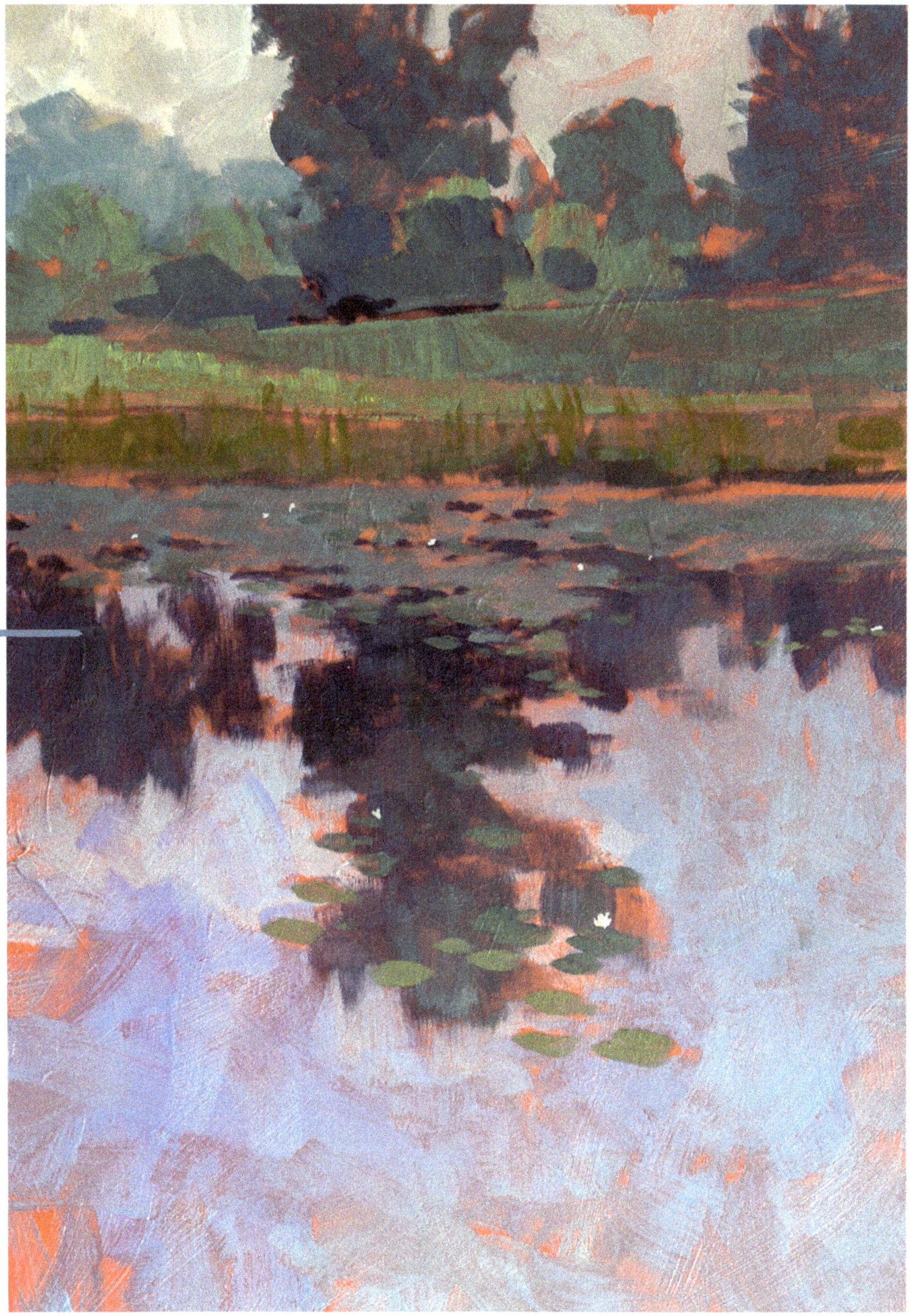

The light was very strong both from above and from behind. In fact, the light was so strong that it washed out some of the color and made the shadows appear almost black. The ground was dirt. The scene looked almost monochromatic—just one color plus black and white. It was very graphic, with hard edges everywhere and lots of value contrast between the lightest light and the darkest dark. I had to paint it!

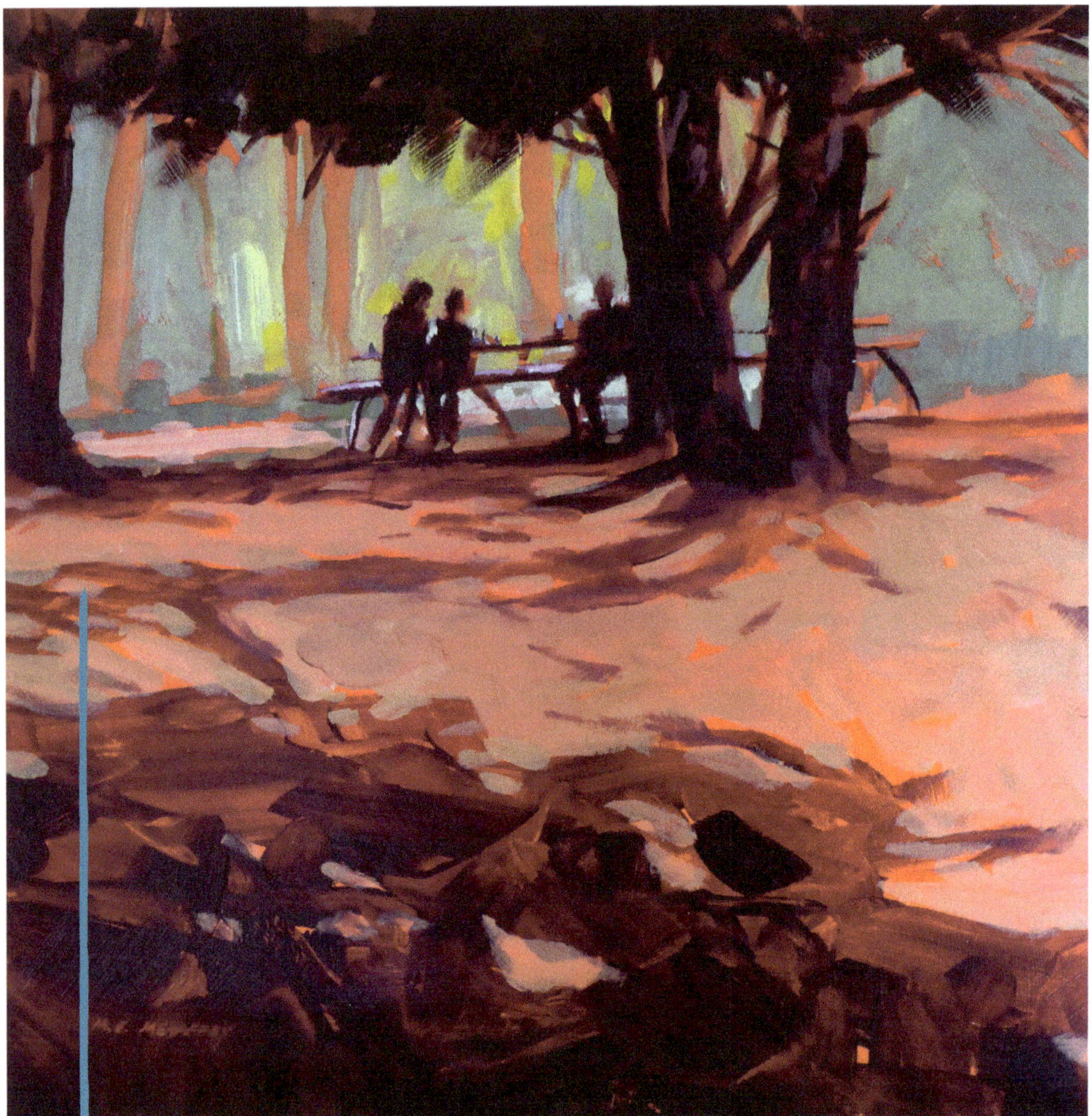

Let's look at two paintings that feature the same composition but were painted two different ways. The result is more or less the way I saw it as I set up. This first painting was done *en plein air*. Even the title of the painting, *Picnic in Color*, alludes to the dark silhouettes of the figures, the trees, and the shadows. It features strong lights and darks, but very little color detail. The composition was sound, with small shapes (the picnic tables and figures) to draw the viewers' attention, while the foreground shadow leads the eye right to the focal area.

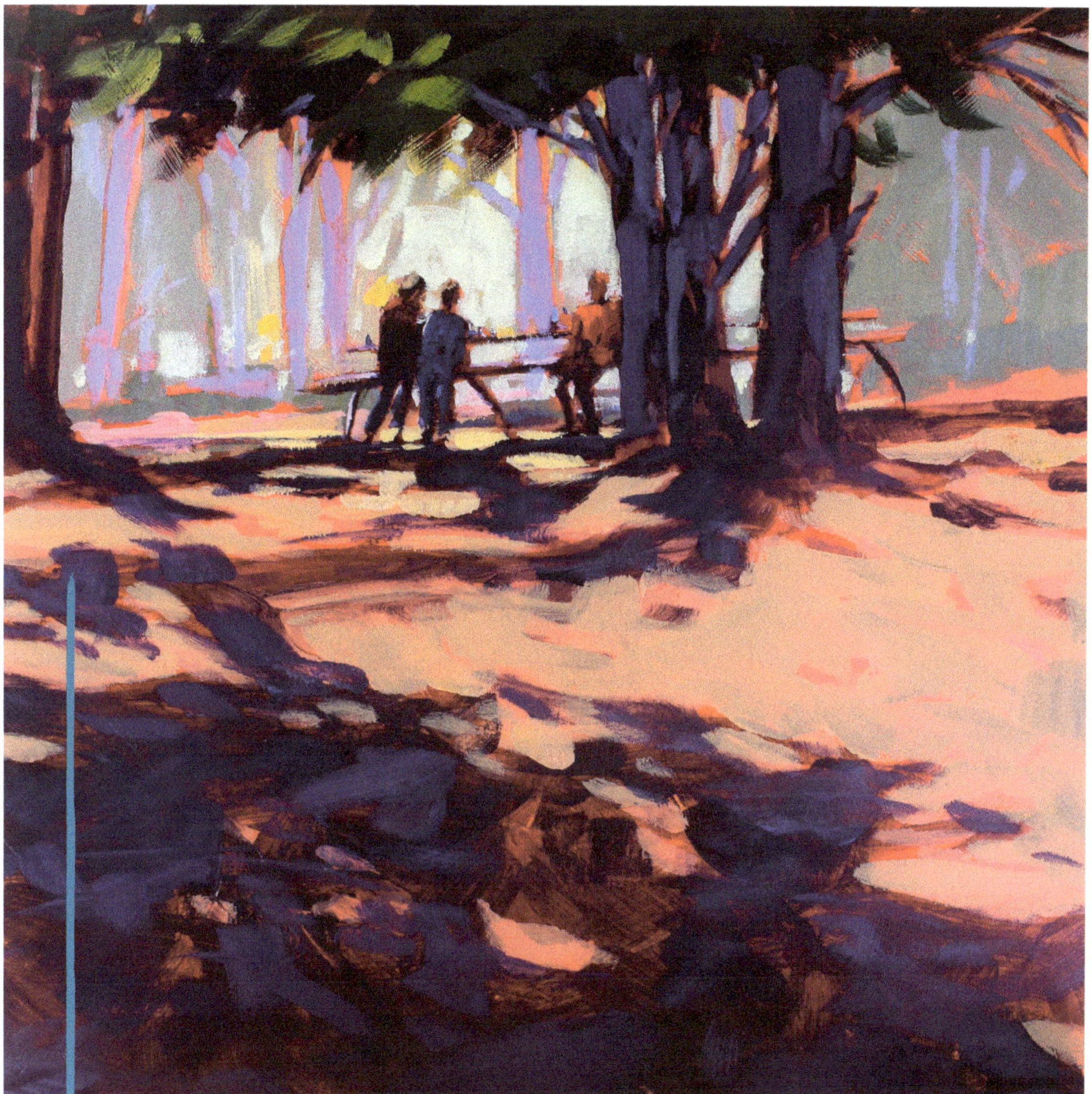

This version of *Picnic in Color* was done in the studio as a counterpoint to the *plein air* work. I liked the design, the brushwork, and the basic value pattern (of lights and darks), but I wanted to see more color and light. The resulting painting has the same arrangement of shapes and the same value contrast between the lightest light and darkest dark, but with added color. To make sure the painting featured brushstrokes, I used the same size 8 nylon flat brush for the whole thing. Using ultramarine blue, a bit of gamboge (deep saffron), and lots of white, I both lightened and cooled the entire background. I used dark blue and violet (a mix of ultramarine blue and alizarin crimson) for the tree and all the shadows. For the strong sunlight, I added a bit more yellow and white. I added green to the pine boughs and red and blue for the figures' shirts, hoping that this added some strength to the focal area.

Painting the Light

Many variables determine the final version of any painting. Location, time, mood, visual problems to solve—the list is endless. The time of day and the atmospheric conditions at the time are also major determinants of how your painting will turn out.

Capturing natural light changes will help you tell your visual story with more clarity. You have two choices: Do your best to paint the light and atmosphere exactly as you perceive it, or artistically alter what you see to make the painting you conceive in your mind's eye (in other words, exercise your artistic license). Both options are entirely valid.

As the day progresses, the angle of the sun and quality of the light change. As *plein air* painters, we can follow this progression. The quality of the light is a combination of these factors: time of day and the relative atmospheric conditions at the time of set up. The atmosphere can vary from day to day—even hour to hour—and change within minutes. When I'm planning to spend a day painting outside, one of the first things I do is check the morning weather report to see what conditions to expect.

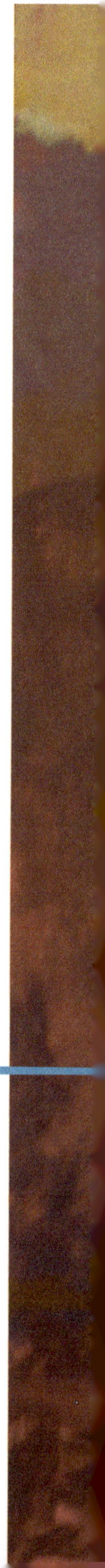

Dawn and dusk provide a lower angle of sunlight and a lower level of light intensity. Humidity in the form of rain, mist, or fog will dramatically change the atmosphere, particularly at those times.

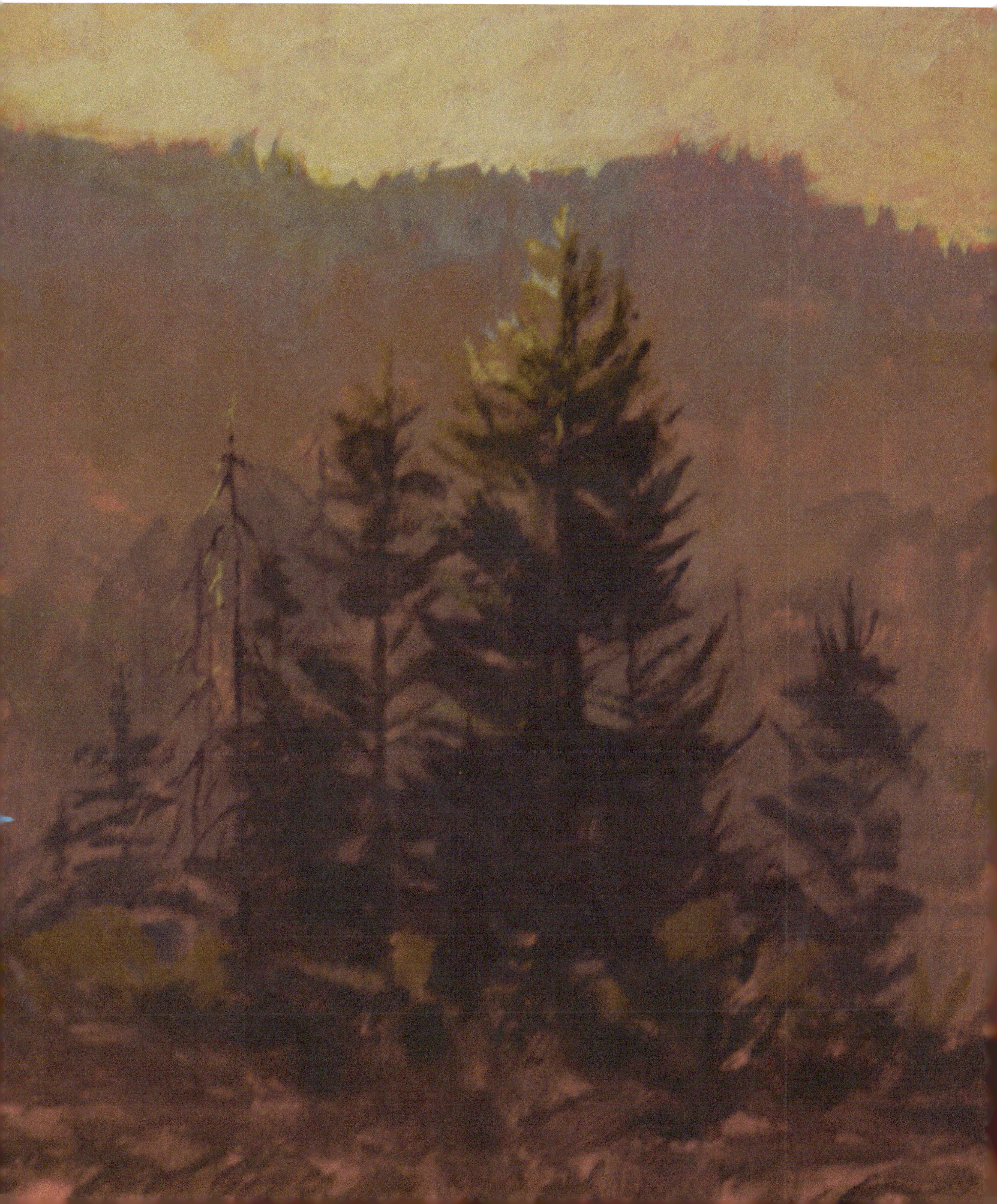

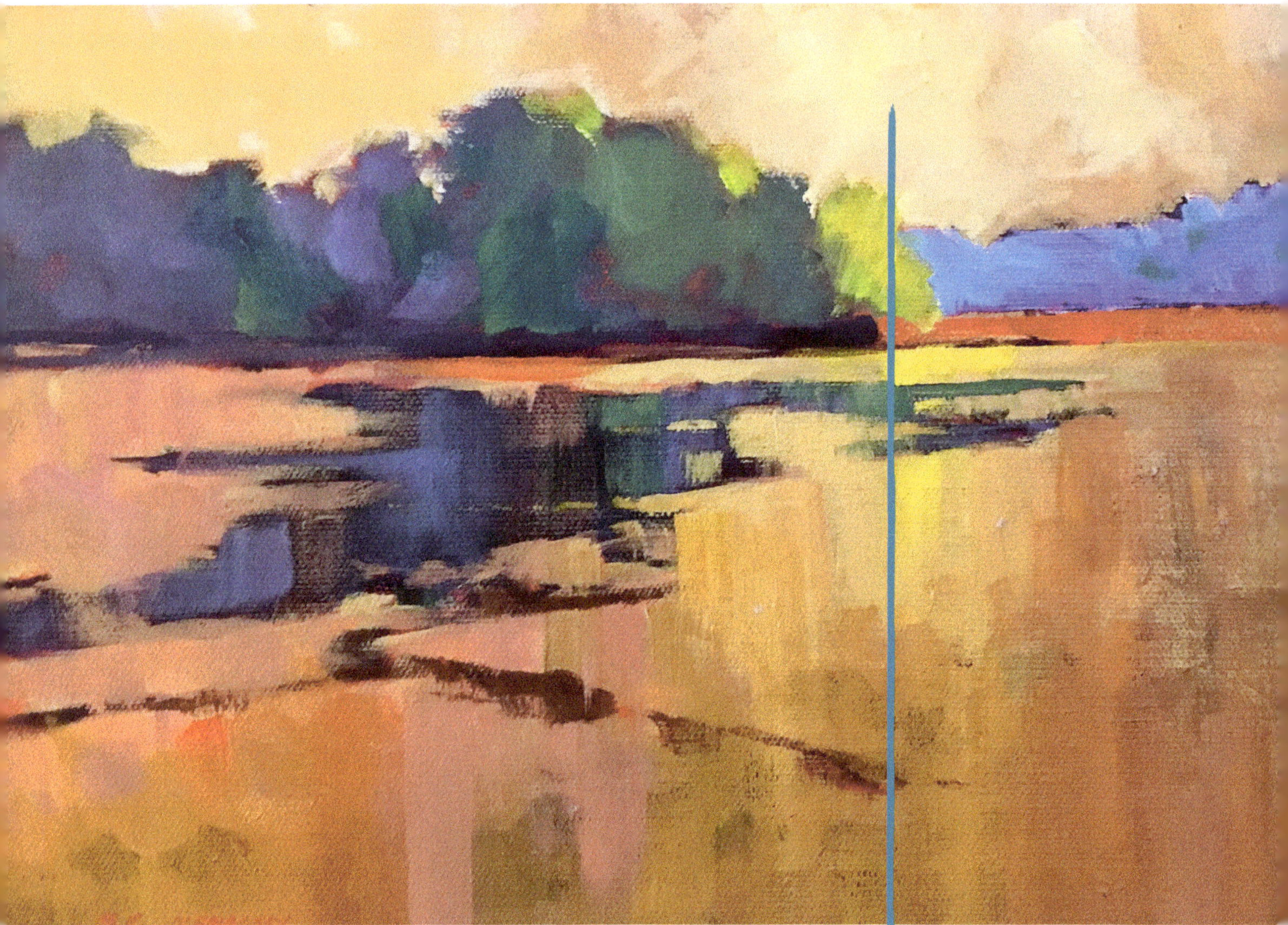

A bright, sunny, cloudless day will be altogether different from a cloudy day. Then again, the conditions will differ considerably between dawn and noon, and the quality of the light will change yet again later in the afternoon. Painting during the middle of the day allows us to come up with a creative solution. We can search for a more complicated scene or one that relies on something other than the lengthy shadows of dawn or dusk.

Later in the day, the shadows begin to lengthen again. Here the late afternoon and evening light is warmer than the light at dawn or early morning. Most of my on-site painting happens in the morning, although I do occasionally get out in the evening.

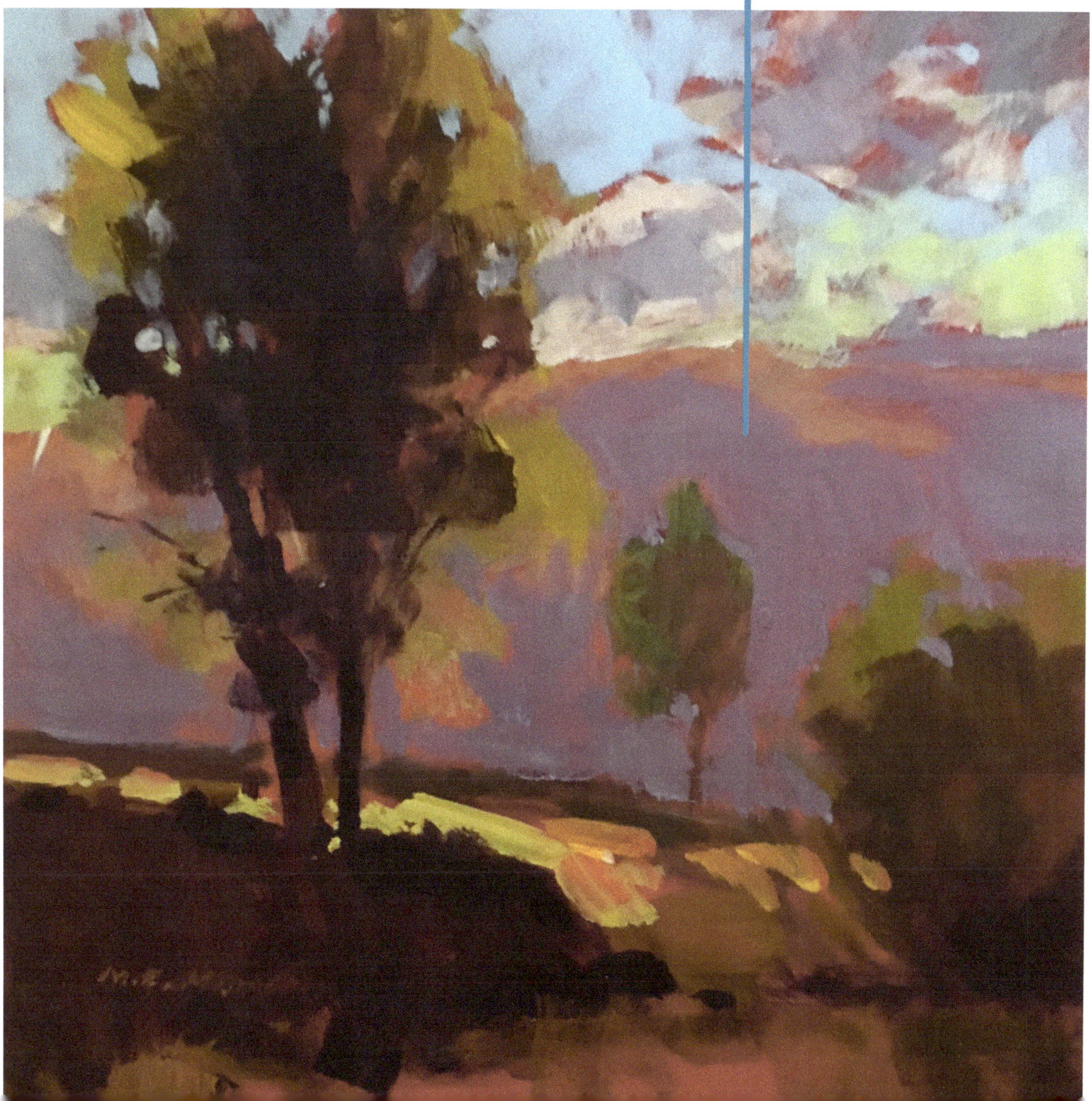

Painting the Seasons

Here in Michigan we fully experience all four seasons: spring, summer, fall, and a four- to six-month winter. If I were to wait for perfect weather, I would not get out to paint much! In the colder months, cloudy skies are the norm, as are chilly and frigid temperatures. Painting outside in Michigan can be a rugged affair, but as long as the outside temperature is above freezing (32°F), I am ready to go.

It is helpful to paint the same area or view in the different seasons. The light changes from season to season, just as it does at different times of the day. The foliage changes as the season progresses, and the amount of light that bounces into the shadows also changes. Take a look at the next four plein air paintings completed from the same location: a stand of trees about two miles from my home (opposite page). They sit on the edge of a farmer's field. All four paintings are small and were completed in under an hour.

This is a photo of one of my favorite places to paint during early spring. The leaves have just started to unfurl and are still a fresh yellow-green. The farmer has been busy preparing the soil for spring planting, and the warm red of the freshly turned soil contrasts nicely with the yellow-green of the new leaves.

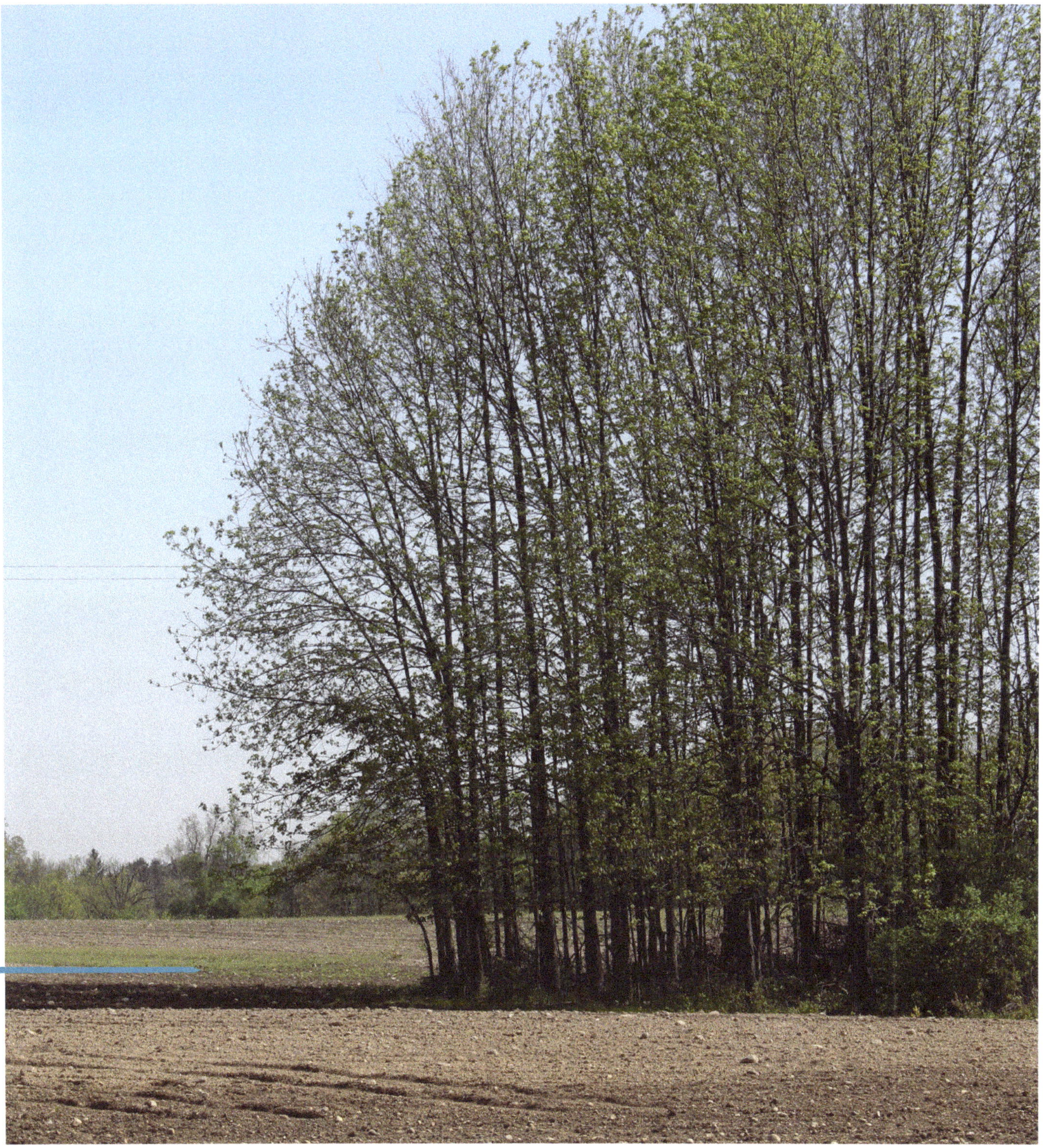

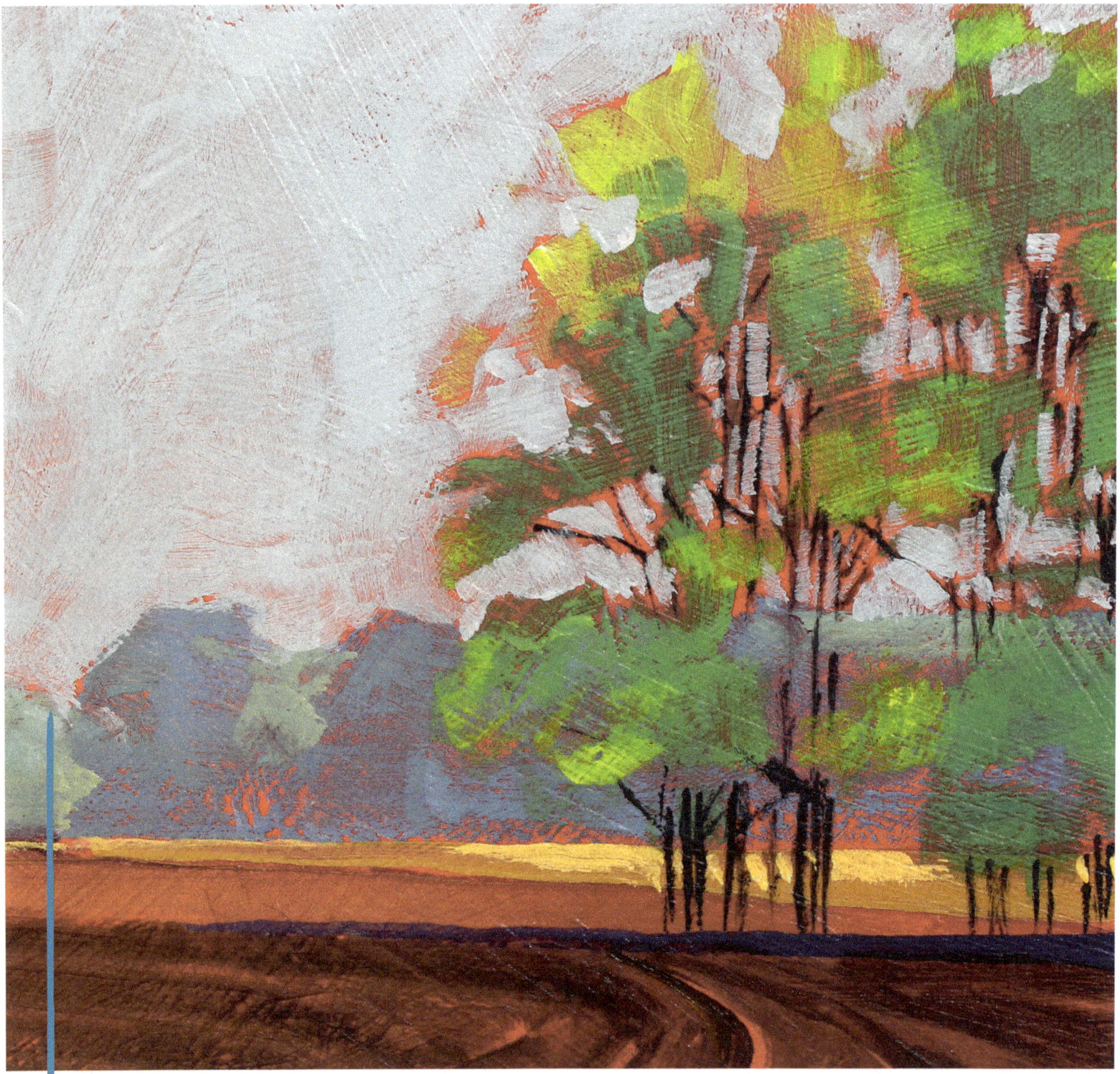

Favorite Place, Spring **(acrylic on panel)**

I used a cadmium red light underpainting and left lots of it showing to indicate the freshly turned soil. I simplified the distant trees and made the bright green of spring a bit bluer to push into the background. I mixed anthraquinone blue and white for most of the trees that form the background. A mixture of anthraquinone blue, alizarin crimson, and a bit of cadmium yellow light created the brown I used to form the furrows made by the farmer's tractor. I used his tracks to lead the eye into the dark tree trunks (a mixture of mostly anthraquinone blue and a bit of alizarin crimson) and then up into saturated yellow-green foliage (a small amount of anthraquinone blue and cadmium yellow light) to convey the freshness of spring.

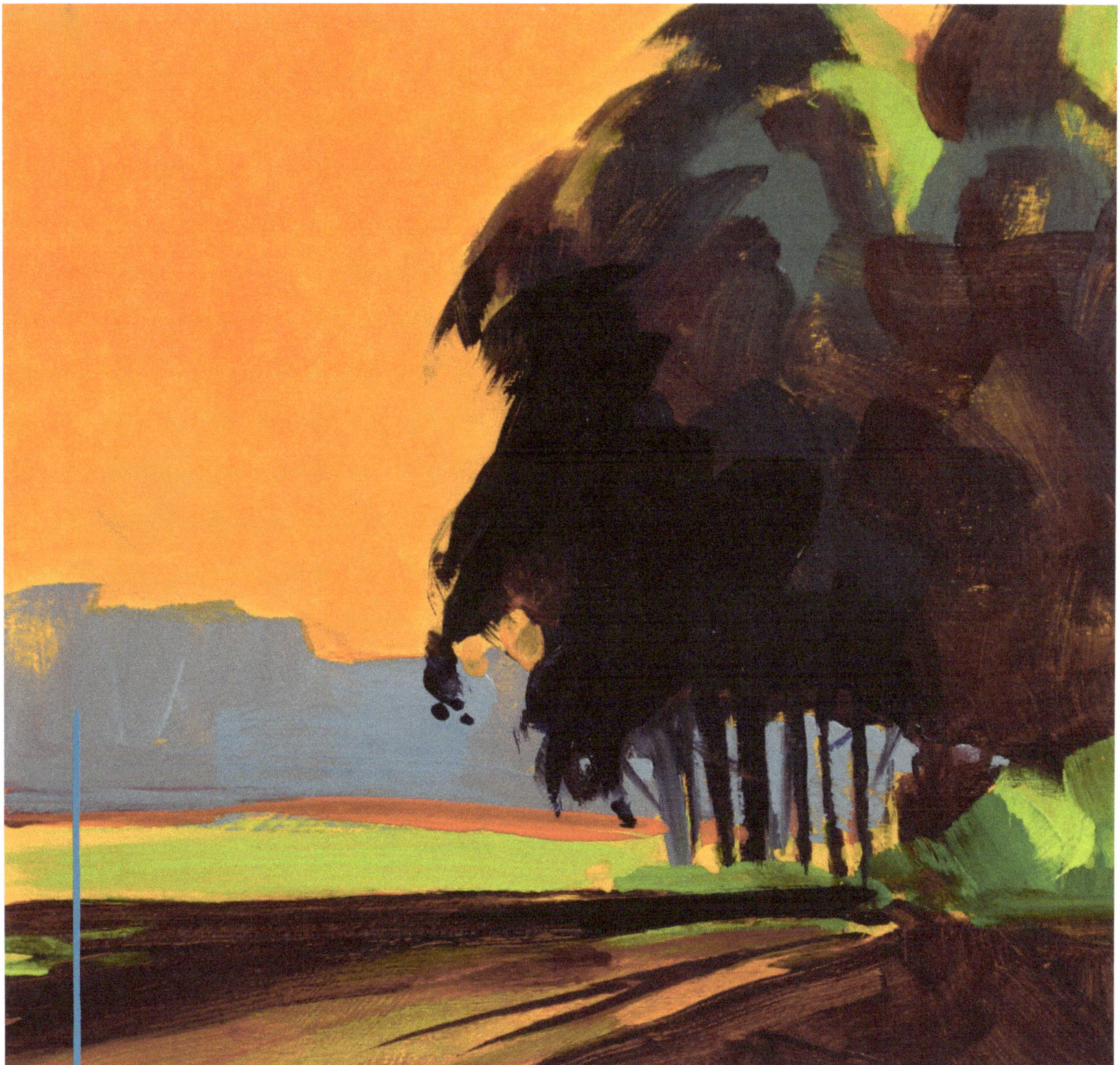

Favorite Place, Summer **(acrylic on panel)**
When the light comes in from the east, the trees throw some dramatic, lengthy shadows into and across the field. To emphasize the warm summer light, I used orange (a mixture of cadmium red light and cadmium yellow deep) for most of the sky and for the light in the foreground. I also greatly increased the dark value of both the trees and their shadows to create more visual drama.

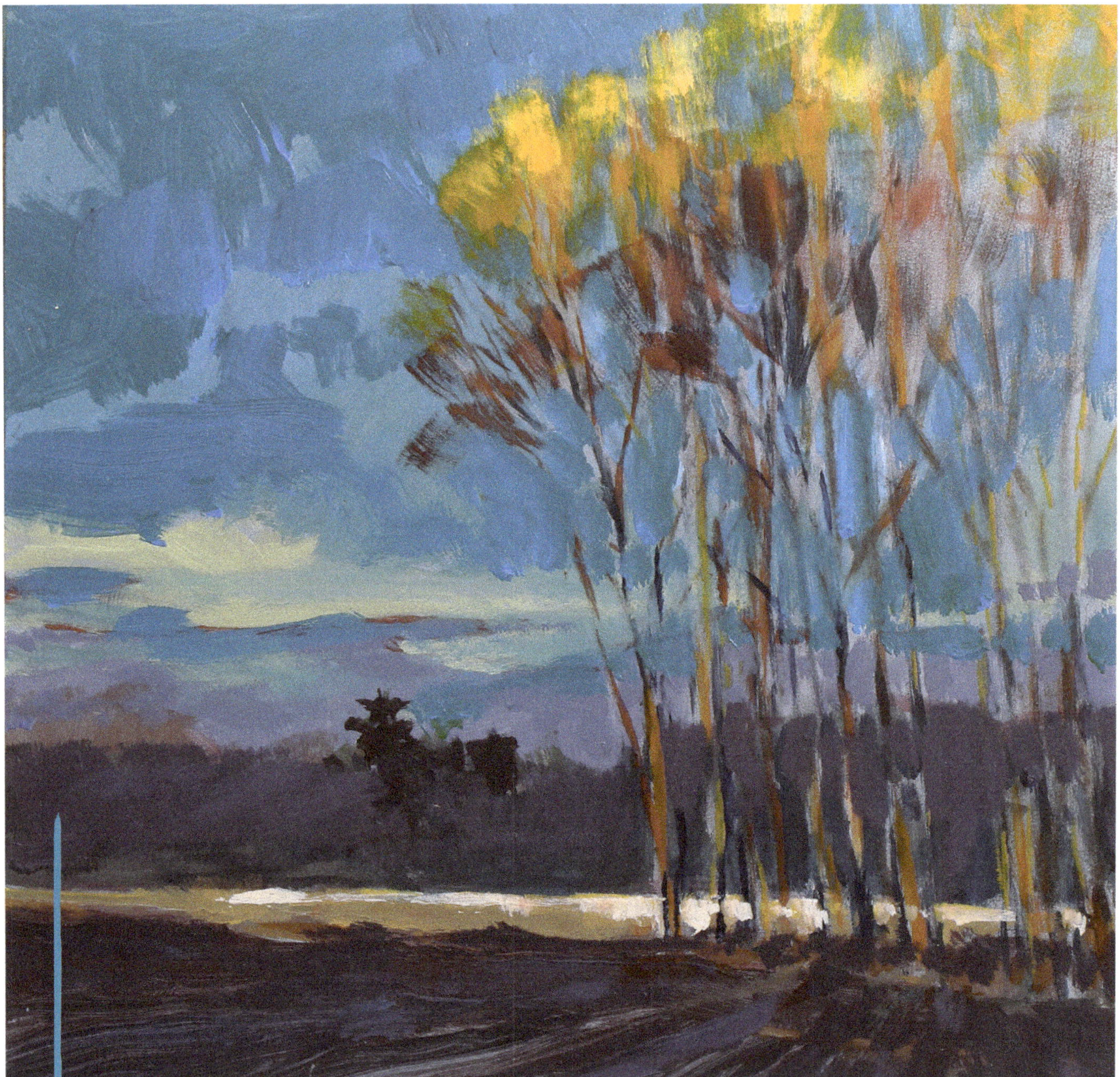

Favorite Place, Fall **(acrylic on panel)**
It's still morning with the light coming in from the east, but now, later in the year, the angle of the sunlight is lower. The morning light was just kissing the tops of the trees with a bit of light. Most of the leaves had dropped, and the fields were plowed under. To make the focus of this piece the light hitting the treetops, I completed the rest of the painting using blues, violets, and neutrals.

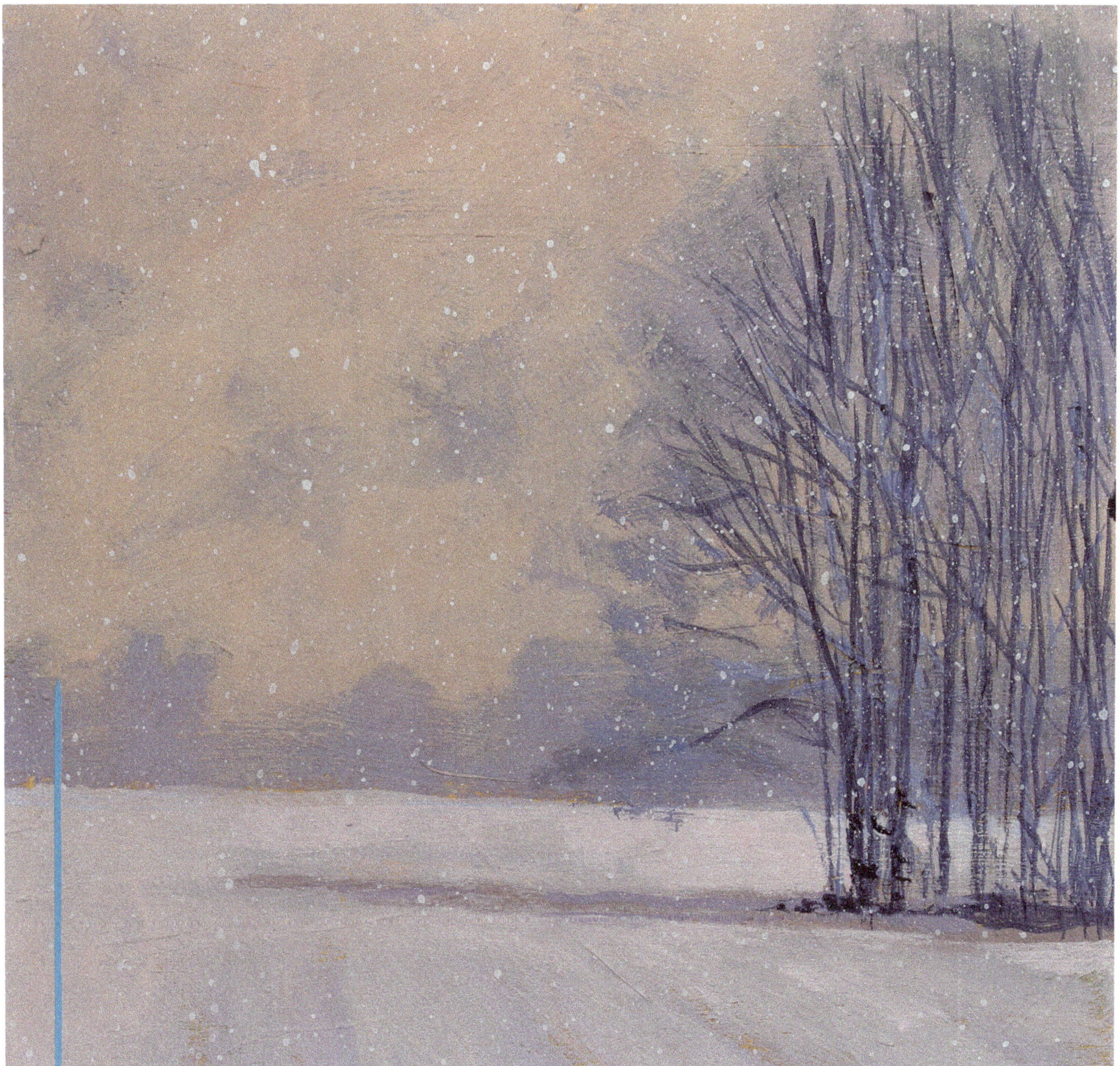

Favorite Place, Winter **(acrylic on panel)**
On this cold day, snowflakes were in the air, and the light was subdued with a heavy cloud cover. I used warm and cool neutrals to keep the mood deliberately somber. I used the edge of my palette knife and a small round brush to indicate the bare trees. Because acrylic dries so quickly, I was able to add spattered, watered down white acrylic for the snowflakes. If you do this, the key is to make different size spatters. The larger dots will appear close, and the small ones will recede into the distance.

Taking Liberties

Sometimes, as we search for subject matter, we spend more time looking for that "perfect spot" than we do actually painting. Instead, use what nature provides and manipulate what you observe to make a better painting. Find one or two interesting things; then build a painting around them. Remember, you are the artist—you can add, subtract, and alter anything you like. Design or arrange the elements in your painting to make a unified whole. Let your initial enthusiasm direct your efforts to make the painting you want to make.

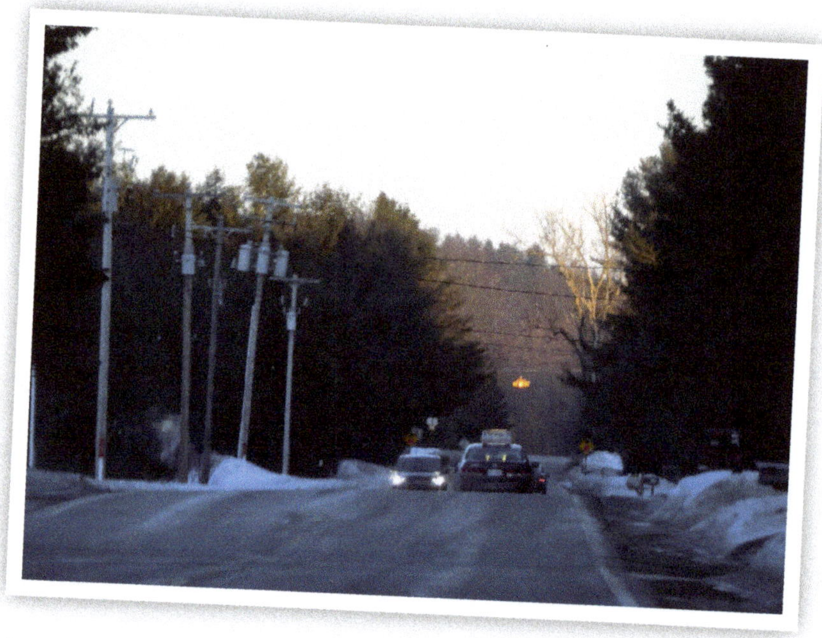

We don't have many sunny days in our Michigan winters. It's cold and snowy for up to six months of the year, and spring comes slowly. I love to go for a drive on those rare occasions when the sun shines. My cameras are always with me: a point-and-shoot with a good telephoto lens and, of course, my cell phone camera.

I was out for an evening drive, and the sun had almost set. There was a warm glow touching the tops of the distant trees. The foreground and middle ground were bathed in shadow. I snapped a photograph (at right) that shows the scene; it also shows too many telephone poles, mailboxes, and traffic.

I used the photo as inspiration, but I did not do the painting outside. It was too cold! Instead, I worked with what nature gave me to make a painting. I kept just three telephone poles, leaning the middle one toward the center of interest—that glow of sunset. I saturated the cool blue of the snow to a bright violet. I also added a cool blue in the sky to replace the warm neutral tone that was washed out by the sun.

Using this cool blue heightened the warm red-orange I chose for the distant tree line. Finally, I changed from a rectangular format to a square composition to put more emphasis on the red-orange trees.

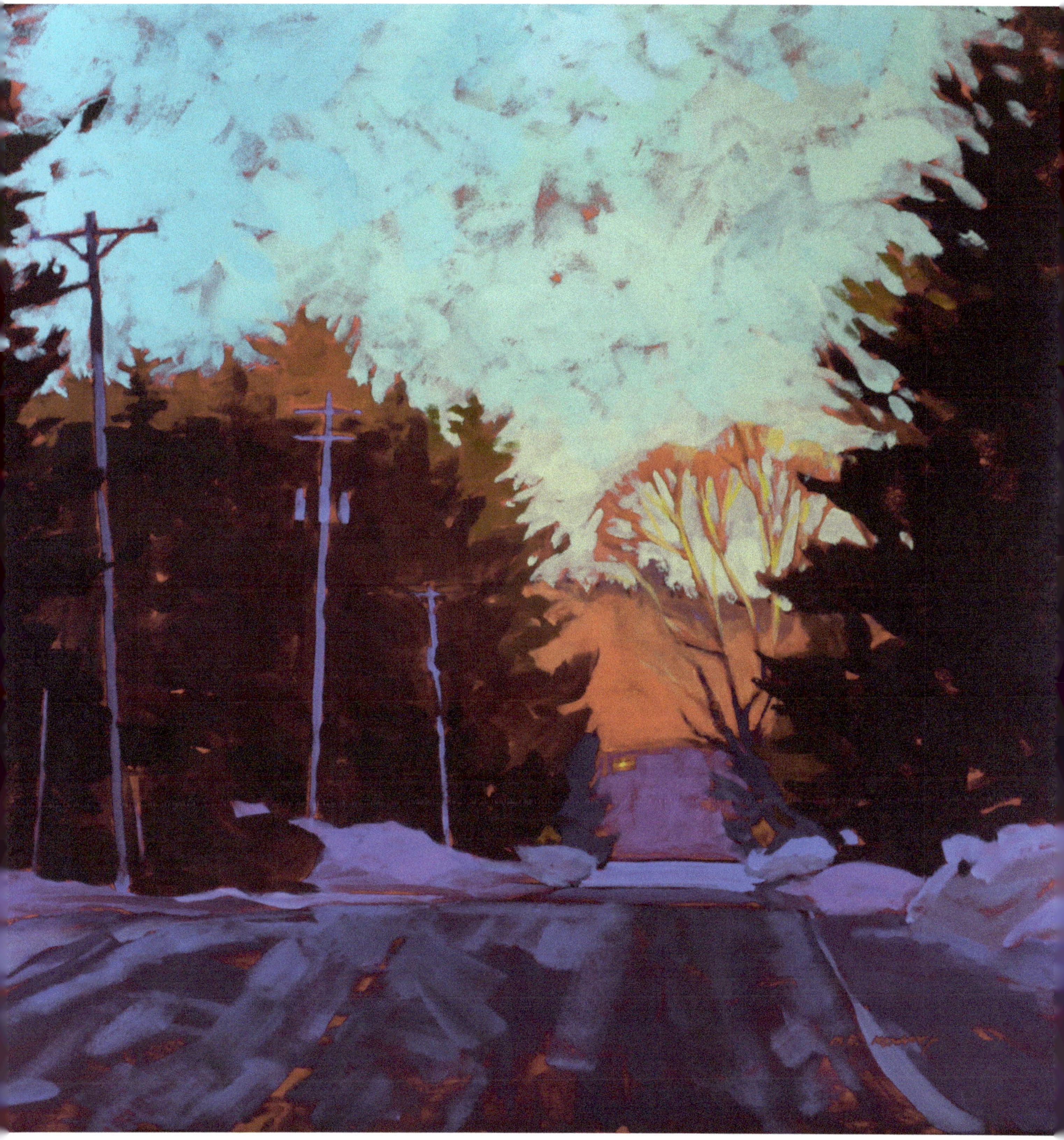

As the artist, you can manipulate what you see and what you paint at any time. It is a realization that allows an enormous amount of freedom for composition.

Here is another example. As I came around a bend, the converging lines that formed the edges of the road captured my interest. This led to a vanishing point of sunlit trees around the bend. I also enjoyed the dance of light across the road and up the snow-covered hill on the right.

I took the photo (below), which gave me enough information to complete the painting in the studio. I wanted to capture the road leading into the distance, the dappled light across the snow, and the deep blue-violet of the shadows.

When working from photographic references, I always consider whether I like the painting more than the photo. In this case, I do. As an artist, you should never feel you are locked into any given scene, colors, or methods. The creative and fun part is to change things to make a great painting!

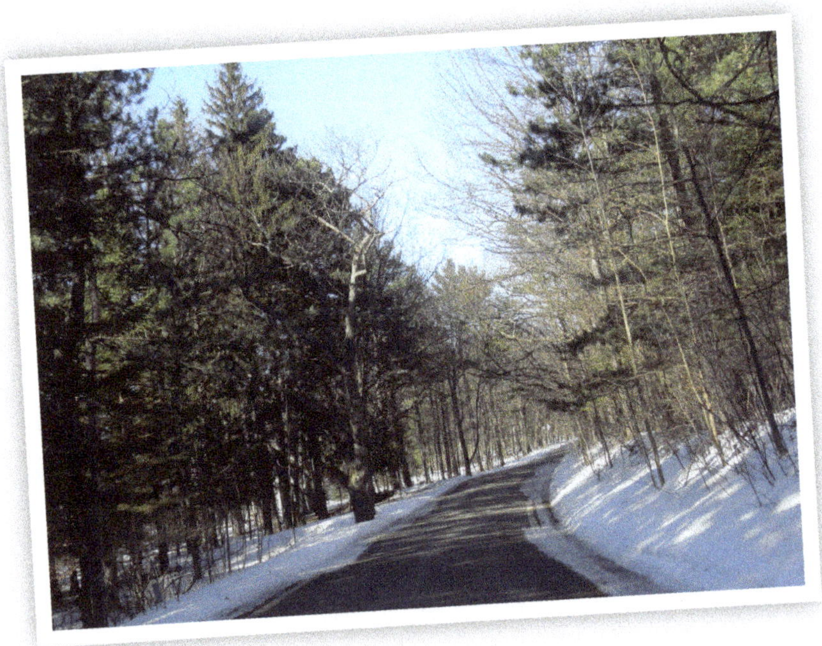

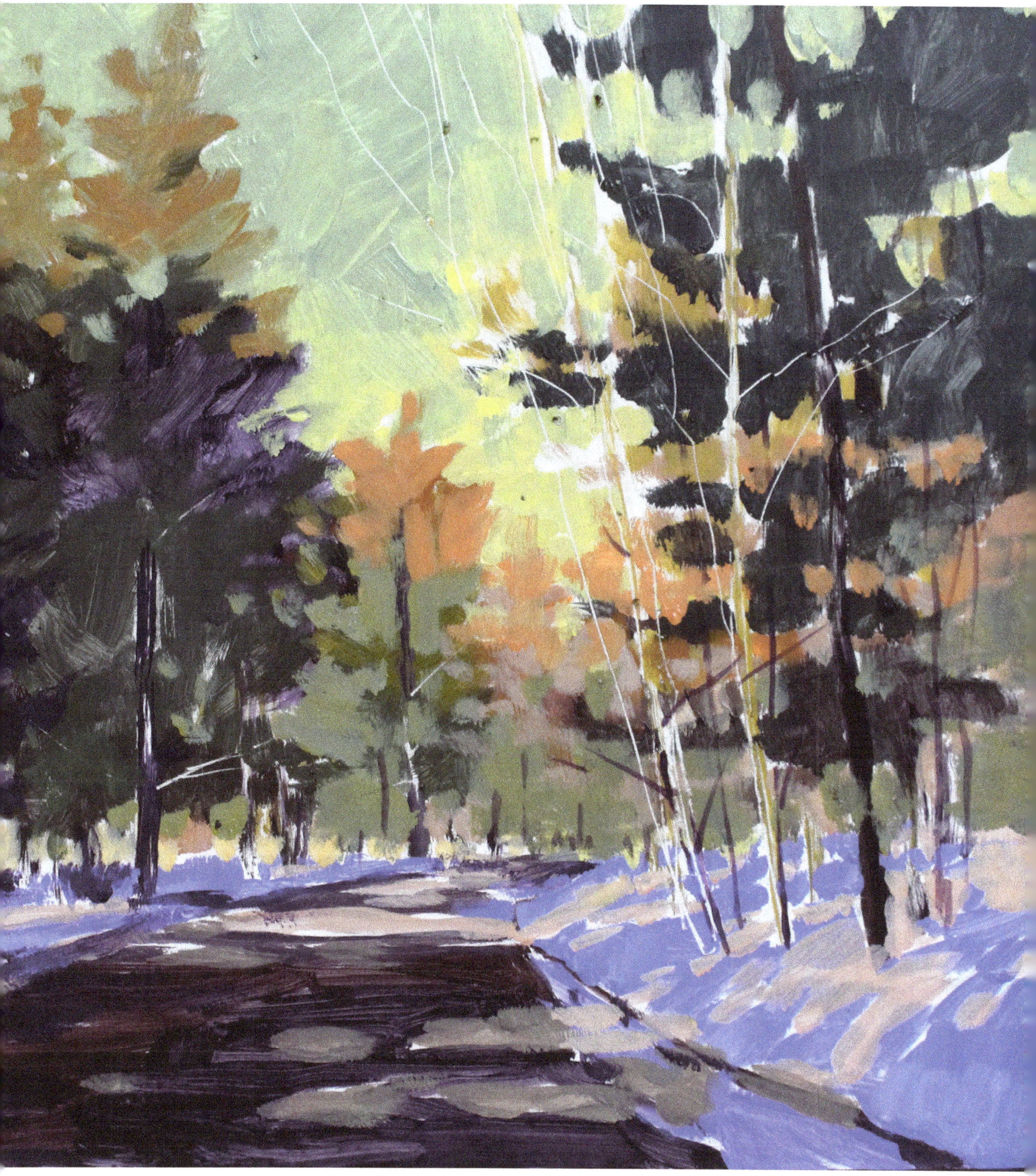

About the Author

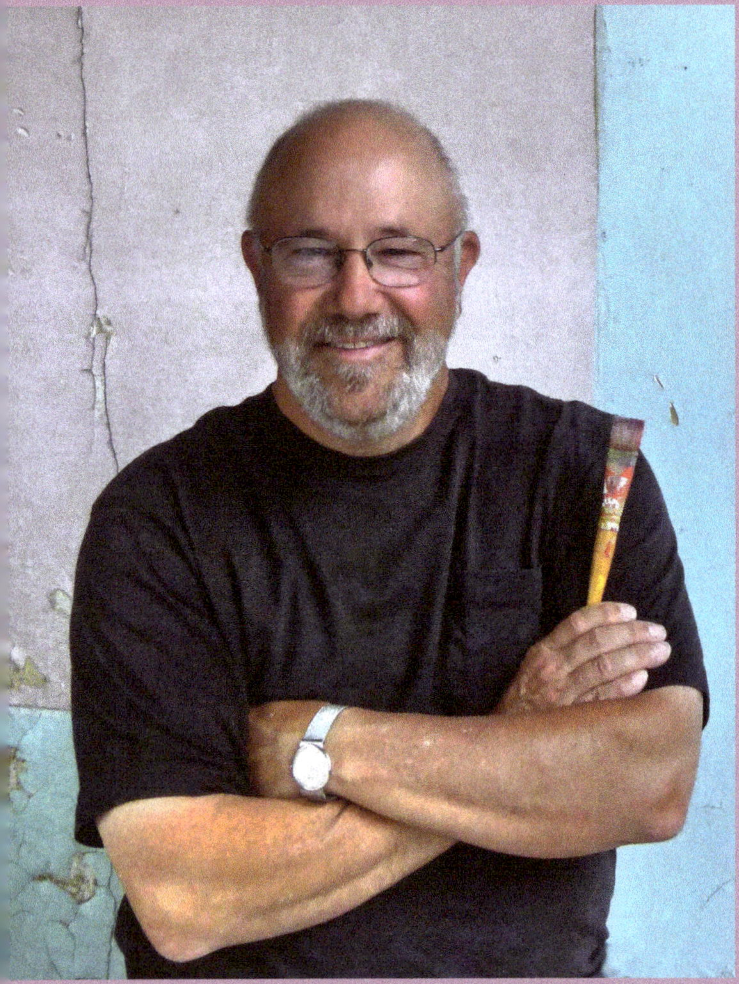

Mark Mehaffey has been painting seriously since the age of 10. Mark was encouraged at this time by a friend's father, his fourth-grade teacher, and most of all, his family, and drawing and painting became part of what he did. He has never stopped.

Mark is a retired public school art instructor, having spent a full career teaching the joys of creating to children of all ages. For close to 30 years he had two full-time jobs; teaching during the day and painting weeknights, weekends, and summers. Since retirement, Mark spends full days in the studio, travels to teach privately, and paints en plein air weekly.

Mark is a signature member of the American Watercolor Society (Dolphin Fellow), National Watercolor Society, Transparent Watercolor Society of America (Distinguished Master), International Society of Acrylic Painters, and International Society of Experimental Artists, among others.

Mark is an avid outdoorsman who enjoys hiking, gardening, fishing, and particularly loves painting en plein air. To see more of Mark's art, visit markmehaffeyfineart.com.

www.ingramcontent.com/pod-product-compliance
Lightning Source LLC
LaVergne TN
LVHW071354200826
846030LV00016B/159